The Films of
Charles Bronson

The Films of
Charles Bronson

by
Jerry Vermilye

The Citadel Press   •   Secaucus, New Jersey

For
Flo & Bill

ALSO BY JERRY VERMILYE

Burt Lancaster
Bette Davis
Cary Grant
Barbara Stanwyck
The Films of Elizabeth Taylor (co-author)
Ida Lupino
The Great British Films

Library of Congress Cataloging in Publication Data

Vermilye, Jerry.
    The films of Charles Bronson.

    1. Bronson, Charles, 1920-

I. Title.
PN2287.B693V4   791.43'028'0924   80-11576
ISBN 0-8065-0695-4

First edition
Copyright © 1980 by Jerry Vermilye
All rights reserved
Published by Citadel Press
A division of Lyle Stuart Inc.
120 Enterprise Ave., Secaucus, N.J. 07094
In Canada: General Publishing Co. Limited
Don Mills, Ontario
Manufactured in the United States of America by
Halliday Lithograph, West Hanover, Mass.
Design and Illustrations by Ramon Luis Vila

Acknowledgments

The author wishes to express his necessarily blind indebtedness to all of those uncredited still-photographers whose efforts make a volume of this sort possible—and to the following distributors for whom these motion pictures were made:

American International; Associated Film Distribution Corp.; Avco Embassy; Columbia Pictures; Emerson Films; GSF Productions; Intercontinental Releasing; International Coproductions & EDP Films; Metro-Goldwyn-Mayer; National General; Paramount Pictures; 20th Century-Fox; United Artists; Universal-International; Warner Bros.; and the following television networks: American Broadcasting Co.; Columbia Broadcasting System and National Broadcasting Co.

The following organizations and individuals were invaluable in the assistance of acquiring stills, credits and general information:

Eddie Brandt's Saturday Matinee; The British Film Institute (National Film Archive/Stills Library); Cabo Productions (Karyn Posner); Judy Caputo; Christopher Denis; Paul Denis; Constance Scrase Dickins; Henry Fera; I.T.C. Entertainment; Jack Kleinhentz; the late Frank Leyendecker; Leonard Maltin; Alvin H. Marill; Albert McFadden; James Robert Parish; Andrea Paskman; Rogers & Cowan (Susan Chavez); Eileen Sauer; Philippe Setbon; Lou Valentino and Steven Whitney.

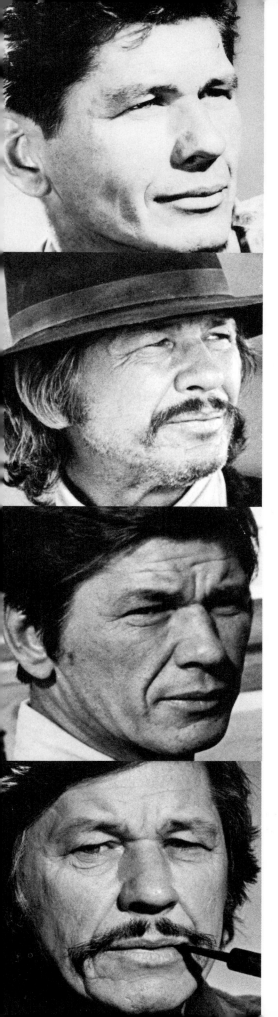

Contents

The Man

The Man

Bronson! There is little need to mention his Christian name. For this movie actor is well on his way to joining that fabled roster — Bogart, Cagney, Gable, etc. — whose last name is enough to elicit instant recognition and a positive response from the vast majority of film audiences. Which is not to presume that Charles Bronson's career boasts the over-all distinction of those luminaries of yesteryear. But, with the demise of the studio system and the passing of the quality-control moguls and producers of 1930s/'40s Hollywood, present-day superstars like Bronson owe the achievements of their often-seesawing careers to sheer luck and good management as much as to intuition, ambition and a keen awareness of their own marketability.

Bronson himself has no illusions about his success, for stardom and its attendant financial rewards came neither early nor easily. For him, the real breakthrough did not transpire until the late Sixties — seventeen years after his first film and when he was past the age of forty-five. And (a source of deep-seated personal bitterness), Bronson had to go to *Europe* to *become* a star. But, by 1975, he was earning a million dollars a picture, plus percentages.

Bronson was always a freelance actor. In the early years of his career, he wanted very much to be placed under contract by one of the major studios. But it never happened. Instead, his rugged face and muscular form helped secure him a place in Hollywood as a solid and reliable character actor, to be counted on for the strong delineation of Indians, gunslingers, convicts, prizefighters and mobsters. From his 1951 movie debut until 1968, Bronson played dozens of roles in support of important stars in major films, and occasionally got a *leading* role in minor "program" pictures. Lack of either personal drive or the backing of a high-powered agent may well have contributed to his failure to rise more quickly in the Hollywood ranks. Few could have predicted that this very capable small-part performer with the rugged face and form would ever be either an important film actor or a leading one. Any notion that he would ever become a top money-making star and world-wide audience favorite would have met with instant ridicule. In 1972, after Bronson and Sean Connery had been named the world's most popular actors by the Hollywood Foreign Press Association's Golden Globe poll of sixty countries, this man of few words summed up his reaction succinctly: "It's a good feeling."

When success comes as belatedly to a performer as it did to Charles Bronson, he usually has the capacity to accept whatever fame or fortune follows without any noticeable upset to his equilibrium.

"When I first began to work in pictures," Bronson recalls, "I tried to attract the attention of film critics." But, more often than not, he was either bypassed in favor of commentary about the leading players or barely mentioned in passing, lumped together with a half-dozen others. In more recent years, Bronson takes the position that he couldn't care less what the movie reviewers think, maintaining that it's only the *paying* members of his public that concern him. "I don't make movies to please them [critics] or myself anymore," he informed an interviewer in 1976. "I look for material that will entertain."

But he's also sufficiently aware to realize his most effective screen image and capitalize on it: and so the indomitable individualist, the neo-primitive survivor, the man of few words but decisive in action and integrity has become the accepted norm in Bronson films. Leathery of skin and nearly expressionless of face, he masks an inner sensitivity beneath a brusquely masculine facade, with only occasional flashes of wry humor to indicate that this somewhat mysterious loner, this athletic man of action, is, in the final breach, a warm human being, capable of love and affection. From time to time, Bronson's macho image has revealed glimpses of this other side of his nature, but mainly in the scenes he has shared with child performers or with his wife, and most frequent co-star, Jill Ireland.

Industry observers have noted that the extraordinary box-office power of Charles Bronson seems to have hit simultaneously with his 1968 marriage to Jill Ireland, and as he began to sign on for films in France, Italy and Spain—of the sort that he had previously rejected. It is a matter of financial record that, from 1968 on, he became the most bankable attraction in the international motion picture market. He frankly credits this success to Jill's help and counsel.

Bronson has built his reputation as a loner, and few claim to have gotten to know him on a movie set, where, when not actively engaged in the business of performing, he is known to remove himself to his dressing-room, avoiding company chitchat and cast/crew fraternization. In his words, "Movie acting is not socializing, it's hard work." Nor does he like publicizing himself or his films, remarking, "The best publicity breaks in the world are your successful pictures—movies that your audience liked well enough to pay three or four dollars a seat, and left the theatre entertained." Indeed, the diversion of his fans appears to have become Bronson's sole professional concern: "I've sustained because I'm sympatico with the material I do, and the other way around. An actor shouldn't just think of doing things he might enjoy doing. I think first of the audience, not of myself, but of the movie fans all around the world who want to be entertained. They pay for it all."

But why is it that so many moviegoers flock to this man's films? Obviously, a combination of factors provides the attraction. One might surmise that men admire Bronson because of the action and violence in his films, while women respond to the animal magnetism of his muscular, ugly/handsome facade. But that's obviously an oversimplification. The Bronson persona is at once obvious and complex: he is beauty and the beast wrapped up in one sleek package. He has referred to himself as a salable commodity, and it's a commodity he carefully maintains. Today, in his late fifties, this now-wealthy actor who can afford several homes and most of life's luxuries for his family, nevertheless keeps in top physical shape with punching-bag and jump rope. On the screen, both sexes admire Bronson, like John Wayne, for his "cool," for that attractive combination of brawn and tautly strung adaptability to any given situation. He may be a man of few words, but he knows how to handle himself. Above all,

In *Hard Times* (1975).

the very quiet of the man—that aura of a simmering pressure-cooker—is the essence of his charisma. In the opinion of makeup man Phil Rhodes, "He is like a hand grenade with the pin pulled." One is never quite sure what he is going to do next, and so to let the eye wander from him might make one miss the explosion, when it happens. His on-screen integrity, courage and resourcefulness add additional appeal.

The poet and novelist James Dickey offers an interesting commentary on this middle-aged superstar: "There is something archetypal about Bronson, no matter how bad his films are. He has never been in the masterpiece that I suspect him capable of carrying off. There are touches in his films, almost all of them, which lead me to believe that, given the right circumstances, his combination of forceful projection and an unexpected male tenderness might produce a truly haunting succession of images in the viewer's mind."

But Bronson himself expresses disdain for such assessments. As he told writer Bill Davidson for a 1974 *New York Times* article: "Don't ask me to explain a mystique. I'm just enjoying all this while it lasts. I'm basically doing the same thing I was doing twenty years ago."

Charles Dennis Bunchinsky was born in the coal-mining town of Ehrenfeld, Pennsylvania, on November 3, 1921 (reputable sources have variously listed the year as 1920 and 1922). Both of his parents were Slavic Catholics: Walter Bunchinsky, a Lithuanian of Russian descent, had, in the 1890s, emigrated to the U.S., where he met and married American-born Mary Valin-

sky. Young Charlie was the fifth son in a prolific succession of offspring that eventually totaled fifteen, several of whom died in infancy. From all reports, his childhood was rough, the family was extremely poor and "Scooptown" (as Ehrenfeld was commonly known) had little to offer a male youngster but the promise of a future in the mines, where conditions made longevity a hopeless dream.

In 1933, when Charlie was twelve, his father died from a combination of the miners' all-too-prevalent black-lung disease and injuries suffered in a mining accident years earlier. Of that awful last summer, the actor recalls: "I remember my father wheezing and choking away his life in a back bedroom. My mother knew nothing could be done. Death was just a matter of time. At the end, he was choking on every breath, and we all pretended we didn't hear anything. How do you explain what that does to you? You never forget it."

"I didn't really know my father well," Bronson later remarked of this man who apparently inspired fear in his children. "I don't know if I loved or hated him."

Because an older brother, Joseph, disliked the sound of their name, it was decided to drop the "n" from Bunchinsky, thus evolving the family's present spelling, with its somewhat softer pronunciation of "Boo-SHIN-ski." It was a name that Charlie would proudly carry into his early years as an actor—until the pressures of the McCarthy era made all Russian-sounding American actors think carefully about changing their status-quo.

His talent for creative artistry started early: "When I was a kid," he recalled in 1974, "I was always drawing things. I'd get butcher paper or grocery bags and draw on them. And at school I was the one who got to draw on the windows with soap. Turkeys for Thanksgiving, that kind of thing. It seemed I just knew how to draw. I had a show of my stuff in Beverly Hills, and it sold out in two weeks—and it wasn't because my name was Charles Bronson, because I signed them Buchinsky."

Bronson's well-known on-the-set aloofness among his Hollywood co-workers stems from boyhood. Despite the natural affection of his mother and many siblings, young Charlie took early to spending more and more time alone, away from both family and friends. Years later, Charles Bronson's movie colleagues would tell reporters about his penchant for solitude and his unsociability during the making of a film. Interestingly enough, the comments of one contemporary who knew him as a boy vary but little: "When Charlie walked by you on the street, he would say hello, but that's all. He would never stop to talk. It's funny; I don't think anybody here ever got close to Charlie."

The boy's high-school graduation, in June of 1939, was a cause for family celebration, because he was the first Buchinsky child to do so. After which, predictably, he went to work for the coal company—not in the mines, but in the processing plant. But still his future was bleak. The pay was small, and there were quite a lot of Buchinskys to help support. Nothing could be saved: "All the money I earned went toward rent and food."

Following the 1941 Japanese attack on Pearl Harbor, Charlie's brothers Joe and Dempsey were drafted, and he became sole support of the family, while the staff-depleted mine accelerated its production quota. Charlie reports having felt an intense anger and frustration, for now he was taken from the comparatively pleasant conditions of the cleaning plant and forced underground. He recalls those years of working in the mines as being "real hell," explaining, "I was terrified with claustrophobia all the time I was underground. At times I got so damned scared, I sued to beat my fists against the walls. You became a man when you went down the pit. I did, but I knew I had to get out."

Charlie Buchinsky had been exempted from military service, because he was officially his family's sole support. But, with the escalation of hostilities, early in 1943 he was drafted into

In *Love and Bullets* (1979).

the Army. For many young American men, military service was a sentence to be endured and (hopefully) survived. But for this impoverished 21-year-old country boy, it marked an escape to a new world of clean beds, fresh clothing—and a full stomach.

After the coal mines, Arizona's Kingman Air Force Base, where part of his training took place, was like a vacation: "It was freedom for me. I discovered the world and the people outside." He also discovered that his fellow recruits did not talk as he did, for his youthful environment had left him with speech patterns so thick-accented and so poorly pronounced as to make him appear foreign-born. The lad's inexperience in the mainstream of American life, added to his speech difficulties, immediately set him apart from the others, producing anger and frustration within. As he later recalled, "I guess I had a chip on my shoulder for awhile. I got into fights. But, in time, I found I could be as good any anyone else. And when you gain confidence, you're no longer insecure."

Contrary to some published reports, Charlie Buchinsky did not spend his entire Army service in Arizona. Although assigned to the 760th Mess Squadron at Kingman, where he drove food delivery trucks, he later transferred to the Pacific Theater of Operations, where he served as a tail gunner aboard a B-29, flying more than twenty-five missions.

In February of 1946, he won an honorable discharge, and returned to Ehrenfeld, where he had no intention of going back into the mines. Veterans had the option of reclaiming their old

In *St. Ives* (1976).

jobs, and were given three months, following discharge, to make their decisions. Charlie had already made that decision, although his future plans remained uncertain. Recalling that period of transition, he has said: "For a year I just lazed around, doing nothing while I collected twenty bucks a week from the government. When the money stopped, I decided to head for New York, but it turned out I only had enough fare to go to Philadelphia, and that's where I wound up."

Because a Veterans Administration aptitude test revealed that Charlie demonstrated a marked talent for creative art, he then took advantage of the GI Bill to enroll at the Hussien Art School, where his training was financed by the government. To pay for room and board, he worked variously as a waiter, bricklayer and baker's assistant. At a local gym, where Charlie went to keep in shape, he met actors from the city's Plays and Players organization. Through them he got involved in such backstage activities as painting scenery, and even gathered enough courage to try out for an acting role—a traumatic experience that temporarily sent him back to the scene-shop. As he later revealed in an interview, "The first time I read for a part the director screamed and yelled and chased me out of the theatre. I had come to the word 'heroine,' and I pronounced it 'her-OY-an.' The director couldn't believe it. 'How dare you audition? You're illiterate! You'll never, never become an actor.'"

Charlie Buchinsky repaired to his backstage activities, as he watched, learned and waited.

Eventually, he did get the opportunity to play bits in a number of their productions, where his rugged face and form made him ideal for certain character roles. And he also met the girl he would eventually marry: teen-aged Harriet Tendler had become a member of the acting company about the time Charlie had begun helping behind the scenes, and they realized an early rapport which carried over beyond his tenure with Plays and Players, which habitually closed operations for the summer months.

In search of a lucrative job to tide him over, the would-be actor went to that New Jersey mecca, Atlantic City, where he began the summer of 1947 by renting deck chairs to sunbathers. Later, he graduated to higher pay on the Hamid Amusement Pier, as barker for the Bingo-like game of Thrill-O (reputedly operated by Atlantic City's mobsters). His Thrill-O colleague was an unemployed New York actor named Jack Klugman, who eventually became his best friend and roommate, both in that resort town and—after Charlie had served another winter with Philadelphia's Plays and Players—in New York.

Earnings from the summer of 1948 enabled the pair to support themselves as unemployed actors during the following winter. They shared a one-room seven-dollar-a-week slum apartment in New York on Broadway and 113th Street, which was used for little other than sleeping. Both managed to derive some income from special-delivery work for the post office. But more exciting was Charlie Buchinsky's Manhattan stage debut (January 1949) in a quite respectable showcase production of Ayn Rand's 1936 courtroom comedy-drama, *The Night of January 16,* in which he had the small role of a witness. Like most such offerings, there was no pay involved, merely a chance to gain experience and, perhaps, be seen by someone who might foster a budding actor's hopes for a career in the theatre. Charlie also had the bit role of a gangster in the 1934 melodrama *Stevedore* with Equity Library Theatre, and recalls having auditioned for the Marlon Brando role of Stanley Kowalski in Tennessee Williams' *A Streetcar Named Desire* — presumably as a possible New York replacement or road-company actor, since that hit play had opened on Broadway in late 1947 while Charlie was still with Play and Players in Philadelphia.

With Jack Klugman's encouragement, Charlie Buchinsky determined to put all his energies into succeeding as an actor and, after working the

14

With Jill Ireland in *Love and Bullets* (1979).

summer of 1949 hawking Thrill-O once again in Atlantic City, he decided on a plan of action: with the aid of the GI Bill, he would prepare properly for his chosen profession at California's then-prestigious Pasadena Playhouse, which had the added advantage of its proximity to Hollywood and the movies.

Charlie's close friendship with Harriet Tendler now took a more serious turn and, despite her family's objection to him on religious grounds, they were married in Atlantic City on September 30, 1949, followed by a pre-California visit to the Buchinsky family in Ehrenfeld. With the modest sum of $250 (his summer savings), they then traveled west by Greyhound bus.

The Buchinskys' first California home was a cramped one-room set-up, in essence a veritable enclosed porch, at the back of a house at 160 North El Molina Avenue in Pasadena. And, while Harriet supported them by selling handbags at Mather's Department Store, Charlie studied his craft (in particular, speech, to improve his diction). "I knew I was going to do character parts," he has said. "I was already identified as a character by my ridiculous speech. At that time, all the leading men were Cary Grant types. They all looked like the guy who got the girl. I didn't look or sound like the guy who got the girl."

At the Playhouse, his natural attributes landed him the role of Killer Mears in the prison drama *The Last Mile*, a part that had once helped make stars of Spencer Tracy and Clark Gable. A Playhouse instructor, Thomas Brown

Henry, was then under consideration for a role in director Henry Hathaway's film *U.S.S. Teakettle*, a Gary Cooper vehicle at 20th Century-Fox, and he recommended that Hathaway consider Charlie Buchinsky for the role of the Polish-American fighter/sailor Wascylewski. As the actor told Rex Reed in a 1972 interview, "I got the role because I could belch on cue." Another tough-looking young actor made his movie bow in that picture: Lee Marvin, who had a much smaller role but who would rise to stardom faster than Charlie Buchinsky, via vicious "heavy" parts.

In his motion-picture debut, Charlie's supporting role provided him with a suitable introduction to the moviegoing public, showing his burgeoning talents to advantage in a character that appeared on and off throughout the length of the film. It also provided him with a trip to Norfolk, Virginia, where location scenes were shot. *U.S.S. Teakettle*, although favorably reviewed, made little money, which moved Fox to re-title it *You're in the Navy Now*, for the remainder of its engagements. Only moderately successful despite Gary Cooper, the movie, predictably, was a great hit in Johnstown, Pa., because of hometown-hero Buchinsky.

On the film's Hollywood set, Charlie also found his first professional representation via Gus Dembling, a small-time agent who was about the best a movie novice could hope for at this stage of his career. Dembling helped Charlie get bit roles in a number of other movies, enabling him to forsake his drama-

In *Hard Times* (1975).

school education for a full-time Hollywood career. But after *Teakettle,* his roles only seemed to grow smaller: a bit in Spencer Tracy's *The People Against O'Hara* at MGM; as a longshoreman walk-on in *The Mob,* a crime yarn starring Broderick Crawford at Columbia; a firefighter in the Richard Widmark-Jeffrey Hunter melodrama, *Red Skies of Montana,* filmed on location for Fox.

While Harriet continued to work (she had decided to give up her own acting career when they married), Charlie enjoyed somewhat more sizable roles as a sarcastic prison inmate in *My Six Convicts,* a modest Stanley Kramer production for Columbia, and in *Pat and Mike,* where he shared scenes with the film's big-league stars, Spencer Tracy and Katharine Hepburn.

Charlie Buchinsky coveted a major-studio contract, for a freelance actor like himself constantly lost out on prospective roles when studio casting directors, quite understandably, felt compelled to hire contract-players over outsiders. But the young actor's professionalism won him the respect of his industry colleagues: he arrived at work on time, he knew his lines and he always "delivered." And directors with whom he worked once habitually hired him again and again.

Not unexpectedly, Charlie Buchinsky soon grew too big for Gus Dembling's small-potatoes management of his career, and he was fortunate enough to find, in Meyer Mishkin, a star-handler willing to gamble with a little-known bit player. Mishkin introduced his new client to the television studios, pulled Charlie from the ranks of movie extras and told him henceforth to refuse all subsequent bit parts.

The ex-coal miner's TV bow appears to have been in the January 10, 1953, episode of *The Doctor,* a thirty-minute NBC anthology series. In a teleplay called "Take the Odds," written and directed by a former RKO clerk named Robert Aldrich, he had a rather good supporting role. Despite favorable results, it was many months before further television work would come Charlie's way. But "Take the Odds," aside from introducing him to the growing medium that was providing movies with such intense competition for audience attention, also established a professional friendship with Robert Aldrich that would prove advantageous to his future.

Through Mishkin, Charlie got the role in *House of Wax* that many recall with pleasure, for in this 3-D horror melodrama his enactment of Vincent Price's sinister, mute sidekick Igor is perhaps his earliest movie characterization easily recalled by the average Charles Bronson fan. *House of Wax* seems to have become more easily accessible, in revival and on TV, than *U.S.S. Teakettle/You're in the Navy Now.* Charlie's grim-visaged, Neanderthal-like wax-museum aide generates dark humor, especially in the scene where he stalks frightened heroine Phillis Kirk by "hiding" among a collection of waxen heads, with his gimlet eyes the only ones to move in pursuit of her.

With Meyer Mishkin's backing, Charlie Buchinsky was on public view frequently during 1954, in a succession of roles presenting him as Indians, gangsters, prizefighters and cowboys. In *Miss Sadie Thompson,* the third movie version of Somerset Maugham's *Rain,* starring Rita Hayworth (in a role originally intended for Jane Russell), he was frequently on muscular view as one of Sadie's marine pals. For that he got a trip to Hawaii. As Charlie's roles grew in size, so naturally did his billing: in the 1954 Burt Lancaster film *Apache,* his name appeared in fourth place.

Charlie Buchinsky first reached the moviegoing public as "Charles Bronson" when Alan Ladd's Western, *Drum Beat,* opened late in 1954 (just ahead of his last Buchinsky-billed performance in *Vera Cruz*). But *Drum Beat* was a milestone for more reasons than the nominal "Bronson" milestone: Mishkin's continued urging had finally convinced his client to consider a name-change, and Hollywood's then-current anti-Red pressures (with complete loss of employment for many a suspected Communist sympathizer) helped speed his decision. Reportedly the "Bronson" name derives from a Hollywood street that came to his attention at the time when he was searching for an alternate to Buchinsky. (Despite the prideful reversion to ethnic original names amongst entertainers of the roots-proud 1970s, it is interesting to conjecture whether "Buchinsky" would today be as big a superstar-name as "Bronson," had he retained it).

Drum Beat not only provided the newly christened Charles Bronson with his best role to date, as the vicious renegade Modoc Indian Captain Jack, but it stole much of the attention away from producer-star Alan Ladd, whose first film this was for his Jaguar production company. In the words of *The Los Angeles Times,* "Charles Bronson is only slightly less than sensational in the part. It is he who dominates the picture."

In *Breakheart Pass* (1976).

Charlie and Harriet had finally moved into a real *house,* and, on February 27, 1955, their first child, Suzanne Frances, was born. Fortunately for this added expense in their lives, the actor continued to get TV roles. He had his first "live" part in the Lux Video Theater production of *A Bell for Adano.* Usually he portrayed con men and killers, with an occasional switch to more positive character traits. On Stage 7's drama *The Time of Day,* he even got to romance Peggy Ann Garner.

During 1955, he was seen to advantage in such action-oriented series as *Public Defender, Man Behind the Badge* and *Treasury Men in Action.* But, despite the power of his *Drum Beat* performance, movie producers did not flood him with offers. In 1955, big-screen watchers saw him play major supporting roles in the grade-B prison melodrama *Big House, U.S.A.* and the grade-B war film *Target Zero.* The following year, he had a small part in the interesting psychological Western *Jubal.* In 1957, he portrayed perhaps the most muscular (and skimpily clad) Indian that movie reviewers had ever seen, opposite chubby Rod Steiger, in *Run of the Arrow,* directed by cult favorite Samuel Fuller. His part in this movie was obtained for him via the Lester Salkow Agency, a smaller organization than Mishkin's, but one to which Bronson had chosen to switch at this time. Not unexpectedly, this change in agents resulted in a temporary falling-off of work, but Salkow soon compensated for this slack period with a deluge of TV roles on the series *Gunsmoke, The Millionaire, Richard Diamond* and *Have Gun,*

17

In *Breakout* (1975).

Will Travel.

Bronson had long continued, as a hobby, his interest in art, and throughout these years he maintained painting as a pastime, variously recording on canvas his memories of the mines of Ehrenfeld and the early years of his daughter Suzanne.

The pattern of Charles Bronson's seven-year motion picture career had become established with small roles in big films and larger ones in lesser ones. Leading parts had altogether eluded him—until he signed to *star* in a pair of black-and-white B-movies,—a crime drama and a Western—to be produced by Harold E. Knox and directed by Gene Fowler, Jr., for 20th Century-Fox's "programmer" division, Regal Films. Released during the first half of 1958, *Gang War* and *Showdown at Boot Hill* were well-made supporting features, presenting Bronson as tough loners seemingly capable of violence when provoked. Neither film had an important big-city opening, but what critical notices they gathered were good ones. Made on modest budgets, both displayed ingenuity and intelligence above the average for their genre.

Another leading role in a grade-B crime story, the title role in quickie-king Roger Corman's *Machine Gun Kelly,* won the actor more favorable notices. But, once again, this melodrama played mostly to the less discriminating, action-oriented audiences that filled "grind" houses and drive-ins, where it shared an American International Pictures double-bill with its female counterpart, *The Bonnie Parker Story,* starring that bargain-basement Doris Day, Dorothy Provine. *Machine Gun Kelly,* characteristic of the production speed attributed to Corman's prodigious film output of the 1950s, was filmed in eight days for less than $200,000. In it, Bronson made a sensational impression in the overseas markets, where this movie was a minor triumph. Ten years before Bronson would become a European cult-figure, his magnetic screen presence was beginning to take hold. Yet seldom has a show-business sensation been less of an "overnight" affair.

In between *Machine Gun Kelly* and the actor's charismatic Continental success in 1968's French-made *Adieu L'Ami (Farewell, Friend),* would be fifteen additional movies. For the most part, these were Hollywood productions, filmed by Bronson on a freelance basis for a variety of different studios, confining him to roles consistent with his well-established reputation as an accomplished and reliable character actor. In predictable fashion, he had leads in minor-league efforts like *When Hell Broke Loose* (1958) and *Master of the World* (1961), while continuing to provide solid support for big-leaguers like Frank Sinatra, Elvis Presley, Robert Mitchum and the Burtons, Richard and Elizabeth. But he was also seen to advantage in three of the Sixties' biggest box-office hits: 1960's exciting Westernization of a Japanese classic, *The Magnificent Seven;* 1963's *The Great Escape,* as the claustrophobic tunnel-digger; and 1967's *The Dirty Dozen,* in which, as one of the twelve, he played second-fiddle to his ex-fellow-bit-player, Lee Marvin (in a role turned down by John Wayne).

John Sturges, who directed Bronson in *The Magnificent Seven* and *The Great Escape,* lauds the actor's professionalism, adding, "His biggest asset on screen is that coilspring attitude. Nobody knows what he's going to do. He looks like a guy who is going to tear everything apart."

Television afforded Bronson continued employment during that period. In 1958, he even had his own action series, *Man with a Camera,* in which, for a season-and-a-half, he portrayed former World War II combat photographer Mike Kovac, who covers Manhattan in aid of the police, shooting with his camera instead of a gun. During the first half of 1963, Bronson played the recurring part of Paul Moreno in the Western series *Empire,* followed by *Jamie McPheeters,* another pioneer saga, in which he was Linc Murdock during the 1963-64 season. Following a role on John Mills' short-lived 1967 series, *Dundee and the Culhane*, Bronson left TV to concentrate on European feature films, and did not return to television until his portrayal of Israeli General Dan Shomron in the fact-based 1977 TV-movie, *Raid on Entebbe*.

The 1960s witnessed yet another change of professional representation for Bronson, as he left the independent Lester Salkow for exclusive handling by that industry giant, MCA. In doing so, he was immediately assured of higher fees for his services. Fortunately so, for the Bronsons were four as of February 19, 1961, when Harriet gave birth to their first son, Anthony Charles. For relaxation, the actor continued to paint — in a workshop he had set up behind his home. As he once told an interviewer, "I paint for the same season I act. It is a form of emotional expression, and I feel gratification working in both mediums."

Returning to the U.S. from Germany, after filming *The Great Escape*, Bronson found himself again without an agent: as part of a conglomerate, MCA was closing out its agency division, leaving former clients to fend for themselves. While on location in Bavaria, he had become close friends with blond British actor David McCallum and his equally blonde actress-wife Jill Ireland, and when the McCallums relocated to the States in the autumn of 1962, Bronson helped them settle in. At the same time, McCallum introduced Bronson to *his* agent, Paul Kohner, and Charlie's professional dilemma was subsequently solved. Kohner has been Bronson's longest-lasting agent.

He then turned down an acting job that only hindsight could reveal as a mistake. For who could expect any great career-reversals to come from starring in an Italian-made Western called *Per un Pugno di Dollari*, to be directed by the obscure Sergio Leone? Fortunately for Clint Eastwood of TV's *Rawhide* series, the profered $15,000 seemed lucrative for *A Fistful of Dollars* (as it was called in the U.S.) made him an international superstar. Why had Bronson rejected Leone's offer? Apparently, he hadn't liked the screenplay, an oversight he was to regret. In retrospect, he reflects, "What I didn't understand was that the script didn't make any difference; it was the way Leone was going to direct it that would make the difference."

During the winter of 1962-63, while Charlie toiled in the *Empire* television series, his mar-

In *Death Wish* (1974).

riage to Harriet reached a shaky state. It was a situation that both parties apparently fought to rectify. Meanwhile, his best Hollywood friends appeared to be the English McCallums, and he was frequently seen about Hollywood in their company, and without Harriet. And, while acting in films for which he had as little regard as *The Sandpiper*, Bronson again turned down a Sergio Leone offer — because this time he didn't want to play second-fiddle to Clint Eastwood in *For a Few Dollars More*. But evil-eyed Lee Van Cleef had no such hang-up, finding, in his acceptance of that role, a revitalized career as a Continental screen favorite. Later still, Bronson again rejected Leone, deferring a role to Eli Wallach in *The Good, the Bad and the Ugly*.

Before 1964 ended, Bronson and his wife had officially split, and he moved out of the house they had shared. In March of 1965, Harriet won an uncontested divorce, as well as custody of

19

In *St. Ives* (1976).

Tony and Suzanne.

Charlie remained close with the McCallums. David had found American fame as Robert Vaughn's co-star in TV's *The Man From U.N.C.L.E.* series, but his own marriage was already in trouble and when, in 1966, it broke up, Jill and Charlie's friendship intensified at the same time the two men's declined. After taking several years away from her own career to give McCallum three children, Jill now resumed acting, in the short-lived *Shane* TV series. And she took steps to divorce McCallum.

There was talk of Bronson joining Paul Newman and Joanne Woodward in a movie that never reached production, while European offers continued to divert him. A part of his former resistance had been motivated by a basically patriotic desire to "make it" in American movies only. But, with the passage of years—and in light of the success already enjoyed abroad by Eastwood and Van Cleef —Bronson accepted the second male lead, as a militant Yaqui Indian leader, in the French-Mexican-Italian co-production of *La Bataille de San Sebastian (Guns for San Sebastian),* starring Anthony Quinn and filmed in the picturesque mountains of Mexico.

When Bronson went to Spain for *Villa Rides,* with Yul Brynner and Robert Mitchum, Jill Ireland had the first of her many roles (albeit here a small one) in Bronson films. It was Charlie's last movie as a supporting actor, for during its shooting he was approached by French producer Serge Silberman to team with Continental favorite Alain Delon in *Adieu L'Ami*

(Farewell, Friend), about the uneasy alliance of a pair of demobilized Algerian War parachutists who drift into a postwar life of larceny in France.

It was at Jill's urging that Bronson accepted Silberman's offer and, in January of 1968, he left for France and a new career. Paul Kohner had worked some clever contractual sleight-of-hand, and instead of the actor's customary $50,000 salary, he would now receive *twice* that sum—and co-star billing with Delon, although the latter's name would appear first. Jill accompanied Charlie to Paris, with the understanding that she was to have the leading female role—eventually played by the blonde former child-star of *Forbidden Games,* Brigitte Fossey.

Bronson didn't care for his *Adieu L'Ami* director, Jean Herman, nor did the French critics, when the film was released later that year. Fortunately, they *did* like the two stars and, even more important, so did the public.

And now Bronson *accepted* Sergio Leone's *fourth* film offer, literally moving directly from the set of *Adieu L'Ami* to Italy for the start of *C'Era una Volta il West (Once Upon a Time in the West).* Leone's most ambitious movie to that date, this five-million-dollar homage to Hollywood Westerns gave Bronson the gun-toting, harmonica-playing heroic lead in a production that teamed him with sexy Claudia Cardinale, Jason Robards and—as the black-clad, most dastardly of villains—Henry Fonda.

Leone pulled out all the proverbial stops for this one, achieving epic proporations with an imaginative use of photography, music, widespread locations (including the actual U.S. Southwest) and much ingenuity. The Europeans loved it, their critics considering it a Western *Gone with the Wind.* And, while *Farewell, Friend* had broken all records in France and caused a sensation, *Once Upon a Time in the West* scored an even greater success all over the Continent. With his ugly/attractive sex appeal and air of simmering mystery, Bronson was compared with popular European stars like Belmondo and Gabin, at the same time creating quite a stir in his own right. Suddenly, Bronson's name was on everyone's lips. And his fame was certain and secure—outside of the U.S.

Paramount Pictures owned the American distribution rights to *Farewell, Friend,* which they chose not to release at all, and *Once Upon a Time in the West,* which they spent little money or energy in promoting. Expectedly, it was a U.S. theatrical flop, and was little seen until sold to television.

Bronson returned to the States in September of 1968 to find his European stardom a virtual secret. On October 5, he and Jill Ireland were married, moving into a lavish, thirty-three room Bel Air mansion with the three McCallum youngsters, of whom Jill had custody.

For a change of pace, Bronson next played opposite young Susan George, in a film variously known as *Twinky* and *Lola,* about the rocky relationship—and marriage—of a middle-aged American writer and a nubile British teen-ager. Despite good performances by the leads, and a distinguished supporting cast, it was a failure.

Jill and Charlie had been working on their own screenplay, whose title has alternately appeared as *98* or *$1.98,* an obviously semi-autobiographical script about a boy's growth to manhood in an impoverished coal-mining town, where he witnesses the death of his father. Reportedly, the screenplay has undergone many revisions. At this writing, it has yet to be produced.

After *Twinky/Lola,* Bronson needed a good film. And this he found in *Le Passager de la Pluie (Rider on the Rain),* a stylish suspense tale directed, in Hitchcock fashion, by Rene Clement *(Purple Noon).* Bronson himself considers this movie his "real beginning" as a star. Although the story centers on Marlene Jobert, as a young Frenchwoman who kills her rapist, Bronson's role as a mysterious American stranger sufficiently impressed the filmmakers (bolstered by the actor's by-now immense Gallic popularity) to bill him alone above the film's title, with unwarranted disregard for Mlle. Jobert.

Again, European movie-house records were broken, with *Rider on the Rain* drawing capacity crowds for the twenty-one weeks of its Paris premiere engagement. In the U.S. Joseph E. Levine released the movie through his Avco Embassy company. But, despite some enthusiastic notices, it was little seen outside of certain major cities, where it enjoyed a temporary art-house prestige—in itself a rarity for a Charles Bronson film.

As Bronson explains, "Jill pushed me in directions I didn't want to go. She made me do *Adieu L'Ami* in France with Alain Delon—which was critically and financially good. After that the same team asked me to do *Rider on the Rain* and I turned it down. Jill was miffed, since she thought the script was great. But I had had an unhappy relationship with the screenwriter, and

In *Once Upon a Time in the West* (1968).

I didn't want to work with him again. Jill convinced me to make *Rider* and, ironically, it was the picture that changed my career. So she was right. As a woman, she saw something I couldn't see—the effect such a film might have on other women."

In Turkey, Bronson joined Tony Curtis for the ill-conceived *Dubious Patriots,* an uninteresting adventure tale of two brawling soldiers-of-fortune, released in 1970 as *You Can't Win 'Em All.* During this period, in an effort to satisfy the audience demand for more Bronson throughout western Europe and the Orient (to which his cult-appeal had spread), TV packagers came up with a pair of instant Western "movies," *Guns of Diablo* and *This Rugged Land,* derived respectively from the actor's old *Jamie McPheeters* and *Empire* series. And overseas, those who owned foreign rights to other U.S. TV series reportedly worked their own cutting-room

In *Guns for San Sebastian* (1968).

wizardry, and emerged with at least another pair of "undiscovered" Bronson films, which they called *The Californian* and *The Bull of the West*. As anticipated, they *all* made money.

With his marriage to Jill, Bronson's once-simple life style changed considerably. When the actor traveled off to a film location, the entire Bronson clan now customarily accompanied him, followed by an entourage of maids, tutors, governesses, animals, chauffeurs, cooks and secretaries—and some sixty-five pieces of luggage. Frequently, this party would require one of a location-hotel's entire floors.

"I hardly ever see my own films," admits Bronson. "I don't like the look of myself or the way I speak. I'm surprised the public likes me." But like him they do, especially overseas, where, despite indifferent quality, vehicles like *You Can't Win 'Em All* and those ersatz TV-movies nevertheless draw enthusiastic crowds.

Most of Bronson's Seventies films have centered on crime and/or the Old West, more often than not with Jill Ireland cast opposite her husband—sometimes to considerable advantage *(From Noon Till Three)*. Yet Bronson has continued to play opposite other actresses —even other *blonde* ones (Lee Remick, Ursula Andress, Kim Novak).

Early in 1979, the actor filmed *Cabo Blanco* in Mexico opposite a *pair* of blonde ladies, *neither* of whom was Jill. But there were various reports in the press that the reason Bronson declined, in 1978, to make *Firepower* opposite Sophia Loren was the producers' refusal to write in a role for *Mrs.* Bronson.

In America, the Seventies have witnessed the belated release of various little-heralded European-made Bronson features *(The Family, Chino, Cold Sweat, Someone Behind the Door)* that have met with scant critical favor. Their rapid journey to TV is likely to please undemanding, died-in-the-wool Bronson addicts. Abroad, these lacklustre motion pictures have, undoubtedly, more than compensated their producers for the now-immense cost of engaging superexpensive superstar Bronson—a member of that rather select multimillion-dollar star category, limited to those few whose box-office earning-power merits it.

Overseas, Bronson's 1971 *Soleil Rouge (Red Sun)* enjoyed a tremendous success not duplicated in the U.S., where its distributor (National General) was on the verge of folding. But the casting alone displays a cunning eye to international commerce, re-teaming Bronson with France's Alain Delon, bolstered by Japan's super-samurai-star Toshiro Mifune, and with the accented pulchritude of Switzerland's Ursula Andress and French-born Capucine. In Europe and the Orient, *Red Sun* won widespread approval from critics and audiences alike, topping all previous records for a Bronson film. Its first-run Tokyo engagement stretched to an all-time record of thirty-five weeks. In a 1975 interview with columnist Liz Smith, the actor named this film and *Rider on the Rain* as his personal favorites.

Chato's Land, the first of several pictures Bronson made with director Michael Winner, was completed just prior to the arrival of the actor's only child by Jill Ireland. Born on August 4, 1971, she was named Zuleika Jill, after the charismatic heroine of Max Beerbohm's novel, *Zuleika Dobson.* Three months after her arrival, the Bronsons purchased an unusual country retreat, an eigthteenth-century farmhouse on a 260-acre estate in West Windsor, Vermont—a suitable location for the antiques Charlie and Jill have collected in their around-the-world travels.

A London report now disclosed that a Reuters news agency poll of sixty countries had designated Charles Bronson as the world's most popular movie actor, bar none! Despite the star's somewhat uncertain status in the cinemas of his native land, his name was synonymous with "box-office" in Italy, France, Japan and South America. In the words of producer-director Michael Winner, Bronson was to the international film world "a totally bankable name."

With 1972's amoral crime melodrama, *The Mechanic,* produced and directed by Winner for the Dino De Laurentiis organization, the film's U.S. distributor United Artists realized the first real profit on a Bronson film in years. This was understandable, since none of the actor's recent movies had enjoyed widespread American distribution. Critics generally disliked *The Mechanic* and its "mindless" violence, but it was a cunningly devised escapist fantasy, and action-movie fans were suitably entertained. Which must have pleased Bronson.

In 1972, close on the heels of Francis Ford Coppola's immensely successful *The Godfather,* Dino De Laurentiis produced *The Valachi Papers,* like its predecessor a Mafia-oriented melodrama. In this case, however, its source was a true-life story, based on the revelations of a petty mobster named Joseph Valachi. But, unlike the fictional Coppola movie, *The Valachi Papers* named names, with the result that De Laurentiis, director Terence Young and company found the New York location filming so intimidating, rife with threats of mob violence, that they quickly repaired to Italy, where the film was completed.

The notion of portraying a real-life Mafioso who would age from his late teens to his early sixties undoubtedly seemed like a fascinating challenge to the actor. But accepting fifty-one-year-old Bronson as a youth was not within the grasp of 1972's critics, who also found the movie generally far below the production standards set forth by *The Godfather.* Nor did script

In *Chato's Land* (1972).

In *Red Sun* (1971).

or direction appear more than pedestrian, despite an earnest stab at characterization by Bronson, whose efforts went unappreciated by many of the reviewers. *The Valachi Papers* made a lot of money, probably due to its controversial subject matter promising an expose of actual organized crime, but again a Bronson vehicle had failed to make him a superstar in his native land.

Nevertheless, De Laurentiis now signed the actor to a contract that would pay him a million dollars for each of three movies. If the U.S. film industry was taken aback by this extreme act of faith, the overseas market accepted it matter-of-factly. In the Orient, Bronson vied with their own Toshiro Mifune as number-one box-office draw. On the Continent, he had no competition for first position. In Spain, he replaced bullfighter El Cordobes as their sex symbol supreme; and in South America, he was dubbed "the World's Sexiest Man." The actor's inscrutable physiognomy and muscular torso loomed large on displays atop foreign cinemas, accompanied by such fond nicknames as Italy's "Il Bruto" and France's "Le Monstre Sacre"—the ultimate tribute indeed.

This adulation confounded Bronson, who countered with "What the hell do they see in me?" He had become a wealthy superstar, almost in spite of himself, and the high-powered fame and acclaim was, for an actor in his fifties, so belated as to produce little more than a secretive smile and an analytic reaction: "I've never imagined young people seeing me as a sex symbol. I think they see me as a father figure. They know about my marriage to Jill, my happy home life, and my love of children. Perhaps I fill the void. Many parents have abdicated so many of their responsibilities towards raising children—maybe they make an idol of someone they feel can give them guidance." A puzzling self-appraisal? Perhaps. Especially in light of his next film. For, with its 1974 release, *Death Wish* (produced by De Laurentiis under the slightly less effective original title of *Sidewalk Vigilante*) finally made Charles Bronson's face, form and macho appeal as familiar to the mainstream of American moviegoers as they had long been elsewhere. His superstardom and his popularity were finally cemented in a highly controversial motion picture that sharply divided the critical fraternity, stirred up a storm of pro-and-con audience reaction and finally rewarded Dino De Laurentiis' faith in Bronson's U.S. potential. It also helped sell, in their

With director Don Siegel on the set of
Telefon (1977).

second-run engagements, a pair of recent but mediocre Bronson-De Laurentiis action features, *The Stone Killer* and *Mr. Majestyk.*

The controversy over *Death Wish* was simple. In it, Bronson portrayed a gentlemanly, upper-middle-class New Yorker whose comfortable life is shattered when three hoodlums invade his home and, in his absence, kill his wife and rape his married daughter, who becomes an institutionalized catatonic. Widower Bronson eventually becomes infamous as Manhattan's anonymous vigilante killer, a situation that evolves out of self-defense. At first, the realization of actually having taken another's life (even out of necessity) literally sickens Bronson. But the slaying of New York's (as here depicted, nearly overwhelming) criminal element becomes his obsessive mission and, neatly attired in suit, tie and overcoat, the man is soon a perfect decoy for every park prowler and subway mugger in the city. Bronson becomes New York's unknown avenger-hero—until a bloodhound-smart police inspector (Vincent Gardenia) uncovers the truth, which he keeps to himself, after informing his quarry that he'd better get himself transferred out of town. As the film concludes, Bronson arrives in Chicago to assume a new post. In the terminal, he witnesses hoodlums victimizing an innocent traveler, and, as they look back at Bronson in their laughing flight, he greets them with a smirk, his index finger in a gunlike gesture. A chillingly amusing finish to a realistic fantasy that must trigger an emotional response from almost every urbanite.

Few other films of the Seventies have enjoyed such consistent reports of cheering in a movie theatre as occurred on each occasion that vigilante Bronson shoots down one of the many knife-and-gun weilders who constantly pursue him in *Death Wish*. At the same time that one laughs in glee as another bad one is shot down frontier-outlaw style, one becomes fully aware of the bald outrageousness of it all. Wish-fulfillment rides high for the film's duration. But those who deplored the movie's power to incite violence-counter-violence seemed overreactive. No resultant urban epidemic of vigilante justice was recorded, although *Death Wish,* admittedly, struck a highly responsive chord everywhere. With its tremendous box-office popularity and emotional impact, *Death Wish* seems likely to be the one film with which Charles Bronson will always be most identified, at least by *American* moviegoers. But, in *all* of the world's film markets, this film was among 1974's most successful. In Tokyo, a billboard of his face stretched the length of a city block and three stories high.

Bronson evidenced surprise at all the commotion over this motion picture. "Violence doesn't pay," he told an interviewer after *Death Wish* burst upon the scene. "My movies show that. People think I'm super-violent, but that's not true."

In defense of *Death Wish,* producer De Laurentiis said, "In no way is the film an invitation to take to the streets with a gun. But it is an invitation—an open invitation to the authorities to come up with remedies to the problem of urban violence, and fast. I do not want people to become Paul Kerseys. I want the proper authorities to take care of the problem."

Nor did Bronson appear either arrogant or conceited with his new-found *American* celebrity status: "I don't let success go to my head. I still feel like the kid who grew up in the school of hard knocks. The bad thing about being famous is people notice you and point you out wherever you go. It scares the hell out of me."

Inevitably, Bronson was announced for prospective films that were never made, among them *Kyle* (for producer Arthur Jacobs), *Relentless* (for Hal Landers) and a remake of *The Last of the Mohicans* (for De Laurentiis). However, he continued to act in two or three movies for each of the next several years, most notably in the off-beat Depression-era street-fighter drama *Hard Times,* a change-of-pace role that won Bronson some critical acclaim, but no awards. To his credit, the actor made several serious attempts to stretch his conventional on-screen image with the black-comedy Western *From Noon Till Three,* as Wild Bill Hickok on a Moby Dickish mission in *The White Buffalo,* and as a neatly attired private-eye in *St. Ives.* But U.S. audiences seemed to prefer the more action-oriented Bronson of *Breakout, Telefon* and *Breakheart Pass.*

Following a surfeit of Bronson movies from 1974 through 1977, there now occurred an inexplicable drop-off in his output. And *Love and Bullets,* made for Britain's Sir Lew Grade and completed early in 1978, wasn't released until the spring of 1979—and then only in Europe—just as his subsequent film, *Cabo Blanco,* was being completed in Mexico. That autumn

Robert Aldrich was announced to direct Bronson and Lee Marvin in *Arctic Rampage,* an action-adventure drama to be shot in Canada, starting in February 1980. At the same time, Paul Kohner, Bronson's agent, was working to set up a motion-picture deal that would reunite the actor with a former co-star, Toshiro Mifune.

While Charles Bronson's undeniable talents continue to please a majority of filmgoers, he has yet to experience that combination of script and direction that might bring him an award for his acting. After some twenty-eight years in the business, his qualifications are beyond question. But will he ever enjoy the good fortune that brought belated Oscars to such rugged predecessors as Bogart, Wayne and Edward G. Robinson?

The late Tom Gries, who directed Bronson in the snowbound mystery-Western *Breakheart Pass,* once offered a wise assessment of his star's enduring appeal: "Charlie represents the quintessential male in the eyes of the audience. The women see strength and toughness mixed with tenderness, while the men see Charlie's power and his ability to prevail over any situation."

As for Bronson himself, his reflective summation is more pragmatic: "I'm only a product—like a cake of soap—to be sold as well as possible."

But, like many another stereotyped actor, he admits to one unfulfilled professional wish: "Some day I would like to have a part where I can lean my elbow against a mantelpiece and have a cocktail."

On the set of *Tennessee Champ* (1954).

The Films of
Charles Bronson

With Gary Cooper and Henry Slate.

U.S.S. Teakettle (You're in the Navy Now)

A 20th Century-Fox Film / 1951

CAST
Lt. John Harkness: Gary Cooper; *Ellie:* Jane Greer; *Larrabee:* Millard Mitchell; *Lt. Bill Barron:* Eddie Albert; *Commander Reynolds:* John McIntyre; *Admiral Tennant:* Ray Collins; *Captain Eliot:* Harry Von Zell; *Ensign Anthony Barbo:* Jack Webb; *Ensign Chuck Dorrance:* Richard Erdman; *Norelli:* Harvey Lembeck; *Chief Engineer Ryan:* Henry Slate; *Commander:* Ed Begley; *Battleship Admiral:* Fay Roope; *Houlihan:* Charles Tannen; *Wascylewski:* Charles Buchinski; *Morse:* Jack Warden; *Crew Members:* Ken Harvey, Lee Marvin, Jerry Hausner, Charles Smith; *Tug Boat Sailor:* Bernard Kates; *New Boy (Sailor):* James Cornell; *Shore Patrolmen:* Glen Gordon, Laurence Hugo; *Doctor:* Damian O'Flynn; *Sailor Messenger:* Biff McGuire; *Admiral's Aide:* Norman McKay; *Admiral's Wife:* Elsa Peterson; *Mess Boy:* Joel Fluellen; *Naval Captain:* Herman Canton; *Lt. Commander:* Rory Mallinson; *C.P.O.:* William Leicester; *Naval Officer:* Ted Stanhope.

CREDITS
Producer: Fred Kohlmar; *Director:* Henry Hathaway; *Screenwriter:* Richard Murphy; *Based on an Article in the* New Yorker *by:* John W. Hazard; *Cinematographer:* Joe MacDonald; *Art Directors:* Lyle Wheeler, J. Russell Spencer; *Set Decorators:* Thomas Little, Fred J. Rode; *Special Effects:* Fred Sersen, Ray Kellogg; *Musical Score:* Cyril Mockridge; *Editor:* James B. Clark; *Technical Adviser:* Joseph Warren Lomax, U.S.N. *Running Time:* 93 minutes.

THE FILM
The naval comedy called *U.S.S. Teakettle* was the first of sixteen movies that Bronson would film under the name of Charles Buchinski —or "Buchinsky," as the spelling appeared to vary from picture to picture. Although it was released to favorable reviews, neither they nor Gary Cooper's starring name managed to draw moviegoers, and 20th Century-Fox wasted little time in devising a new sales campaign, as well

as a new and more commercial title, *You're in the Navy Now*. No longer would there be doubt as to its genre.

The film was released in February of 1951. Only a year earlier, Bronson had been newly enrolled as a first-year student at the Pasadena Playhouse. Aged twenty-nine and married, he was then as atypical as an aspiring movie actor could be, with his homely prizefighter's face and unrefined speech. But the Playhouse staff was apparently impressed with his presence, for they gave him roles no first-year student had reason to hope for—like the lead in *Command Decision*, an all-male war play.

Eight months after Bronson's admission to the Playhouse, they were contacted by Hollywood agent Gus Demling, who was trying to cast a film role with a difficult requisite—an actor who would resemble "a cross between Humphrey Bogart and John Garfield." Charles Buchinsky was thus sent to audition for director Henry Hathaway.

His face helped secure him the part. And since it was that of a Polish-American sailor called "Wascylewski," the name Buchinsky was hardly a deterrent. Nor were the requirements that he be able to box—and belch on cue. This modest black-and-white World War II comedy accorded the novice film actor fifteenth

place in its cast list and gave him several scenes with Gary Cooper, who portrayed the inexperienced skipper of a problem-plagued patrol craft manned by "90-day wonders." For Buchinsky, it was a good movieland beginning. The film required little of him but his natural presence, and it got him noticed by the press, as well as the moviemaking community. After its release, *U.S.S. Teakettle* brought the actor enough small-part film offers to make him decide to leave the Pasadena Playhouse and settle in Hollywood.

In this film's supporting cast, it's interesting to note the name of another non-glamor-boy "character actor," destined, like Bronson, for belated stardom—Lee Marvin.

CRITICS' CORNER
"Mr. Hathaway has a wonderfully able cast, headed up by Gary Cooper as the skipper of the teakettle tub. As assorted crew members of the bucket, Jack Warden, Harvey Lembeck, Henry Slate, Charles Tannen and Charles Buchinski deserve particular mention here. Through 20th Century-Fox, which made this sparkler, they are contributing the best comedy of the year."
Bosley Crowther, *The New York Times*

With Damian O'Flynn, Gary Cooper, Richard Erdman, Jack Webb and Eddie Albert.

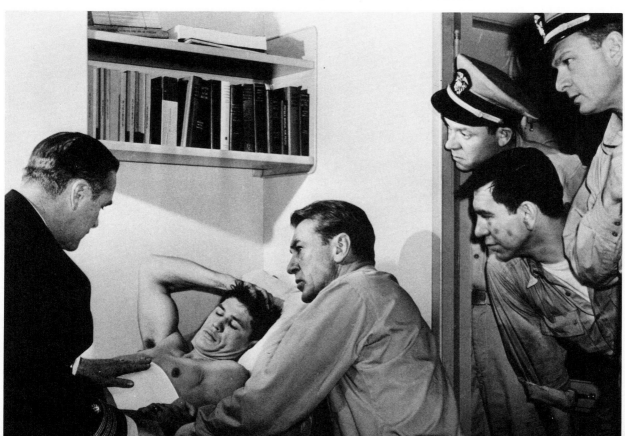

With Richard Bartlett, Spencer Tracy, Bill Fletcher, Peter Mamakos, Celia Lovsky, and Lawrence Tolan.

The People Against O'Hara

A Metro-Goldwyn-Mayer Picture / 1951

CAST
James P. Curtayne: Spencer Tracy; *Virginia Curtayne:* Diana Lynn; *Vince Ricks:* Pat O'Brien; *Louis Barra:* John Hodiak; *Knuckles Lanzetta:* Eduardo Ciannelli; *John O'Hara:* James Arness; *Frankie Korvac:* William Campbell; *Sven Norson:* Jay C. Flippen; *Carmilita Lanzetta:* Yvette Duguay; *Jeff Chapman:* Richard Anderson; *Judge Keating:* Henry O'Neill; *Mr. O'Hara:* Arthur Shields; *Mrs. O'Hara:* Louise Lorimer; *Betty Clark:* Ann Doran; *Capt. Tom Mulvaney:* Emile Meyer; *Fred Colton:* Regis Toomey; *Mrs. Sheffield:* Katherine Warren; *Howie Pendleton:* Paul Bryar; *James Korvac:* Peter Mamakos; *Gloria Adler:* Perdita Chandler; *Al:* Frank Ferguson; *Monty:* Don Dillaway; *George:* C. Anthony Hughes; *Emmet Kimbaugh:* Lee Phelps; *Vince Korvac:* Lawrence Tolan; *Clerk:* Jack Lee; *Little Wolfie:* Tony Barr; *Girls:* Jay Kayne, Virginia Hewitt; *Sailor:* Richard Landry; *Judge:* Ned Glass; *Angelo Korvac:* Charles Buchinski; *Mrs. Korvac:* Celia Lovsky; *Receptionist:* Mae Clarke; *Uniformed Detective:* Jack Kruschen.

CREDITS
Producer: William H. Wright; *Director:* John Sturges; *Assistant Director:* Herbert Glazer; *Screenwriter:* John Monks, Jr.; *Based on the Novel by:* Eleazar Lipsky; *Cinematographer:* John Alton; *Art Directors:* Cedric Gibbons, James Basevi; *Set Decorators:* Edwin B. Willis, Jacque Mapes; *Special Effects:* A. Arnold Gillespie, Warren Newcombe; *Musical Score:* Carmen Dragon; *Editor:* Gene Ruggiero.
Running Time: 102 minutes.

THE FILM
Bit parts would frequently be Bronson's lot during the first two years of his movie career. In this 1951 Spencer Tracy vehicle, the novice was again acting with one of the giants of the business—and under the direction of John Sturges, who would later put Bronson to better use in *Never So Few, The Magnificent Seven* and *The Great Escape.* But in *The People Against O'Hara* Bronson was little more than set-dressing as a member of the blue-collar family that criminal lawyer Tracy visits during his investigation of a murder case.

CRITICS' CORNER
"The picture is a curiously old-fashioned courtroom drama with the star portraying a criminal lawyer who against all odds manages to save an innocent boy from the chair. The studio has padded the proceedings with an interesting cast—and a half-dozen competent bit players. John Sturges' smooth and level-handed direction is all that could be asked."

Howard Thompson, *The New York Times*

Broderick Crawford and Richard Kiley.

The Mob

A Columbia Picture / 1951

CAST
Johnny Damico: Broderick Crawford; *Mary Kiernan:* Betty Buehler; *Thomas Clancy:* Richard Kiley; *Lt. Banks:* Otto Hulett; *Smoothie:* Matt Crowley; *Gunner:* Neville Brand; *Joe Castro:* Ernest Borgnine; *Sgt. Bennion:* Walter Klavun; *Peggy:* Lynne Baggett; *Doris:* Jean Alexander; *Police Commissioner:* Ralph Dumke; *Tony:* John Marley; *Culio:* Frank de Kova; *Russell:* Jay Adler; *Radford:* Duke Watson; *Gas Station Attendant:* Emile Meyer; *District Attorney:* Carleton Young; *Plainclothesman:* Fred Coby; *Police Officer:* Ric Roman; *Talbert:* Michael McHale; *Paul:* Kenneth Harvey; *Bruiser:* Don Megowan; *Gunman:* Robert Foulk; *Joe:* Al Mellon; *Cigar Store Owner:* Joe De Leo; *Crew Member:* Ernie Venneri; *Mate:* Robert Anderson; *Officer:* Art Millan; *Chauffeur:* Richard Irving; *Fred:* Peter Prouse; *Policemen:* Sidney Mason, David McMahon; *Mason:* Jess Kirkpatrick; *Jack:* Charles Buchinski; *Nurses:* Mary Alan Hokanson, Virginia Chapman; *Daniels:* Harry Lauter.

CREDITS
Producer: Jerry Bresler; *Director:* Robert Parrish; *Screenwriter:* William Bowers; *Based on the* Collier's *magazine story* "Waterfront" *by:* Ferguson Findley; *Cinematographer:* Joseph Walker; *Art Director:* Cary Odell; *Musical Score:* George Duning; *Editor:* Charles Nelson. *Running Time:* 87 minutes.

THE FILM
This well-made little gangland melodrama, with Broderick Crawford (an Oscar winner two years earlier for *All the King's Men*) as an undercover detective on the trail of a waterfront mobster, again relegated Bronson to the bottom of the cast list in a bit role that made him virtually blend with the movie's seamily realistic backgrounds. It all marked his initial alliance with the element with which his career would eventually become nearly synonymous — violence.

CRITICS' CORNER
"A bold melodrama, it makes no attempt to be pretty, and its violence is as exciting and as fast-paced as you could ask for. But even with a stereotyped tale, the cast and the director managed to come out head and shoulders above any other crime films around town. What it offers, precisely, is an hour and a half of physical mayhem, served up hot with pistols and blackjacks."

Oscar Godbout, *The New York Times*

Aldo Ray and Judy Holliday.

The Marrying Kind

A Columbia Picture / 1952

CAST
Florence Keefer: Judy Holliday; *Chet Keefer:* Aldo Ray; *Judge Carroll:* Madge Kennedy; *Joan Shipley:* Sheila Bond; *Howard Shipley:* John Alexander; *George Bastian:* Rex Williams; *Mrs. Derringer:* Phyllis Povah; *Emily Bundy:* Peggy Cass; *Pat Bundy:* Mickey Shaughnessy; *Charley:* Griff Barnett; *Ellen:* Susan Hallaran; *Joey, Age 4:* Barry Curtis; *Joey Age 6:* Christie Olsen; *Newhouse:* Wallace Acton; *Marian:* Elsie Holmes; *Dancer:* Joan Shawlee; *Mr. Jenner:* Thomas B. Henry; *Mr. Quinn:* Frank Ferguson; *Roy:* Don Mahin; *Benny:* Larry Blake; *Cliff:* Tom Farrell; *Steve:* Gordon Jones; *Minister:* John Eliott; *Bus Driver:* Joe McGuinn; *Lawyer:* Richard Gordon; *Child:* Patrick Butler; *Charlotte:* Malan Mills; *Eddie:* Charles Buchinski; *Edie:* Nancy Kulp; *Musicians:* Robert Hartley, Charles Brewer, Johnnie Kiado.

CREDITS
Producer: Bert Granet; *Director:* George Cukor; *Screenwriters:* Ruth Gordon, Garson Kanin; *Cinematographer:* Joseph Walker; *Art Director:* John Meehan; *Set Decorator:* William Kiernan; *Musical Score:* Hugo Friedhofer; *Editor:* Charles Nelson.
Running Time: 93 minutes.

THE FILM
This realistic comedy-drama, extensively punctuated with flashbacks and dream sequences, served to unite director George Cukor with his Oscar-winning *Born Yesterday* star, Judy Holliday, in the story of a failing marriage. It also marked the promising leading-man debut of Aldo Ray, as the husband.

Parts of the film were shot on location in New York City.

In perhaps the briefest role of his film career, Bronson flashed by as "Eddie," a fellow worker in the post office that employs Ray.

CRITICS' CORNER
"The simple domestic problems of a young married couple in New York . . . have been treated with cheerfulness and wisdom in the clever and facile script Ruth Gordon and Garson Kanin have written. And the wonderfully fluent talents of that grand actress, Judy Holliday, and an equally potent new actor by the name of Aldo Ray have been put by director George Cukor to the incarnation of this script into what will undoubtedly stand up as one of the happiest entertainments of the year."

Bosley Crowther, *The New York Times*

With Robert Osterloh, Henry Kulky, Warren Stevens, Larry Dobkin, Richard Widmark, Ann Morrison, and bit players.

Red Skies of Montana (Smoke Jumpers)

A 20th Century-Fox Film / 1952
In Technicolor

CAST
Cliff Mason: Richard Widmark; *Peg:* Constance Smith; *Ed Miller:* Jeffrey Hunter; *Dryer:* Richard Boone; *Steve:* Warren Stevens; *Boise:* James Griffith; *Pop Miller:* Joe Sawyer; *Randy:* Gregory Wolcott; *Noxon:* Richard Crenna; *Felton:* Bob Nichols; *Piney:* Ralph Reed; *Winkler:* William Murphy; *Neff:* Charles Buchinsky; *Spotter:* Larry Dobkin; *McMullen:* Robert Adler; *Kenner:* Mike Mahoney; *Lewisohn:* John Close; *Sabinson:* Grady Galloway; *Dawson:* Henry Kulky; *Philippe:* Harry Carter; *Pilot:* Charles Tannen; *Grayson:* Ron Hargrave; *Dispatcher:* Robert Osterloh; *Foreman:* Ted Ryan; *Telegraph Operator:* John Kennedy; *Doctor:* Parley Baer; *Nurse:* Barbara Woodell; *Inspectors:* Ray Hyke, Wilson Hood; *Mrs. Miller:* Ann Morrison.

CREDITS
Producer: Samuel G. Engel; *Director:* Joseph M. Newman; *Screenwriter:* Harry Kleiner; *Based on a Story by:* Art Cohn; *Cinematographer:* Charles G. Clarke; *Art Directors:* Lyle Wheeler, Chester Gore; *Set Decorator:* Thomas Little; *Musical Score:* Sol Kaplan; *Editor:* William Reynolds. *Running Time:* 89 minutes.

THE FILM
Bronson returned to 20th Century-Fox, the scene of his movie debut, for another bit role in a second male-oriented story, *Red Skies of Montana,* his first color film. This time the milieu was that of the smoke-jumping U.S. Forestry Service firefighters whose dangerous profession centers on the timberlands of the American Northwest. In the film's leading roles were Richard Widmark and Richard Boone, the studio's tough action performers of the early fifties, and handsome, blue-eyed young Jeffrey Hunter—in 1952, as likely a prospect for glamour stardom as Bronson/Buchinsky appeared set for a career of pug-ugly, supporting character roles. And again Bronson helped decorate the mountain wilderness location settings with his steely-eyed macho image, while rubbing shoulders with, and learning the working habits of, some of Hollywood's top professionals.

But Fox executives appeared nervous about *Red Skies of Montana,* a title more suggestive of a Roy Rogers-Dale Evans Western than the very respectable action-adventure yarn offered here. In some areas, they called it *Smoke Jumpers,* a no-nonsense title under which *The New York Times* ran its review.

CRITICS' CORNER
"Richard Widmark, Jeffrey Hunter, Constance Smith and a handful of Fox contract players are marking time—and how!—in a story by Art Cohn that has the two men feuding in a training station for firefighters. The others stand around and watch and a few random fires smolder, for the most part, in the distance (beyond the budget, we suspect)."

Howard Thompson, *The New York Times*

35

With Frank Mitchell, Dick Curtis, John Beal, and bit players.

My Six Convicts

A Columbia Picture / 1952

CAST

James Connie: Millard Mitchell; *Punch Pinero:* Gilbert Roland; *Doc:* John Beal; *Blivens Scott:* Marshall Thompson; *Clem Randall:* Alf Kjellin; *Dawson:* Henry Morgan; *Steve Kopac:* Jay Adler; *Dr. Gordon:* Regis Toomey; *Warden Potter:* Fay Roope; *Capt. Haggerty:* Carleton Young; *Knotty Johnson:* John Marley; *Dr. Hughes:* Russ Conway; *Doc Brint:* Byron Foulger; *Jocko:* Charles Buchinsky; *Higgins:* Jack Carr; *Mrs. Randall:* Carol Savage; *Convicts:* Peter Virgo, George Eldredge, Paul Hoffman, Dick Cogan, Allen Mathews, H. George Stern, Danny Jackson, Joe Haworth, Chester Jones, Vincent Renno, Frank Mitchell; *Big Benny:* Joe McTurk; *Banker:* Harry Stanton; *Store Detective:* Fred Kelsey; *Guard on Dump Truck:* Edwin Parker; *Convict Driver:* Joe Palma; *Baker Foreman:* Barney Philips; *Guards:* Dick Curtis, John Monaghan.

CREDITS

Producer: Stanley Kramer; *Director:* Hugo Fregonese; *Screenwriter:* Michael Blankfort; *Based on a Story by:* Donald Powell Wilson; *Cinematographer:* Guy Roe; *Art Director:* Edward

Ilou; *Musical Score:* Dimitri Tiomkin; *Editor:* Gene Havlick.
Running Time: 104 minutes.

THE FILM
This respectable little prison drama was produced with an eye to 1950's "authenticity" (utilizing San Quentin locations) by Stanley Kramer, who had been steadily building a socially-responsible Hollywood reputation with such down-to-earth, semidocumentary subject matter as *Home of the Brave, Champion* and *The Men.*

The focus here is on Doc (John Beal), a young psychologist, who recalls his experiences with the inmates of "Harbor State Prison," a fictitious stand-in for Leavenworth, the actual locale of Donald Powell Wilson's published memoir.

Coming fourteenth in the movie's cast list, Bronson lends a tough, understandably authentic presence to the prison yard, but his role is minimal and his utterances are confined to a few terse comments and wisecracks. Nor is he even one of the titled half-dozen cons to whose reform potential the Beal character devotes his energies.

CRITICS' CORNER
". . . penology, psychology and crime have been blended into a compassionate, thoughtful, incisive and, above all, genuinely humorous account of life behind prison walls."
        A. H. Weiler, *The New York Times*

With John Marley.

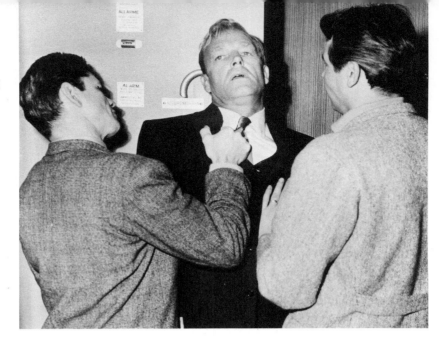

With James Millican and Michael Ansara.

Diplomatic Courier

A 20th Century-Fox Film   /   1952

CAST

Mike Kells: Tyrone Power; *Joan Ross:* Patricia Neal; *Col. Cagle:* Stephen McNally: *Janine:* Hildegarde Neff; *Ernie:* Karl Malden; *Sam Carew:* James Millican; *Platov:* Stefan Schnabel; *Arnov:* Herbert Berghof; *Max Ralli:* Arthur Blake; *Airline Stewardess:* Helene Stanley; *Ivan:* Michael Ansara; *Chef de Train:* Sig Arno; *Cherenko:* Alfred Linder; *M.P. at Trieste:* Lee Marvin; *Watch Officer:* Tyler McVey; *Zinski:* Peter Coe; *Intelligence Clerk:* Dabbs Greer; *Brennan:* Carleton Young; *French Ticket Agent:* Charles La Torre; *Cherney:* Tom Powers; *French Stewardess:* Monique Chantal; *Jacks:* Lumsden Hare; *Bill:* Russ Conway; *Russians:* Charles Buchinski, Mario Siletti.

CREDITS

Producer: Casey Robinson; *Director:* Henry Hathaway; *Screenwriters:* Casey Robinson, Liam O'Brien; *Based on the Novel* Sinister Errand *by:* Peter Cheyney; *Cinematographer:* Lucien Ballard; *Art Directors:* Lyle Wheeler, John De Cuir; *Set Decorators:* Thomas Little, Stuart Reiss; *Musical Score:* Sol Kaplan; *Special Effects:* Ray Kellogg; *Editor:* James B. Clark; *Narrator:* Hugh Marlowe.
Running Time: 97 minutes.

THE FILM

Among the mediocre films that 20th Century-Fox's handsome contract star Tyrone Power was assigned in the early 1950's was this confused and confusing spy tale about a U.S. State Department messenger in Trieste to uncover the Russians' secret timetable for their invasion of Yugoslavia.

Bronson's bit role here is as one of the two Soviet hit-men who, aboard a Continental train, quite successfully silence Carew (James Millican), the American ambassador to Bucharest, before he can transmit an important document to courier Power. Bronson's grim Slavic countenance was, of course, visually perfect casting for the part.

CRITICS' CORNER

"The fault seems to lie in the writing. Casey Robinson and Liam O'Brien, who did the script from a novel by Peter Cheyney, have assembled an impressive array of melodramatic occurrences. But they haven't concocted a story that has clarity and suspense, and Mr. Hathaway hasn't been able to direct it so that it looks like anything on the screen."

Bosley Crowther, *The New York Times*

With Spencer Tracy, Katharine Hepburn and George Mathews.

Pat and Mike

A Metro-Goldwyn-Mayer Picture   /   1952

CAST

Mike Conovan: Spencer Tracy; *Pat Pemberton:* Katharine Hepburn; *Davie Hucko:* Aldo Ray; *Collier Weld:* William Ching; *Barney Grau:* Sammy White; *Spec Cauley:* George Mathews; *Mr. Beminger:* Loring Smith; *Mrs. Beminger:* Phyllis Povah; *Hank Tasling:* Charles Buchinski; *Sam Garsell:* Frank Richards; *Charles Barry:* Jim Backus; *Police Captain:* Chuck Connors; *Harry McWade:* Owen McGiveney; *Waiter:* Lou Lubin; *Bus Boy:* Carl Switzer; *Pat's Caddy:* William Self; *Caddies:* Billy McLean, Frankie Darro, Paul Brinegar, "Tiny" Jimmie Kelly; *Women Golfers:* Mae Clarke, Elizabeth Holmes, Helen Eby-Rock; *Commentator:* Hank Weaver; *Sportscaster:* Tom Harmon; *Line Judge:* Charlie Murray; *Themselves:* Don Budge, Helen Dettweiler, Betty Hicks, Beverly Hanson, Babe Didrikson Zaharias, Gussie Moran, Alice Marble, Frank Parker; *Reporters:* Kay English, Jerry Schumacher, Sam Pierce, Bill Lewin, A. Cameron Grant; *Troopers:* John Close, Fred Coby, Russ Clark; *Shooting Gallery Proprietors:* Tom Gibson, Kay Deslys; *Tennis Players:* Barbara Kimbrell, Elinor Cushingham; *Railway Conductor:* Louis Mason; *Linesman:* King Mojave; *Chairman:* Frank Sucack; *Tennis Umpire:* Crauford Kent; *Lawyer:* Sam Hearn.

CREDITS

Producer: Lawrence Weingarten; *Director:* George Cukor; *Assistant Director:* Jack Greenwood; *Screenwriters:* Ruth Gordon, Garson Kanin; *Cinematographer:* William Daniels; *Art Directors:* Cedric Gibbons, Urie McCleary; *Set Decorators:* Edwin B. Willis, Hugh Hunt; *Musical Score:* David Raskin; *Special Effects:* Warren Newcombe; *Editor:* George Boemler.
Running Time: 95 minutes.

THE FILM

Brief as had been his bit in director George Cukor's *The Marrying Kind,* Bronson had impressed himself upon the famed director with his tough, sinister visage. Which resulted in his being cast for the role of the Runyonesque thug Hank Tasling in *Pat and Mike,* the sports-oriented 1952 comedy that reunited the incomparable team of Spencer Tracy and Katharine Hepburn for the seventh time.

In an ill-fitting gray suit and fedora, Bronson finally had a character role in which he could really impress, handling the Garson Kanin-Ruth Gordon dialogue with a natural skill that perfectly satirized the gangster-film genre. With poker face and sandpaper voice, he proudly held his own in the formidable company of Tracy and Hepburn—even neatly dispatched by the latter in a hilariously unexpected show of Judo.

The "Buchinski" billing isn't very prominent in *Pat and Mike's* credits list, but his several scenes made their mark on the critics, as well as the movie's considerable audiences.

CRITICS' CORNER

". . . it is smoothly directed by George Cukor and slyly, amusingly played by the whole cast, especially by its duo of easy, adroit, experienced stars.

"George Mathews and Charles Buchinski are also fun as 'the kind of types that have been known to act very hot-headed in their day and age.'"

Bosley Crowther, *The New York Times*

With Wally Vernon, Scott Brady,
Edwin Max, and George E. Stone.

Bloodhounds of Broadway

A 20th Century-Fox Film / 1952
In Technicolor

CAST
Emly Ann Stackerlee: Mitzi Gaynor; *Robert "Numbers" Foster:* Scott Brady; *Tessie Sammis:* Mitzi Green; *Yvonne:* Marguerite Chapman; *Inspector McNamara:* Michael O'Shea; *Poorly Sammis:* Wally Vernon; *Dave, the Dude:* Henry Slate; *Ropes McGonigle:* George E. Stone; *Look-out Louie:* Edwin Max; *Curtaintime Charlie:* Richard Allan; *Little Elida:* Sharon Baird; *Frankie Ferraccio:* Ralph Volkie; *Pittsburgh Philo:* Charles Buchinski; *Crockett Pace:* Timothy Carey; *Uncle Old Fella:* William (Bill) Walker; *Theo Pace:* Paul Wexler; *Foy Pace:* Alfred Mizner; *Skipper:* Emile Meyer.

CREDITS
Producer: George Jessel; *Director:* Harmon Jones; *Assistant Director:* Stanley Hough; *Screenwriter:* Sy Gomberg; *Based on a Story by:* Damon Runyon; *Adaptation:* Albert Mannheimer; *Cinematographer:* Edward Cronjager; *Art Directors:* Lyle Wheeler, J. Russell Spencer; *Songs:* Eliot Daniel, Ben Oakland, Paul Webster; *Musical Director:* Lionel Newman; *Musical Settings:* Joseph C. Wright; *Musical Numbers Directed by:* Robert Sidney; *Editor:* George A. Gittens.
Running Time: 90 minutes.

THE FILM
Damon Runyon's writings once had quite an influence on Hollywood writers and producers, from 1933's *Lady for a Day* to the 1956 Marlon Brando-Frank Sinatra film version of Broadway's musical hit, *Guys and Dolls.* In 1952, George Jessel produced an unpretentious, original screen musical oddly entitled *Bloodhounds of Broadway,* based on a Runyon story and designed to help 20th Century-Fox's singing-dancing starlet, Mitzi Gaynor, on her way to becoming the TV and night-club musical star she remains.

By this time, Bronson was all too obvious a choice to populate the cast of any tale about gangsters, whether funny or serious. And so we have him present in *Bloodhounds of Broadway,* not singing or dancing but offering deadpan humorous support to the bottom half of the cast roster as a character bearing the typically Runyonesque name of "Pittsburgh Philo." And, although the actor has his amusing moments, the movie is not in the same league with *Pat and Mike.*

CRITICS' CORNER
"Whether Damon Runyon cultists will recognize the master's genuine touch in the film version of *Bloodhounds of Broadway* is a matter of some conjecture. What 20th Century-Fox has done to turn Mr. Runyon's obscure fiction into the stuff of a musical film is obviously not calculated to preserve the late writer's racy style."

Bosley Crowther, *The New York Times*

Red Skelton, Billy Barty, and Tim Considine.

The Clown

A Metro-Goldwyn-Mayer Picture / 1953

CAST

Dodo Delwyn: Red Skelton; *Dink Delwyn:* Tim Considine; *Paula Henderson:* Jane Greer; *Goldie:* Loring Smith; *Ralph Z. Henderson:* Philip Ober; *Little Julie:* Lou Lubin; *Dr. Strauss:* Fay Roope; *Joe Hoagley:* Walter Reed; *Television Director:* Edward Marr; *Floor Director:* Jonathan Cott; *Gallagher:* Don Beddoe; *Young Man:* Steve Forrest; *Danny Dayler:* Ned Glass; *Maitre D'Hotel:* Steve Carruthers; *Midget:* Billy Barty; *Girl:* Lucille Knoch; *Silvio:* David Saber; *Bunny:* Sandra Gould; *Dundee:* Gil Perkins; *Herman:* Danny Richards, Jr.; *Lefty:* Mickey Little; *Jackson:* Charles Calvert; *Blonde:* Karen Steele; *Twins:* Jack Heasley, Bob Heasley; *Miss Batson:* Helene Millard; *Pawnbroker:* Forrest Lewis; *Eddie:* Charles Buchinsky; *Al Zerney:* Robert Ford; *Counterman:* John McKee; *Women:* Jan Wayne, Vici Raaf; *Sergeant:* Jesse Kirkpatrick; *Neighbor:* Martha Wentworth; *Secretary:* Inge Jolles; *Hogarth:* Harry Staton; *Judy:* Linda Bennett; *Wardrobe Man:* Wilson Wood; *Charlie:* Frank Nelson; *Clancy:* Thomas Dillon; *Young Man:* Paul Raymond; *Men:* James Horan, Al Freeman; *Vendor:* Tom Urray; *Heavy Girl:* Mary Foran; *Girl:* Sharon Saunders; *TV Page Boy:* David Blair; *Stagehand:* Brick Sullivan; *Makeup Man:* Cy Stevens; *Mr. Christenson:* G. Pat Collins; *Mrs. Blotto:* Shirley Mitchell; *Counterman:* Robert R. Stephenson; *Ad-Libbers:* Jimmie Thompson, Allen O'Locklin, Tony Merill; *Dice Players:* Al Hill, Jerry Schumacher, Barry Regan; *George:* Lennie Bremen; *Sergeant:* Lee Phelps; *Attendants:* Joe Evans, Walter Ridge, George Boyce, Donald Kerr, Mickey Golden; *Man with Hogarth:* Roger Moore; *Dancers:* Jules Brock, Eve Martell, Neva Martell.

CREDITS

Producer: William H. Wright; *Director:* Robert Z. Leonard; *Screenwriter:* Martin Rackin; *Based on the 1931 movie "The Champ," written by:* Leonard Praskins and Frances Marion; *Cinematographer:* Paul C. Vogel; *Art Directors:* Cedric Gibbons, Wade B. Rubottom; *Musical Score:* David Rose; *Editor:* Gene Ruggiero. *Running Time:* 92 minutes.

THE FILM

Comedian Red Skelton's career as an MGM star was very much on the wane, prior to his television hedyday, when this remake of the Wallace Beery-Jackie Cooper hit, *The Champ* (1931), was released early in 1953. But its story, about a once-great Ziegfeld star reduced to playing fairground clowns because of his addiction to gambling and alcohol, proved an unwise choice for funnyman Skelton, whose fans weren't ready for a tearjerker about a dying father's soap-operatic relationship with his little boy.

Bronson's brief appearance here occurs in a garage where he shoots craps—and a few lines of dialogue—with Skelton's compulsive gambler.

CRITICS' CORNER

"This is the poor man's *Limelight*. It takes most of the principal dramatic elements in Chaplin's picture and proceeds to demonstrate how not to handle them. Sentimentality in its sloppiest form abounds. This is not good Skelton."

Monthly Film Bulletin

With Vincent Price and Paul Cavanagh.

House of Wax

A Warner Bros. Picture / 1953
In Natural Vision 3-Dimension and WarnerColor

CAST
Prof. Henry Jarrod: Vincent Price; *Lt. Tom Brennan:* Frank Lovejoy; *Sue Allen:* Phyllis Kirk; *Cathy Gray:* Carolyn Jones; *Scott Andrews:* Paul Picerni; *Matthew Burke:* Roy Roberts; *Mrs. Andrews:* Angela Clarke; *Sidney Wallace:* Paul Cavanagh; *Igor:* Charles Buchinsky; *Leon Averill:* Ned Young; *Sgt. Jim Shane:* Dabbs Greer; *Barker:* Reggie Rymal; *Bruce Allison:* Philip Tonge.

CREDITS
Producer: Bryan Foy; *Director:* Andre de Toth; *Screenwriter:* Crane Wilbur; *Based on a Story by:* Charles Belden; *Cinematographers:* Bert Glennon, Peverell Marley; *"Natural Vision" Supervisor:* M. L. Gunsburg; *Art Director:* Stanley Fleischer; *Musical Score:* David Buttolph; *Editor:* Rudi Fehr.
Running Time: 88 minutes.

THE FILM
In the early 1950s, television's inroads into stealing away Hollywood's motion-picture audiences were sufficient to warrant developing means of retaliation. One of these was 3-Dimensional movies, inaugurated by *Bwana Devil* (1953), an inferior safari adventure in color. This was closely followed by the minor black-and-white thriller called *Man in the Dark.* In the former, spears and wild animals "attacked" the film's patrons, who were obliged to wear uncomfortable cardboard spectacle-frames outfitted with red-and-blue polaroid lenses.

With the opening of *House of Wax,* in April of 1953, the critical consensus was that it was 3-D's finest hour to date. Faint praise, in light of that film's low-grade predecessors.

For *House of Wax,* Warner Bros. resuscitated a familiar horror-movie plot from the *Phantom of the Opera* school: an innocent man loses his immediate livelihood—and his sanity—in a terrible fire, which not only scars him horribly but makes of him a homicidal maniac. Ultimately, he's unmasked by a potential (female, of course) victim who's rescued in the nick of time. And the villain meets his death.

Warners filmed it first in 1932 as *The Mystery of the Wax Museum,* employing primitive, two-color Technicolor and offsetting the story's thrills with an irritating reliance on wisecracking "comedy relief." Although this was wisely omitted with its 1953 resurrection as *House of Wax,* the basic plot was now padded out, in the interests of three-dimensional gimmickery, with can-can girls and bouncing paddle-balls. Nonetheless, the movie remains a fairly exciting thriller of its kind, even as seen, necessarily without its extra visual attractions, on contemporary TV.

Bronson received only ninth billing in this popular thriller, but his background role is as colorfully sinister as it is amusing. And, as "Igor," the deaf-mute assistant to the story's murderous central figure (portrayed with hammy relish by Vincent Price), Bronson is an arresting figure of menace, with his close-cropped Neanderthalian appearance, slit-eyed, stony mask of a face and muscular torso.

Whether disposing of unwanted intruders behind the scenes of the museum (where the waxen images are actually wax-coated corpses) or carrying out the nefarious orders of his suave employer, Bronson makes an arresting impression here. Especially memorable is that sequence in which he stalks the film's suspicious heroine (Phyllis Kirk) through the deserted museum, lending his primitive features to such hokum as posing (quite effectively) among a shelf-full of wax heads, contributing a wonderfully amusing bit of scary fun.

For Buchinsky/Bronson, *House of Wax* remains a milestone, the earliest performance for which he is well remembered. For Vincent Price, it opened a whole new career of elegant menace, type-casting him to new heights of fame and fortune.

CRITICS' CORNER
"A synthetic spine-chiller."
The New York Daily News
"What hath the Warner Brothers wrought? For this mixture of antique melodrama, three-dimensional photography, ghoulish sensationalism and so-called directed sound (which means noises coming at you from all parts of the theatre) raises so many serious questions of achievement and responsibility that a friend of the motion picture medium has ample reason to be baffled and concerned."
Bosley Crowther, *The New York Times*

With Phyllis Kirk.

Miss Sadie Thompson

A Beckworth Corporation Production / 1953
A Columbia Picture
In 3-D and Technicolor

CAST

Sadie Thompson: Rita Hayworth; *Alfred Davidson:* Jose Ferrer; *Sgt. Phil O'Hara:* Aldo Ray; *Dr. Robert MacPhail:* Russell Collins; *Ameena Horn:* Diosa Costello; *Joe Horn:* Harry Bellaver; *Governor:* Wilton Graff; *Mrs. Margaret Davidson:* Peggy Converse; *Griggs:* Henry Slate; *Hodges:* Rudy Bond; *Edwards:* Charles Buchinsky; *Mrs. MacPhail:* Frances Morris; *Chung:* Peter Chong; *Reverend:* John Grossett; *Marines:* Billy Varga, Teddy Pavelec, Frank Stanlow, Harold T. Hart, Ben Harris, Ted Jordan, Eduardo Cansino, Jr., John Duncan; *Native Children:* Clifford Botelho, Erlynn Botelho, Elizabeth Bartilet, Dennis Medieros; *Dispatcher:* Robert C. Anderson; *Native:* Joe McCabe; *Secretary:* Al Kikume; *Messenger:* Fred Letuli.

CREDITS

Producer: Jerry Wald; *Director:* Curtis Bernhardt; *Assistant Director:* Sam Nelson; *Screenwriter:* Harry Kleiner; *Based on W. Somerset Maugham's story "Miss Thompson," and "Rain," the dramatization by* John Colton and Clemence Randolph; *Cinematographer:* Charles Lawton, Jr.; *Art Director:* Carl Anderson; *Set Decorator:* Louis Diage; *Musical Score:* George Duning; *Songs by:* Lester Lee, Ned Washington, Allan Roberts; *Vocals for Rita Hayworth Sung by:* Jo Ann Greer; *Choreographer:* Lee Scott; *Editor:* Viola Lawrence. *Running Time:* 91 minutes.

THE FILM

The oft-told tale of South Seas harlot Sadie Thompson, W. Somerset Maugham's vivid 1920s literary creation, reached the screen for the third time in 1953, as impersonated by fading sex goddess Rita Hayworth. Unexpectedly, she brought to this meaty role (a challenge, even in this watered-down version), a fiery spirit and a nervous intensity that stood her Sadie in good stead when pitted against the sternly moralistic Davidson of stage-trained Jose Ferrer. Hayworth never had a better dramatic role than this and, under Curtis Bernhardt's direction, she acted circles around Oscar-winner Ferrer. It remains, undoubtedly, her finest performance.

Filmed in Hawaii, *Miss Sadie Thompson* is an odd movie. Originally, it was conceived as a musical adaptation of *Rain,* but the final product can better be termed only a *semi*-musical.

Its several songs and musical numbers uncertainly establish the lighthearted mood of a post-World War II Pacific atoll, where life for the marines stationed thereon is considerably brightened when "cabaret entertainer" Sadie Thompson is stranded there. As in the original stage play *Rain* (it hardly *ever* rains in this version), Sadie clashes with a self-styled reformer (Ferrer), who lusts for her beneath a pious exterior. And, despite 1950s censorship, it ramains fairly clear that Davidson (offscreen) rapes Sadie before committing suicide (also offscreen). At the story's close, Sadie is heading for San Francisco to turn herself in for complicity on an old murder case.

Miss Sadie Thompson was released to New York theatres as a 3-D attraction, but the film was so obviously a strong enough draw in its own right that Columbia decided it needed no such gimmicks to sell it, and subsequent engagements were projected "flat," without a need for polaroid glasses. The sensational 3-D fad had waned almost as quickly as it had snowballed to success.

Once again, Bronson's tough mug and sinewy body provide little more than atmospheric set

With Rita Hayworth, Aldo Ray, and Henry Slate.

dressing. But he's on view in so many of the scenes involving Hayworth and Ray that audiences are constantly reminded of his potent presence. Ironically, only a year before he would change his name to "Bronson," his public was connecting that familar face with "Buchinsky."

CRITICS' CORNER
"I never though I'd live to see the day when Rita Hayworth would steal acting honors from Jose Ferrer. But that's exactly what she does in this sanitary version of Somerset Maugham's classic short story about a bad woman and a clergyman-bigot in the South Seas."

Jesse Zunser, *Cue*

"For the most part, *Miss Sadie Thompson,* as Columbia has brought it to the screen, is a Technicolor fable of the visit of an American party girl to a South Pacific island populated largely by a garrison of howling marines. This lady becomes the center of attraction the moment she arrives, and continues so, with interruptions, right up to the moment she leaves."

Bosley Crowther, *The New York Times*

With Henry Slate, Aldo Ray, and Rudy Bond.

With Phyllis Kirk and Gene Nelson.

Crime Wave (The City Is Dark)

A Warner Bros. Picture / 1953

CAST
Det. Sgt. Sims: Sterling Hayden; *Steve Lacey:* Gene Nelson; *Ellen:* Phyllis Kirk; *"Doc" Penny:* Ted de Corsia; *Ben Hastings:* Charles Buchinsky; *"Dr." Otto Hessler:* Jay Novello; *Daniel O'Keefe:* James Bell; *Gus Snider:* Dub Taylor; *Kelly:* Gayle Kellogg; *Sully:* Mack Chandler; *Johnny:* Timothy Carey; *Mark:* Richard Benjamin; *Hastings' Girl:* Iris Adrian; *Zenner:* James Hayward; *Man:* Fritz Feld.

CREDITS
Producer: Bryan Foy; *Director:* Andre de Toth; *Assistant Director:* James McMahon; *Screenwriter:* Crane Wilbur; *Adapters:* Bernard Gordon, Richard Wormser; *Based on a Story by:* John and Ward Hawkins; *Cinematographer:* Bert Glennon; *Art Director:* Stanley Fleischer; *Musical Score:* David Buttolph; *Editor:* Thomas Reilly. *Running Time:* 74 minutes.

THE FILM
In the successful wake of their *House of Wax*, the team of producer Bryan Foy, director Andre de Toth and screenwriter Crane Wilbur turned to this underworld yarn, retaining Bronson's services and elevating him, in direct ratio to the importance of his casting, to fifth billing.

But *Crime Wave* (or *The City Is Dark*, as it was filmed—and shown in Britain) hardly achieved the popularity of its predecessor, for all of its semidocumentary on-location filming and realistic dialogue. Its modest length, production budget and cast (Sterling Hayden, Gene Nelson and Phyllis Kirk) best qualified this underworld melodrama for the bottom half of Warner Bros. double-bills. Which, of course, lessened the impact of Bronson's largest featured role at that time.

He portrayed the sadistic, leather-jacketed member of a trio of San Quentin escapees who seek refuge in the home of parolee Nelson and wife Kirk. When law officer Hayden comes close to discovering their whereabouts, Bronson kills informer Jay Novello. With sidekick gunman Timothy Carey now dead of gunshot wounds, Bronson and his slickly dressed buddy, Ted de Corsia, take the couple as hostages and hide out in Los Angeles' Chinatown, from where they plan a bank robbery. But a clue left behind by Nelson tips off Hayden, thus foiling the heist. Both hoods are killed and Nelson is exonerated of collaborating with them.

With Gene Nelson, Phyllis Kirk, and Ted de Corsia.

Bronson's role obviously isn't *Crime Wave's* largest or most important. But in a small cast he stands out, his dangerous presence impresses greatly, and his future potential appears undeniable. It is a chilling character performance, as much for what he does and says as for what he doesn't. It is the smouldering intensity behind those cold killer's eyes and Slavic-simian features that marks the indelible Buchinsky/Bronson persona and makes producers and directors continue to feature him in their films.

CRITICS' CORNER
"Average-to-good crime story, which starts excitingly, loses grip in the middle, but revives at the end with a gripping bank hold-up. Actual Los Angeles settings are well used, and the police procedure is unflatteringly realistic. The film is very competently acted except for one overdrawn characterization of a 'different' moronic gangster."

Monthly Film Bulletin

"By shuffling some standard ingredients with quiet competence, *Crime Wave* manages to look a good deal better than it is.

"Dancing shoes aside, Mr. Nelson gives his best performance to date in his dramatic debut. Miss Kirk is also effective, as are Ted de Corsia, Charles Buchinsky, Jay Novello and James Bell."

Howard Thompson, *The New York Times*

With Timothy Carey, Ted de Corsia, James Bell, and Gene Nelson.

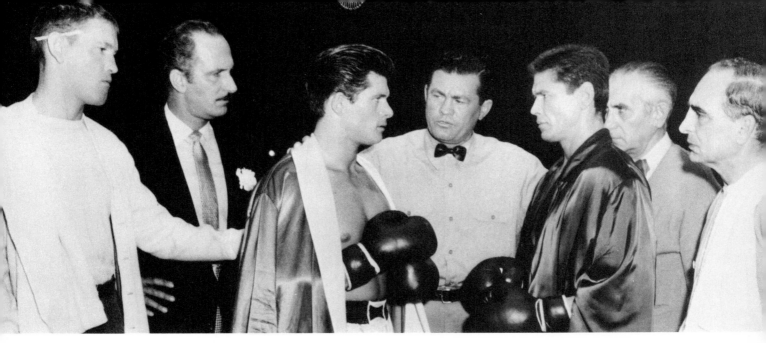

With Earl Holliman, Keenan Wynn, Dewey Martin, Charles Sullivan, William Newell, and Dave White.

Tennessee Champ

A Metro-Goldwyn-Mayer Picture / 1953
In Ansco Color

CAST
Sarah Wurble: Shelley Winters; *Willy Wurble:* Keenan Wynn; *Daniel Norson:* Dewey Martin; *Happy Jackfield:* Earl Holliman; *Luke MacWade:* Dave O'Brien; *Sixty Jubel:* Charles Buchinsky; *Blossom:* Yvette Dugay; *J. B. Backett:* Frank Richards; *Andrews:* Jack Kruschen; *Referee:* Johnny Indrisano; *Sam:* Alvin J. Gordon; *Poker Players:* Paul Hoffman, Bruno Ve Sota, John Damler; *Ring Announcer:* William Newell.

CREDITS
Producer: Sol Baer Fielding; *Director:* Fred M. Wilcox; *Assistant Director:* Marvin Stuart; *Screenwriter:* Art Cohn; *Based on "The Lord in His Corner" and Other Stories by:* Eustace Cockrell; *Cinematographer:* George Folsey; *Art Directors:* Cedric Gibbons, Daniel B. Cathcart; *Musical Score:* Conrad Salinger; *Editor:* Ben Lewis. *Running Time:* 73 minutes.

THE FILM
This little 73-minute boxing yarn was deemed so unimportant at MGM that they released it throughout the country on double-bills and in drive-ins. But it wasn't given a regular New York City opening, with the result that there were few critical notices accorded this movie—which may have pleased MGM, after all.

In the title role, Metro contract player Dewey Martin portrays a religious-minded young boxer, whose avaricious glib manager (Keenan Wynn) is responsible for the "fixed" fights and other scrapes that the youth gets into. In the end, its pugilist-hero finally appears to be headed for the ministry.

Bronson, here afforded sixth billing in the cast list, plays a hard-as-rocks fighter sporting the colorful name of "Sixty Jubel," who makes a formidable ring adversary for the film's idealistic central character.

CRITICS' CORNER
"This mixture of boxing and religion is likely to seem in somewhat doubtful taste. The opening shots, a card game sequence, have some atmosphere but, in general, the film is an undistinguished piece of work."

Monthly Film Bulletin

With Dub Taylor, Wayne Morris, and bit players.

Riding Shotgun

A Warner Bros. Picture / 1954
In WarnerColor

CAST
Larry Delong: Randolph Scott; *Tub Murphy:* Wayne Morris; *Orissa Flynn:* Joan Weldon; *Tom Biggert:* Joe Sawyer; *Dan Marady:* James Millican; *Pinto:* Charles Buchinsky; *Doc Winkler:* James Bell; *Fritz:* Fritz Feld; *Walters:* Richard Garrick; *Bar-M Rider:* Victor Perrin; *Hughes:* John Baer; *Col. Flynn:* William Johnstone; *Ben:* Kem Dibbs; *Johnny:* Alvin Freeman; *Manning:* Ned Young; *Bob Purdee:* Paul Picerni; *Lewellyn:* Jack Lawrence; *Hardpan:* Jack Woody; *Blackie:* Richard Benjamin; *Red:* Boyd Red Morgan; *Cynthia Biggert:* Mary Lou Holloway; *Ellie:* Lonnie Pierce; *Eddie:* Dub Taylor; *Dance Hall Girls:* Evan Lowe, Holly Brooke; *Mrs. Fritz:* Allegra Varron.

CREDITS
Producer: Ted Sherdeman; *Director:* Andre de Toth; *Assistant Director:* James McMahon; *Screenwriter:* Tom Blackburn; *Based on a Story by:* Kenneth Perkins; *Cinematographer:* Bert Glennon; *Art Director:* Edward Carrere; *Set Decorator:* Benjamin S. Bone; *Musical Score:* David Buttolph; *Editor:* Rudi Fehr;
Running Time: 75 minutes.

THE FILM
Bronson once again joined the cast of an Andre de Toth film—playing in his first Western—when the veteran director guided this 1954 Randolph Scott vehicle. Here, the monolithic Scott plays a stagecoach's shotgun guard who, discredited in the eyes of his townspeople and like Gary Cooper in *High Noon,* finds himself fighting a band of outlaws single-handed. As "Pinto," Bronson is the right-hand man of badman James Millican, who robs stagecoaches only to divert the law from his main goal—a lucrative gambling casino.

Flint-eyed Bronson gives Scott and deputy sheriff Wayne Morris plenty of trouble himself, before being gunned down, with the other villains, in the climactic casino shoot-out.

CRITICS' CORNER
"If Randolph Scott's assignment in *Riding Shotgun* calls for anything he hasn't done before, it's not apparent. Produced by Ted Sherdeman in rather faded-looking WarnerColor, this tired, bony little offering of frontier violence and justice remains about as ordinary as they come."

Howard Thompson, *The New York Times*

With John McIntire.

Apache

A Hecht-Lancaster Production
for United Artists / 1954
In Technicolor

CAST
Massai: Burt Lancaster; *Nalinle:* Jean Peters; *Al Sieber:* John McIntire; *Hondo:* Charles Buchinsky; *Weddle:* John Dehner; *Santos:* Paul Guilfoyle; *Clagg:* Ian MacDonald; *Lt. Col. Beck:* Walter Sande; *Dawson:* Morris Ankrum; *Geronimo:* Monte Blue.

CREDITS
Producer: Harold Hecht; *Director:* Robert Aldrich; *Assistant Director:* Sid Sidman; *Screenwriter:* James R. Webb; *Based on the Novel "Bronco Apache" by:* Paul I. Wellman; *Cinematographer:* Ernest Laszlo; *Art Director:* Nicolai Remisoff; *Set Director:* Joseph Kish; *Musical Score:* David Raksin; *Editor:* Alan Crosland, Jr.
Running Time: 91 minutes.

THE FILM
Not all of the critics found Burt Lancaster and Jean Peters believably cast as Apache Indians in this 1954 production from Burt's Hecht-Lancaster organization. But it was generally conceded that the customary Hollywood stereotypes were refreshingly missing from this action yarn about a real-life brave (Lancaster) who became a legend for waging a one-man war against the encroaching U.S. Army in the 1880s.

For Bronson, it marked the first of his numerous excursions into Indian territory. For his primitive face with its high cheekbones and deep-set crags lent itself naturally to the long-haired black wig and headband in which the actor appeared so much at home here in his subsidiary, fourth-billed role of "Hondo," the uniformed

With Jean Peters, Burt Lancaster, and John McIntire.

Apache soldier.

Subsequently, Robert Aldrich, would direct Bronson's performances in a trio of male-oriented adventure films: *Vera Cruz, 4 For Texas* and *The Dirty Dozen*.

CRITICS' CORNER
"Robert Aldrich, making his second start as feature film director, handles cast and action well, waste movement being eliminated and only essentials to best storytelling being retained.

"On white side of cast, John McIntire, chief scout out to capture or kill Lancaster, is very good, underplaying neatly. John Dehner, cruel Indian agent, also shows up well and excellent assists are provided by Charles Buchinsky's Indian soldier; Paul Guilfoyle, Walter Sande and Morris Ankrum."

Variety

with Jean Peters.

52

As Hondo.

With Alan Ladd.

Drum Beat

A Jaguar Production
for Warner Bros. Pictures / 1954
In CinemaScope and WarnerColor

CAST

Johnny MacKay: Alan Ladd; *Nancy Meek:* Audrey Dalton; *Toby:* Marisa Pavan; *Bill Satterwhite:* Robert Keith; *Scarface Charlie:* Rodolfo Acosta; *Captain Jack:* Charles Bronson; *General Canby:* Warner Anderson; *Crackel:* Elisha Cook, Jr.; *Manok:* Anthony Caruso; *Dr. Thomas:* Richard Gaines; *Jesse Grant:* Edgar Stehli; *Gen. Grant:* Hayden Rorke; *Modoc Jim:* Frank de Kova; *Bogus Charlie:* Perry Lopez; *Gen. Gilliam:* Willis Bouchey; *Lt. Goodsall:* Peter Hansen; *Capt. Alonzo Clark:* George Lewis; *Lily White:* Isabel Jewell; *Mr. Dyar:* Frank Ferguson; *Mrs. Grant:* Peggy Converse; *O'Brien:* Pat Lawless; *William Brody:* Paul Wexler; *Meek:* Richard Cutting; *Scotty:* Strother Martin.

CREDITS

Producer: Alan Ladd (uncredited); *Director-Screenwriter:* Delmer Daves; *Assistant Director:* William Kissel; *Cinematographer:* J. Peverell Marley; *Art Director:* Leo K. Kuter; *Set Decorator:* William L. Kuehl; *Special Effects:* H. F. Koenekamp; *Musical Score:* Victor Young; *Editor:* Clarence Kolster; *Technical Advisers:* Ben Corbett, George Ross.
Running Time: 111 minutes.

THE FILM

Drum Beat, written and directed by Delmer Daves for Alan Ladd's newly formed Jaguar Productions, was the film that literally provided Charles Bronson with his real break-through role as a screen actor. For this part, the actor had his first billing under the "Bronson" name, with only one film, the earlier-made but later-released *Vera Cruz,* remaining to show audiences a last glimpse of his ethnic origin in its credits.

Drum Beat is an Alan Ladd Western, but the actor who, quite understandably, made the more indelible impression on both critics and audiences was the newly christened "Charles Bronson," in the colorful role of the movie's renegade Indian "heavy." It's interesting to note, however, that the film's ad campaign, emblazoning Ladd's star-name in letters the same size as the title, includes only four other names—but not Bronson's! One imagines that perhaps executive producer Ladd did not fully appreciate Bronson's scene-stealing talents *or* the generous amount of close-ups allowed his thespian

With Alan Ladd and bit players.

adversary by the movie's suitably impressed director, Delmer Daves.

The setting for this fact-based story is Oregon (represented by location shooting in Northern Arizona's Coconino National Forest) in the 1869-70 period. Experienced Indian fighter Johnny MacKay (Ladd) is presidentially appointed as Peace Commissioner, assigned to effect a treaty, without resort to arms, with the Modoc Indians of the Oregon-California border. the Modoc majority leans toward the hoped-for peace, but a renegade band strongly resists, under the self-appointed leadership of the vicious Captain Jack (Bronson), whose men ravage the area and skirmish with the soldiers of Fort Klamath. In the film's exciting climax, MacKay personally tracks down Jack and battles him in hand-to-hand combat on a rocky mountainside. The renegade leader is defeated, brought to trial and is hanged.

CRITICS' CORNER

"In a better-than-average story, Alan Ladd is again the strong, silent character to whom actions come quicker than words. The script gives him every opportunity, but his performance is dwarfed by that of Charles Bronson as Captain Jack. Jack is the one to remember—proud, ruthless, magnificent, a good fighter fighting in all sincerity to retain lands his ancestors have ruled for centuries. When finally he is brought captive to the army camp, his braves scattered or dead, his arms bound to his side, the hangman's noose that greets him signifies not only his personal defeat by Johnny, but also the collapse of the Indian cause. Thus *Drum Beat,* more than the usual Western, is a comment on American history."

Peter Baker, *Films and Filming*

"Captain Jack, the renegade redskin, is forcefully played by Charles Bronson."

Variety

"Alan Ladd is an authority on such roles as MacKay, though he has little chance here to employ any but routine effects. Of the supporting players, however, only Charles Bronson as

Captain Jack rises superior to the script."

Monthly Film Bulletin

"Charles Bronson (formerly Buchinsky) is probably the most muscular Indian ever to have brandished a rifle before a camera."

A. H. Weiler, *The New York Times*

"Marisa Pavan and Charles Bronson can be singled out for especial notice, having contributed enormously in their roles of a friendly Modoc leader, and a vicious renegade Indian."

The Film Daily

As Captain Jack.

Vera Cruz

A Hecht-Lancaster Production
for United Artists / 1954
In SuperScope and Technicolor

CAST
Benjamin Trane: Gary Cooper; *Joe Erin:* Burt Lancaster; *Countess Marie Duvarre:* Denise Darcel; *Marquis de Labordere:* Cesar Romero; *Nina:* Sarita Montiel; *Emperor Maximilian:* George Macready; *Donnegan:* Ernest Borgnine; *Danette:* Henry Brandon; *Pittsburgh:* Charles Buchinsky; *General Aguilar:* Morris Ankrum; *Little Bit:* James McCallion; *Charlie:* Jack Lambert; *Tex:* Jack Elam; *Abilene:* James Seay; *Ballard:* Archie Savage; *Reno:* Charles Horvath; *Pedro:* Juan Garcia.

CREDITS
Producer: James Hill; *Director:* Robert Aldrich; *Screenwriters:* Roland Kibbee, James R. Webb; *Based on a Story by:* Borden Chase; *Cinematographer:* Ernest Laszlo; *Art Director:* Al Ybarra; *Musical Score:* Hugo Friedhofer; *Editor:* Alan Crosland, Jr.
Running Time: 94 minutes.

THE FILM
In his last motion picture carrying the "Buchinsky" billing, Bronson was relegated to a sideline role as tough, gunslinging "atmosphere" in this rugged outdoor tale, directed by Robert Aldrich for the Harold Hecht-Burt Lancaster company.

For this one, Burt took second billing to Westerns veteran Gary Cooper in this story of an outlaw who joins forces with a former Confederate to guide a shipment of gold through 1866 Mexico. Vivacious Denise Darcel appears as a colorful but doublecrossing French Countess traveling from Maximilian's Mexico City to Vera Cruz, and Mexican favorite Sarita Montiel is the fiery Juarista follower whose sensuality draws lustful aggression from Bronson's peripheral tough-guy, "Pittsburgh." Generally, the actor has little to do here, but in one brief scene, he comes on strong with Montiel, begins to manhandle her, and gets a swift knee to the groin for his amorous efforts. This causes a scuffle in which Bronson is knocked into the dust. In this Mexican-filmed box-office hit, it's his biggest moment—a fitting swansong for "Charles Buchinsky."

CRITICS' CORNER
"The Borden Chase story, expertly fashioned for the screen by Roland Kibbee and James R. Webb, is of the high romance school that responds aptly to the vigorous direction given it by Robert Aldrich. The stress is mostly on the violence and suspenseful action bred during Mexico's revolutionary period when the Juaristas were trying to free the country of the French-supported Emperor Maximilian."

Variety

"Surely one of the most exhilarating adventure stories ever filmed."

Derek Hill, *Films and Filming*

". . . a film which sets out to entertain, and succeeds admirably."

Monthly Film Bulletin

With James Seay, Gary Cooper, Jack Elam, Ernest Borgnine, Burt Lancaster, and Archie Savage.

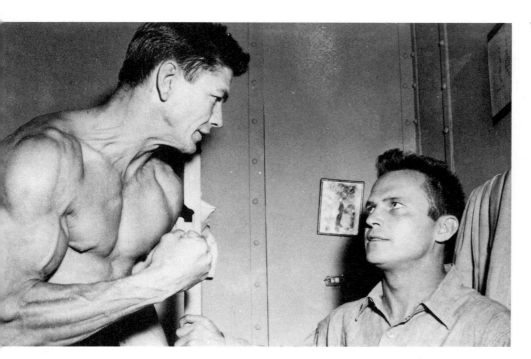

Big House, U.S.A.

A Bel-Air Production / 1955
for United Artists

CAST
Rollo Lamar: Broderick Crawford; *Jerry Barker:* Ralph Meeker; *James Madden:* Reed Hadley; *Nurse Emily Evans:* Randy Farr; *Machinegun Mason:* William Talman; *Alamo Smith:* Lon Chaney; *Benny Kelly:* Charles Bronson; *Danny Lambert:* Peter Votrian; *Chief Ranger Erickson:* Roy Roberts; *Robertson Lambert:* Willis B. Bouchey.

CREDITS
Producer: Aubrey Schenk; *Director:* Howard W. Koch; *Screenwriter:* John C. Higgins; *Cinematographer:* Gordon Avil; *Musical Score:* Paul Dunlap; *Editor:* John F. Schreyer.
Running Time: 82 minutes.

THE FILM
The pseudo-documentary style in which this uneven program melodrama was made failed to disguise the disjointedness of its narrative. This case history of a crime begins in the great outdoors (locations were filmed in Colorado's Royal Gorge Park) when a young boy (Peter Votrian) runs away from camp, only to be kidnapped by the man (Ralph Meeker) who "helps" him, then blackmails the lad's wealthy father. But the boy accidentally dies in a fall from the forest lookout tower where he was confined, and, for lack of other evidence, his kidnapper can only be convicted on an extortion charge. The story then shifts gears entirely, turning to prison drama (filmed at the Cascabel Island facility) as the plot now focuses on four cutthroat convicts (Broderick Crawford, William Talman, Lon Chaney and Charles Bronson) with whom the "extortionist" is thrown in. A breakout is planned, with their target the hidden $200,000 ransom money. The escape is successful, but there is a falling-out among the gang members, and one is killed. A gun battle ensues between the convicts, Federal authorities and rangers, as justice, not unexpectedly, wins out.

As Benny Kelly.

After his big break opposite Alan Ladd in *Drum Beat,* Bronson was relegated to the sort of supporting "heavy" role he had done so often before in this black-and-white supporting feature. As in *My Six Convicts,* his tough physiognomy lends itself well to the inside of a prison. But scriptwriter John C. Higgins and director Howard W. Koch give him the short end of it by killing off Bronson's character, once the prison escape has been effected. His death is a particularly grisly one, as Broderick Crawford, in an effort to distract the police, kills Bronson and uses a blowtorch on his face and fingers to obliterate means of identification. If the scene recalls similar horrors in the 1947 prison movie *Brute Force,* it also signifies the elements that will continue to be most closely associated with Bronson's career—male machismo and, above all, relentless violence!

CRITICS' CORNER
"*Big House, U.S.A.* is an idea for a good crime melodrama gone wrong."
Howard Thompson, *The New York Times*

"The characters here depicted are so brutal as to anaesthetize all sympathy, and their savagery is minutely explored by the director, Howard W. Koch, in a manner that leaves one shocked yet disinterested. The playing is indifferent, and the film as a whole singularly distasteful."
Monthly Film Bulletin

"The melodrama provides a fair amount of entertainment. Plenty of violence is featured throughout in some rather chilling scenes, but fits the tough characters with which the story deals. Performances are in keeping, with Meeker doing a good job of a cold-blooded crook nick-named 'The Iceman.' Crawford, Talman, Chaney and Bronson also are okay heavies."
"Brog.," *Variety*

With William Talman, Ralph Meeker, and Lon Chaney.

With Richard Conte.

Target Zero

A Warner Bros. Picture / 1955

CAST
Lt. Tom Flagler: Richard Conte; *Ann Galloway:* Peggie Castle; *Sgt. Vince Gaspari:* Charles Bronson; *Sgt. David Kensemmit:* Richard Stapley; *Pvt. Feliz Zimbalist:* L.Q. Jones; *Pvt. Moose:* Chuck Connors; *Cpl. Devon Enoch:* John Alderson; *Pvt. Harry Fontenoy:* Terence de Marney; *P.F.C. George:* John Dennis; *Sue:* Angela Loo; *Pvt. Geronimo:* Abel Fernandez; *Pvt. Ma*

Koo Sung: Richard Park; *Pvt. Stacey Zorbados:* Don Oreck; *Dan O'Hirons:* Strother Martin; *Strangler:* Aaron Spelling; *Priest:* George Chan; *Soldier:* Joby Baker; *Colonel:* Leo K. Kuter; *Marine Officer:* Hal Sheiner.

CREDITS
Producer: David Weisbart; *Director:* Harmon

Jones; *Assistant Director:* Oren Haglund; *Screen-writer:* Sam Rolfe; *Based on a Story by:* James Warner Bellah; *Cinematographer:* Edwin DuPar; *Art Director:* Leo K. Kuter; *Set Decorator:* G.W. Berntsen; *Musical Score:* David Buttolph; *Editor:* Clarence Kolster.
Running Time: 92 minutes.

THE FILM
For his only other 1955 film, Bronson now returned to the genre with which he had first entered movies, the war story, this time donning G.I. combat gear for a Korean War yarn in which he received third billing after *Target Zero's* nominal stars, Richard Conte and Peggie Castle. With a character name like Sgt. Vince Gaspari (actor L.Q. Jones portrays the curiously titled "Pvt. Feliz Zimbalist"), it's obvious that Bronson is here helping fulfill Hollywood's customary war-film quota of ethnic types. It is a quirk of casting that Bronson will find himself frequently faced with over the ensuing decade.

The film's plot, concerning a handful of men separated from the remainder of their unit behind enemy lines, suspends disbelief when it introduces a stranded, blonde U.N. biochemist, in the person of the vapidly sexy Peggie Castle (who, of course, falls in love with the movie's star, Richard Conte, in between battle skirmishes). In addition to her, the men are joined by three members of a British tank squad. Their destination, reached after various battles with the enemy, is the American mountain outpost, where they find the entire company killed. Ordered to hold this position, the small band, with the aid of naval guns and aerial bombardments, eventually wipes out the opposition.

CRITICS' CORNER
"After a few tentative attempts at individual characterization, the film soon deteriorates into routine battle exploits culminating in one of the most cold-blooded massacres yet seen in an American war film. The romance between the tough, ruthless commander and the highly unlikely U.S. biochemist appears peculiarly repellent against this background of carefully contrived bloodshed."

Monthly Film Bulletin

"The stars and other cast members answer capably the not too taxing demands of the plot. Charles Bronson is good as a Yank sarg, and Richard Stapley does okay as the prejudiced Britisher."

"Brog.," *Variety*

"That sanguinary business in Korea was unquestionably grim and wearying. But it certainly was not wearying in the way that it is made to be in this film."

Bosley Crowther, *The New York Times*

With Peggie Castle, Abel Fernandez, and Richard Conte.

With Valerie French and Felicia Farr on the location of *Jubal*.

Jubal

A Columbia Picture / 1956
In CinemaScope and Technicolor

CAST

Jubal Troop: Glenn Ford; *Shep Horgan:* Ernest Borgnine; *Pinky:* Rod Steiger; *Mae Horgan:* Valerie French; *Naomi Hoktor:* Felicia Farr; *Shem Hoktor:* Basil Ruysdael; *Sam:* Noah Beery, Jr.; *Reb Haislipp:* Charles Bronson; *Carson:* John Dierkes; *McCoy:* Jack Elam; *Dr. Grant:* Robert Burton; *Jake Slavin:* Robert Knapp; *Charity Hoktor:* Juney Ellis; *Jim Tolliver:* Don C. Harvey; *Cookie:* Guy Wilkerson; *Bayne:* Larry Hudson; *Tolliver Boys:* Mike Lawerence, Robert Henry; *Matt:* William Rhinehart; *Cowboy:* Bob Cason; *Rancher:* John Cason; *Girl:* Ann Kunde.

CREDITS

Producer: William Fadiman; *Director:* Delmer Daves; *Screenwriters:* Russell S. Hughes and Delmer Daves; *Based on the Novel "Jubal Troop" by:* Paul I. Wellman; *Cinematographer:* Charles Lawton, Jr.; *Art Director:* Carl Anderson; *Musical Score:* David Raksin; *Editor:* Al Clark.
Running Time: 101 minutes.

THE FILM

Jubal, filmed under the title *Jubal Troop* (the name of its leading character, played by Glenn Ford), returned Bronson to the West and the

With Valerie French, John Dierkes, Glenn Ford, Ernest
Borgnine, and Rod Steiger.

As Reb Haislipp.

company of director Delmer Daves, with whom he had made *Drum Beat*. Cast as a ranchhand friend of Ford's in the employ of Ernest Borgnine, Bronson helps save Ford from a lynching and contributes his natural masculine presence to this psychological Western. A rancher's wanton wife (Valerie French) spins the plot by her attentions to the disinterested cowboy Jubal, which further stirs up the surly range rider (Rod Steiger) with whom she had previously been carrying on an affair, unbeknownst to her good-natured husband (Borgnine). The resultant outbursts of sex, jealousy and revenge make of *Jubal* a rather powerful and engrossing piece of adult entertainment.

CRITICS' CORNER
"The strong point of the William Fadiman pro-

duction, along with ace performances and an overall plot line that grips tightly, is a constantly mounting suspense. Delmer Daves' direction and the script he wrote with Russell S. Hughes from Paul I. Wellman's novel carefully build towards the explosion that's certain to come, taking time along the way to make sure that all characters are well-rounded and understandable.

"Oddly enough, much of the footage is free of actual physical violence, but the nerves are stretched so taut that it's almost a relief when it does come."

"Brog.," *Variety*

With Ernest Borgnine and Glenn Ford.

With H.M. Wynant and Rod Steiger.

Run of the Arrow

A Globe Enterprises Production / 1957
for R.K.O.
Released by Universal-International
   In RKO-Scope and Technicolor

CAST
O'Meara: Rod Steiger; *Yellow Moccasin:* Sarita Montiel (Voice dubbed by Angie Dickinson); *Capt. Clark:* Brian Keith; *Lt. Driscoll:* Ralph Meeker; *Walking Coyote:* Jay C. Flippen; *Blue Buffalo:* Charles Bronson; *Mrs. O'Meara:* Olive Carey; *Crazy Wolf:* H. M. Wynant; *Lt. Stockwell:* Neyle Morrow; *Red Cloud:* Frank de Kova; *Gen. Allan:* Col. Tim McCoy; *Col. Taylor:* Stuart Randall; *Ballad Singer:* Frank Warner; *Silent Tongue:* Billy Miller; *Corporal:* Chuck Hayward; *Sergeant:* Chuck Roberson; *Doctor:* Carleton Young; *Vinci:* Don Orlando; *Sgt. Moore:* Bill White, Jr.; *Gen. Lee:* Frank Baker; *Gen. Grant:* Emile Avery.

CREDITS
Producer-Director-Screenwriter: Samuel Fuller; *Assistant Director:* Ben Chapman; *Cinematographer:* Joseph Biroc; *Art Directors:* Albert D'Agostino, Jack Okey; *Set Decorator:* Bert Granger; *Musical Score:* Victor Young; *Editor:* Gene Fowler, Jr.
Running Time: 86 minutes.

THE FILM
Originally, writer-director-producer Samuel Fuller had entitled this Western drama *The Last Bullet:* "That's what started me thinking about the whole story; what happened to the last cartridge fired in the Civil War." But the

With Rod Steiger, Sarita Montiel, and H.M. Wynant.

movie was eventually shown as *Run of the Arrow*, with reference to the Sioux Indian endurance test in which the story's white hero is obliged to participate.

Fuller's screenplay centers on O'Meara (Rod Steiger), a Confederate soldier whose last bullet of the war wounds Driscoll (Ralph Meeker), a Union Army lieutenant. O'Meara makes a keepsake of that cartridge and, refusing to accept Southern defeat, he finds acceptance in the Sioux nation, after successfully negotiating the aforementioned "run." He later becomes

the Indians' official agent, after the Government signs a treaty with them, and is married by Chief Blue Buffalo (Charles Bronson) to a beautiful squaw, Yellow Moccasin (Sarita Montiel, a Mexican actress whose accent was deemed unacceptable, and whose lines were redubbed by Angie Dickinson, then an RKO contract player).

But trouble is stirred up by the appropriately named Chief Crazy Wolf (H. M. Wynant), the treaty is broken and it's war between the Sioux and hot-headed Lieutenant Driscoll. When the latter is captured and brutally tortured by the Indians, O'Meara commits a mercy killing and permanently leaves the Sioux to lead Driscoll's wounded troops to Fort Laramie.

Bronson is once again lending his considerable "presence" and muscular physique to the periphery of an outdoor drama. For the most part, he is merely called upon to display his body and lend strength to the Technicolor scenics of this film, which—completed at the time of RKO's formal demise as a producing-releasing organization—officially became a Universal-International picture, when that studio took over RKO's remaining product.

CRITICS' CORNER
"The Sioux Indians and the United States Cavalry are mixing it up again in Samuel Fuller's *Run of the Arrow*. The blood and warpaint look good in color. The plot looks pretty much as it always has. Mr. Fuller, who wrote, produced and directed, has in no way broken the familiar mold."
Bosley Crowther, *The New York Times*

"Samuel Fuller's films have now achieved some notoriety for their use of excessive violence; in *Run of the Arrow,* killings, butcherings, beatings and arrow-pierced flesh are used as deliberate shock tactics, often quite gratuitous to the confused and rambling narrative. The climactic scene of torture, with the Cavalry officer being cut to pieces by vengeful Indians, remains a disturbing experience.

"Rod Steiger plays O'Meara with an affected Irish brogue that is sometimes difficult to understand; and there are some rather odd performances by white actors in Indian roles."
Monthly Film Bulletin

With Rod Steiger and bit players.

Suzy Parker and Gary Cooper.

Ten North Frederick

A 20th Century-Fox Film / 1958
In CinemaScope

CAST
Joe Chapin: Gary Cooper; *Ann Chapin:* Diana Varsi; *Kate Drummond:* Suzy Parker; *Edith Chapin:* Geraldine Fitzgerald; *Mike Slattery:* Tom Tully; *Joby Chapin:* Ray Stricklyn; *Lloyd Williams:* Philip Ober; *Paul Donaldson:* John Emery; *Charley Bongiorno:* Stuart Whitman; *Peg Slattery:* Linda Watkins; *Stella:* Barbara Nichols; *Dr. English:* Joe McGuinn; *Arthur McHenry:* Jess Kirkpatrick; *Harry Jackson:* Nolan Leary; *Marian Jackson:* Helen Wallace; *Robert Hooker:* John Harding; *Lt. Gen. Coates:* Mack Williams; *Waitress:* Beverly Jo Morrow; *Bill:* Buck Class; *Salesgirl:* Rachel Stephens; *Farmer:* Bob Adler; *Peter:* Linc Foster; *Red Wallace:* Dudley Manlove; *Board Chairman:* Vernon Rich; *Nurse:* Mary Carroll; *Waiter:* George Davis; *Taxi Driver:* Joey Faye; *Hoffman:* Fred Essler; *Wife:* Irene Seidner; *Hope:* Melinda Byron; *Sax Player:* Sean Meany; *Men:* John Indrisano, Michael Pataki, Michael Morelli and Charles Bronson.

CREDITS
Producer: Charles Brackett; *Director-Screenwriter:* Philip Dunne; *Based on the Novel by:* John O'Hara; *Cinematographer:* Joe MacDonald; *Art Directors:* Lyle R. Wheeler, Addison Hehr; *Set Decorators:* Walter M. Scott, Eli Benneche; *Special Effects:* L. B. Abbott; *Musical Score:* Leigh Harline; *Editor:* David Bretherton. *Running Time:* 102 minutes.

THE FILM
At this juncture in his career, Bronson's bit role in this Gary Cooper film can only be explained by his loyalty to that actor, with whom he had become friendly during the filming of *U.S.S. Teakettle* and *Vera Cruz.* His flash appearance in this unsuccessful mixture of politics and tortured family relationships, from the John O'Hara best-seller, must have been performed for a lark, and as a good-luck salute to Cooper, during a visit by Bronson to the Fox set.

CRITICS' CORNER
"A fairly interesting study of a man who is the victim of his own virtues."

"Land.," *Variety*

"A strangely superficial, rarely engrossing film."

Cue

With Susan Cabot.

Machine Gun Kelly

An El Monte Production / 1958
for American International Pictures

CAST

Machine Gun Kelly: Charles Bronson; *Flo:* Susan Cabot; *Fandango:* Morey Amsterdam; *Howard:* Jack Lambert; *Maize:* Wally Campo; *Vito:* Bob Griffin; *Lynn:* Barboura Morris; *Apple:* Richard Devon; *Teddy:* Ted Thorp; *Harriet:* Mitzi McCall; *Harry:* Frank de Kova; *Martha:* Shirley Falls; *Ma:* Connie Gilchrist; *Clinton:* Mike Fox; *Drummond:* Larry Thor; *Frank:* George Archambeault; *Philip Ashton:* Jay Sayer.

CREDITS

Executive Producers: James H. Nicholson, Samuel Z. Arkoff; *Producer-Director:* Roger Corman; *Assistant Director:* Jack Bohrer; *Screenwriter:* R. Wright Campbell; *Cinematographer:* Floyd Crosby; *Art Director:* Daniel Haller; *Set Decorator:* Harry Reif; *Musical Score:* Gerald Fried; *Editor:* Ronald Sinclair.
Running Time: 84 minutes.

THE FILM

Charles Bronson's first film, at the age of 37, as a full-fledged star quite prophetically anticipated the kind of role with which he would later become so closely associated—that of the cold, brooding killer, more easily attuned to physical action than mental. Producer-director Roger Corman, who had been establishing a prolific career as a maker of movies in the action-exploitation field, achieved uncannily accurate casting in *Machine Gun Kelly,* for the assignment fit Bronson's talents to a tee. His role, of course, was a big one. Unfortunately, this 84-minute black-and-white programmer was not planned as a "prestige" film. There were no fancy big-city openings and no coverage by the more prestigious critics. Instead, its distributor, American International, packaged *Machine Gun Kelly* on a double-bill with director William Witney's female counterpart, *The Bonnie Parker Story* (starring Dorothy Provine), and booked them into drive-ins and grind-house theatres.

Like most of the cinematic bio-bilms about real-life gangsters, *Machine Gun Kelly's* adherence to the true facts of George R. Kelly's criminal life (1897-1954) was negligible. But its impact as a modest underworld thriller cannot be overlooked, either in the career of cult-favorite Roger Corman or as a Bronson milestone. For this is an excellent example of the well-made little "quickie," filmed in a remarkable eight days!

As Machine Gun Kelly.

The film's tough non-hero is shown to have earned his nickname from his dexterity with every aspect of the machine gun, and somehow the firearm appears to compensate for an inferiority complex as well as his morbid superstitions. Corman emphasizes Kelly's neuroticism during a well-orchestrated bank robbery which Kelly spoils when he's faced with a coffin (one of his superstitions) being transported across his path. Susan Cabot's characterization of Kelly's unpleasantly aggressive moll, as written and directed by Corman, lent an interesting variation to the standard depiction of gangsters' girlfriends. Plotwise, *Machine Gun Kelly* blended the standard elements of 1930s bank-heist melodramas and justice-triumphant endings. But it was the felicitous blend of interesting characterization and behind-the-scenes artistry that saved the picture. A decade later, French star Alain Delon would recall *Machine Gun*

Kelly's impact—and the performance of its star—when seeking an appropriately strong team-mate for *his* next motion picture. However, in 1958, *Machine Gun Kelly* did not immediately lead to bigger and better film roles for Charles Bronson.

CRITICS' CORNER

"The pace of the action is so fast as to be almost frantic and the acting is more than adequate to the occasion—particularly by the two principals. But this apart, the film is in all other respects highly unpleasant."

Monthly Film Bulletin

"Roger Corman, who produced and directed, has taken a good screenplay by R. Wright Campbell, and made a first-rate little picture out of the depressing but intriguing account of a badman's downfall.

"Charles Bronson plays Kelly, shown as an undersized sadist who grows an extra foot or so as soon as he gets a submachine gun tucked under his arm. His exploits, proceeding from penny-ante robbery to bigtime kidnapping, are adroitly and swiftly shown, leading inevitably to the moment when he is surrounded and captured by the police.

"Campbell's script is remarkable for the crisply color flavor of his dialog, putting additional interest in scenes that of themselves might otherwise have been merely repetitive. Corman also takes the trouble to sketch briefly but effectively, minor characters and incidents that give weight and meaning to the otherwise sordid story.

"Bronson gives a brooding, taut performance that somehow takes the curse off the character without lessening the horror of the casual slayings. Susan Cabot is good as the woman behind his deeds, and Morey Amsterdam contributes an offbeat portrayal of a squealer who has the final revenge of turning Kelly in.

"Gerald Fried, using piano taps for an unusual and striking combination, has done a fine progressive jazz score, and Floyd Crosby's photography penetrates the motivations of these unlovely characters."

"Powe.," Variety

"Bronson has the depth and the artistic intelligence of a very fine actor—too fine for the low budgets."

The Los Angeles Times

With Susan Cabot and bit player.

As Luke Welsh.

Showdown at Boot Hill

A Regal Film / 1958
for 20th Century-Fox
In RegalScope

CAST

Luke Welsh: Charles Bronson; *Sloane:* Robert Hutton; *Doc Weber:* John Carradine; *Jill:* Carole Mathews; *Sally:* Fintan Meyler; *Judge:* Paul Maxey; *Con Maynor:* Thomas Brown Henry; *First Cowhand:* William Stevens; *Second Cowhand:* Martin Smith; *Mr. Creavy:* Joseph McGuinn; *Charles Maynor:* George Douglas; *Patton:* Michael Mason; *Sheriff:* George Pembroke; *Mrs. Bonaventure:* Argentina Brunetti; *Brent:* Ed Wright; *Bartender:* Dan Simmons; *Mrs. Maynor:* Barbara Woodell; *Photographer:* Norman Leavitt.

CREDITS

Producer: Harold E. Knox ; *Director:* Gene Fowler, Jr.; *Assistant Director:* Nat Merman; *Screenwriter:* Louis Vittes; *Cinematographer:* John M. Nickolaus, Jr.; *Art Director:* John Mansbridge; *Set Decorators:* Walter M. Scott, Maurice Mulcahy; *Musical Score:* Albert Harris; *Editor:* Frank Sullivan.
Running Time: 71 minutes.

THE FILM

In theory, *Showdown at Boot Hill* provides an excellent starring showcase for Bronson's talents. Unfortunately, its budget is small, its cast little-known and its release patterns, like *Machine Gun Kelly*'s limited to fast play-offs as a supporting programmer at action-oriented theatres. And, like Corman's gangster film, this one received no influential critical notices. And so Charles Bronson's early "stardom" was both temporary and only a signal of the Hollywood status that would continue to elude him, on cinema screens, for another decade. But, in the late 1950s, perhaps moviegoers weren't yet ready for as untraditional and unglamorous-looking a "star" as Bronson. For him, as well as such colleagues as young character-actors Lee

Marvin and James Coburn, it would continue to be a period of waiting—until the public could accept them as its new heroes.

In *Showdown at Boot Hill*, Bronson's "heroism" is rather dubious, despite the indisputability of his leading-man status. For U.S. Marshal Luke Welsh is a relentless bounty hunter. In the movie's early scenes he tracks and kills Con Maynor (Thomas Brown Henry), a wanted criminal. But when Luke tries to collect his reward, he discovers that Maynor was so popular with his fellow townsmen that they turn against Luke, denying him his bounty by refusing to identify the body. His only allies

With Fintan Mayler, Barbara Woodell, and Paul Maxey.

With Carole Mathews.

are barber-undertaker Doc Weber (John Carradine) and Sally (Fintan Meyler), the hotel waitress and daughter of the town madam (Carole Mathews). Under Sally's gentle influence, Luke softens and, after some gunfighting, he wins the townspeople's support and the love of Sally, with whom he leaves town to begin a new life.

CRITICS' CORNER
"Though it promises to be a study of the psychology of a man who kills for money, the film degenerates into a sentimental and clumsily acted story of a man who decides that not all problems can be solved by violence. In endeavoring to excite and entertain, the filmmakers decline their own invitation to study Luke as a man and the film remains just another Western."
Monthly Film Bulletin

"*Showdown at Boot Hill* is a low-budget picture and does not have the production values or star names to make it a top attraction, but it's a well-directed and well-acted film done with taste and imagination.

"Louis Vittes' screenplay is the familiar one of a stranger in a Western frontier town who finds himself at odds with the community. But Vittes' dialog and his plotting make up for familiarity of situation, because the language is pungent and striking, and the frail story is given meaning and interest through characterization and lively scenes.

"Gene Fowler, Jr. shows his editing background in his cohesive direction. The performances are uniformly excellent, with Bronson, Carradine, Miss Mathews, Miss Meyler and Michael Mason most important.

"Fowler and John M. Nickolaus, Jr. employ the RegalScope projection for a number of interesting compositions and the rest of the staff has shown that they realized they were doing something more than a routine program picture."
"Powe.," *Variety*

With Fintan Meyler.

As Alan Avery.

Gang War

A Regal Film for
20th Century-Fox / 1958
In Regalscope

CAST

Alan Avery: Charles Bronson; *Bryce Barker:* Kent Taylor; *Marie:* Jennifer Holden; *Maxie Matthews:* John Doucette; *Edie Avery:* Gloria Henry; *Marsha Brown:* Gloria Grey; *Sam Johnson:* Barney Phillips; *Axe Duncan:* Ralph Manza; *Sgt. Ernie Tucker:* George Eldredge; *Mr. Tomkins:* Billy Snyder; *Joe Reno:* Jack Reynolds; *Bob Cross:* Dan Simmons: *Little Abner:* Larry Gelbmann; *Johnny:* Jack Littlefield; *Henchman No. 1:* Ed Wright; *Nicki:* Shirle Haven; *Capt. Finch:* Arthur D. Gilmore; *Mike Scipio:* Don Giovanni; *Police Sargeant:* Jack Finch; *Hood No. 1:* Stephen Masino; *Millie:* Stacey Marshall; *Diane Barker:* Lynn Guild; *Slick Connors:* Lenny Geer; *Street Girl:* Helen Jay; *Agnes:* Marion Sherman; *Mark:* Whit Bissell.

CREDITS

Producer: Harold E. Knox; *Director:* Gene Fowler, Jr.; *Assistant Director:* Frank Parmenter; *Screenwriter:* Louis Vittes; *Based on the Novel "The Hoods Take Over" by:* Ovid Demaris; *Cinematographer:* John M. Nickolaus, Jr.; *Art Director:* John Mansbridge; *Set Decorators:* Walter M. Scott, Bertram Granger; *Musical Score:* Paul Dunlap; *Editor:* Frank Baldridge. *Running Time:* 75 minutes.

THE FILM

For his second 1958 movie for the low-budget Regal Films organization, Bronson re-teamed with producer Harold E. Knox, director Gene Fowler, Jr., and screenwriter Louis Vittes on *Gang War.*

In this uncanny foretaste of Bronson's 1974 *Death Wish,* he portrays Alan Avery, a Los Angeles high-school teacher whose problems begin when he happens to witness a gangland killing and agrees to identify the murderers. In retaliation, underworld boss Maxie Matthews (John Doucette) is responsible for Avery's pregnant wife's death, understandably inciting the instructor to vengeance. But a gangland battle ensues between Matthews' boys and hit

With Gloria Henry, George Eldridge, and Jack Finch.

men from a national syndicate. When Avery infiltrates Maxie's estate and discovers the mobster chief going berserk, he decides to leave him to the justice of a higher court.

CRITICS' CORNER
"The stock characters that might take part in a gang war—the big boss, the dumb dame, the punch-drunk fighter, the 'bought' cop, and the gangland attorney—take parts in *Gang War,* a Regal production that holds up a bang-bang opus with more than enough excitement for a second-feature life.

Charles Bronson, in underplaying his role of the teacher, keeps a sympathetic interest centered on himself."

"Ron.," *Variety*

"This gangster story is soundly developed and has been treated without undue emphasis on its violence. It is spoiled by some stereotyped characterization. . . the gangster's dumb-blonde moll learning 'culture' at his insistence. . . but the leading player, well acted by Charles Bronson, is a much more convincing figure.
Monthly Film Bulletin

". . . a good gangster meller. The story is plausibly worked out and well paced."
The Film Daily

With Eddie Foy III.

When Hell Broke Loose

A Dolworth Production / 1958
  for Paramount Pictures

CAST
Steve Boland: Charles Bronson; *Ilsa:* Violet Rensing; *Karl:* Richard Jaeckel; *Ludwig:* Arvid Nelson; *Jonesie:* Robert Easton; *Capt. Melton:* Dennis McCarthy; *Capt. Grayson:* Bob Stevenson; *Brooklyn:* Eddie Foy III; *Ruby:* Kathy Carlyle; *Myra:* Ann Wakefield; *Chaplain:* John Morley; *Bertie:* Ed Penny

CREDITS
Producers: Oscar Brodney, Sol Dolgin; *Director:* Kenneth G. Crane; *Assistant Director:* Hal Klein; *Screenwriter:* Oscar Brodney; *Based on Articles by:* Ib Melchior; *Cinematographer:* Hal McAlpin; *Set Decorator:* G. W. Bernstein; *Special Effects:* Jess Davidson; *Musical Score:* Albert Glasser; *Editor:* Asa Clark; *Technical Adviser:* Ib Melchoir. *Running Time:* 78 minutes.

THE FILM
Bronson finished out 1958 with another leading role in another modest program picture, *When Hell Broke Loose,* a Dolworth production released by Paramount.

In this World War II story, he's an irresponsible bookie named Steve Boland, who's forced to join the Army to avoid a jail sentence. He spends

With John Morley.

With Violet Rensing and Robert Easton.

much of the war in the guardhouse, but when he's transferred to Germany, Steve is reformed by the love of a Fraulein, Ilsa (Violet Rensing), whose brother Karl (Richard Jaeckel) turns out to be a member of the Werewolves, a group of Nazis plotting to kill General Eisenhower. With Ilsa's help, Steve and Captain Melton locate the Werewolves' hideout, but are surprised by Karl. In an escape attempt, the girl is killed. Steve retaliates with gunfire, slaying a number of the Werewolves before M.P.s arrive and capture the survivors.

Aside from Jaeckel, Bronson appears to have been the only familiar face in this movie's cast. Indeed, this appears to be the one and only film most of them ever made, including leading lady Violet Rensing, then enjoying her big moment of disputable Hollywood glory.

In reviewing this trivial war yarn, one writer, Dorothy Masters, likened Bronson to John Garfield, calling him "less handsome, but somewhat reminiscent in style and characterization."

CRITICS' CORNER
"When this meandering story reaches its climax —a machine-gun scuffle in the woods—the moment comes as a disappointment. A number of documentary inserts do little to help the realism of a totally unreal film. The plot is slight, and a capable cast can do little with the feeble script."
Monthly Film Bulletin

"Uninspired. The fact that two of the characters are named 'Brooklyn' and 'Jonesie' tells a great deal about the inventiveness of this war melodrama. Although the film is said to be based on factual material, it fails to convince or to entertain.

"The cast try to give some vitality to their shapeless characterizations. Kenneth G. Crane, who edited as well as directed, succeeds in the first capacity better than the second."
"Powe.," Variety

With Dennie McCarthy, Ed Penny, and Bob Stevenson.

As John Danforth.

Never So Few

A Canterbury Production / 1959
  for Metro-Goldwyn-Mayer
In CinemaScope and Metrocolor

CAST
Capt. Tom C. Reynolds: Frank Sinatra; *Carla Vesari:* Gina Lollobrigida; *Capt. Grey Travis:* Peter Lawford; *Bill Ringa:* Steve McQueen; *Capt. Danny de Mortimer:* Richard Johnson; *Nikko Regas:* Paul Henreid; *Gen. Sloane:* Brian Donlevy; *Sgt. Jim Norby:* Dean Jones; *Sgt. John Danforth:* Charles Bronson; *Nautaung:* Philip Ahn; *Col. Fred Parkson:* Robert Bray; *Margaret Fitch:* Kipp Hamilton; *Col. Reed:* John Hoyt; *Capt. Alofson:* Whit Bissell; *Mike Island:* Richard Lupino; *Billingsly:* Aki Aleong; *Nurse:* Maggie Pierce.

CREDITS
Producer: Edmund Grainger; *Director:* John Sturges; *Assistant Director:* Robert E. Relyea; *Screenwriter:* Millard Kaufman; *Based on the Novel by:* Tom T. Chamales; *Cinematographer:* William H. Daniels; *Art Directors:* Hans Peters, Addison Hehr; *Set Decorators:* Henry Grace, Richard Pefferle; *Special Effects:* Robert R. Hoag, Lee LeBlanc; *Musical Score:* Hugo Friedhofer; *Editor:* Ferris Webster.
Running Time: 124 minutes.

THE FILM
Busy with television acting, Bronson now made few appearances in feature films. During 1959, he acted in the big-budgeted war film *Never So Few,* starring Frank Sinatra and Gina Lollobrigida. A routine mixture of unbelievable romance and

jungle skirmishes, the movie is highlighted by William H. Daniels' photography of such exotic locations as Burma, Thailand and Ceylon—and the gorgeous Gina, in an unlikely (for the setting) array of revealing Helen Rose gowns, and a titillating bathtub scene.

The movie's importance to Bronson's career was not, at first, apparent. Billed ninth, he even followed young newcomer Dean Jones. But his director here was John Sturges, who would later remember Bronson when casting the male-oriented *The Magnificent Seven* and *The Great Escape,* two of the actor's best films, as well as huge box-office hits.

CRITICS' CORNER
"What might have been an explosive and searching drama turns out to be just another war adventure film."

Arthur Knight, *Saturday Review*

"There is no way to measure this picture with a yardstick of pure intelligence. It is a romantic fabrication by which intelligence is simply repelled. The war scenes are wild and lurid, the dilly-dallying in the Calcutta bars and palatial hangouts of the wealthy is make-believe from an Oriental dream. Although based on a good book by Tom Chamales, the content of Millard Kauf-

Frank Sinatra and Gina Lollobrigida.

With Frank Sinatra.

man's script has the unsubstantiality of Hollywood hashish. And John Sturges has directed it for kicks. Those who will get them are the youngsters who can be lightly carried away by the juvenile brashness of Mr. Sinatra, by the swashbuckling antics of his pals, played almost beyond comprehension by Richard Johnson, Peter Lawford and Steve McQueen, and by the flamboyance of the fighting and the loving that are done in the same mood of violent bravura. Most sober people will just sit there appalled."
Bosley Crowther, The New York Times

"Anybody who sees this picture may be forgiven a profound sigh of assent when one actor remarks: 'You know, this war seems to go on forever.'"
Time

With Frank Sinatra, Philip Ahn, Steve McQueen, and Peter Lawford.

The Magnificent Seven

A Mirisch Company Production / 1960
  for United Artists
In Panavision and DeLuxe Color

CAST
Chris: Yul Brynner; *Calvera:* Eli Wallach; *Vin:* Steve McQueen; *Chico:* Horst Buchholz; *O'Reilly:* Charles Bronson; *Lee:* Robert Vaughn; *Harry Luck:* Brad Dexter; *Britt:* James Coburn; *Old Man:* Vladimir Sokoloff; *Petra:* Rosenda Monteros; *Hilario:* Jorge Martinez de Hoyos; *Chamlee:* Whit Bissell; *Henry:* Val Avery; *Robert:* Bing Russell; *Sotero:* Rico Alaniz; *Wallace:* Robert Wilke.

CREDITS
Executive Producer: Walter Mirisch; *Associate Producer:* Lou Morheim; *Producer-Director:* John Sturges; *Assistant Directors:* Robert Relyea, Jaime Contreras; *Screenwriter:* William Roberts; *Based on the Japanese Film "The Seven Samurai"* (1954); *Cinematographer:* Charles Lang, Jr.; *Art Director:* Edward Fitzgerald; *Set Decorator:* Rafael Suarez; *Special Effects:* Milt Rice; *Musical Score:* Elmer Bernstein; *Editor:* Ferris Webster.
Running Time: 126 minutes.

THE FILM
This Hollywood-Western adaptation of *The Seven Samurai,* director Akira Kurosawa's notable 1954 adventure melodrama, marked Charles Bronson's only 1960 big-screen appearance. But it was a notable one, making him an important contributor to a worthwhile team effort, a vital cog, as it were, in a well-constructed wheel. For, rather than suffering in comparison to what has become a Japanese classic, this Mirisch Company production is an acclaimed and deservedly popular Western classic in its own right.

A good script by William Roberts helped, as did excellent contributions by cinematographer Charles Lang, Jr., and editor Ferris Webster, underscored at all time by Elmer Bernstein's rousing, if somewhat noisy, background music. But film is a director's medium, and *The Magnificent Seven's* ultimate success rests on the capable talents of John Sturges, who had built his reputation on such 1950s popular outdoor suspense yarns as *Bad Day at Black Rock* and *Gunfight at the O.K. Corral.* Here, Sturges is as mindful of the scenic benefits of his Mexican locations as of the film's audience-grabbing plot elements—and he's fully up to the problems of handling a rather sprawling cast of strongly individual characters, without allowing the slightest degree of viewer confusion or ennui.

MS # 78 (462)

As Bernardo O'Reilly.

With Horst Buchholz and Yul Brynner.

Some of *The Magnificent Seven's* critics found the film difficult to accept in light of their affection for its Oriental predecessor, but most expressed appreciation for its virtues—and audiences made a great success of it at the box office.

Bronson's role made him an integral part of the film's title, centering on seven strangers, professional gunslingers hired by the elders of a Mexican village to put an end to the periodic bandit raids that have plagued them and their livelihood for years. Bronson portrays "Bernardo O'Reilly,"

With Yul Brynner, Steve McQueen, Horst Bucholz, Robert Vaughn, Brad Dexter, and James Coburn.

who explains his curious name to their leader, Chris (Yul Brynner), with "Mexican on one side, Irish on the other—and me in the middle!"

William Roberts' dialogue occasionally permits Bernardo's character a rather arch sense of humor, behind his brawny-flint exterior. After witnessing an unusual display of temperament by young Chico (Horst Buchholz), the Mexican-Indian destined to become their seventh member, Bernardo and Harry Luck (Brad Dexter) are riding along together. When the latter remarks, distractedly, "I keep thinking of that kid back there," Bernardo cracks wryly, "If you can't forget him, why not ride side-saddle?"

Bronson and Dexter, along with Robert Vaughn and James Coburn, are among the protagonists killed off in the movie's ultimate shoot-out between bandits and gunmen.

The Magnificent Seven's success spawned three sequels of downward-spiralling merit: Return of the Seven (1966, again starring Yul Brynner), Guns of the Magnificent Seven (1969) and, last and least of all, The Magnificent Seven Ride (1972).

CRITICS' CORNER
"There is a heap of fine acting and some crackling good direction by John Sturges, mostly in the early stages. Brynner exhibits anew the masculine charm that has won him so many femme fans. McQueen, an actor who is going places, brings an appealing ease and sense of humor to his role. Buchholz makes an auspicious screen bow in this country. Bronson fashions the most sympathetic character of the group."

"Tube.," Variety

"Kurosawa's film has been paralleled without being slavishly copied. William Roberts' script with its terse, elliptical and often superb, dialogue, has kept pretty closely to the original story, but adapted without damaging—while the completely new episodes show a high level of imagination. More importantly, Sturges' direction is as admirable a virtuoso display as was Kurosawa's.

"The acting is entirely without weakness, a series of beautifully delineated characterizations from the seven gunmen, each emerging as a definite character yet never swamping the others with personal idiosyncrasies. This is American film acting at its very best, and deserving of some sort of collective Academy Award."

Richard Whitehall, Films and Filming

"When the action takes over, Sturges guides it with a firm hand and a sharp eye for pictorial excitement. And, for a polyglot cast he draws uniformly strong performances."

Arthur Knight, Saturday Review

". . . the supporting performances are of an unusually high standard. Particularly notable are Charles Bronson as the neolithic-looking strong man with tender paternal instincts, James Coburn as the tensely commanding knife expert, Steve McQueen as the most relaxed of the group, and Robert Vaughn as the one whose black gloves and nightmares serve as a constant reminder that The Magnificent Seven, unlike The Seven Samurai, is also and perhaps sadly a Freudian Western."

Monthly Film Bulletin

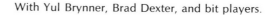

With Yul Brynner, Brad Dexter, and bit players.

With Vincent Price.

Master of the World

An American International Picture / 1961
In MagnaColor

CAST
Robur: Vincent Price; *Strock:* Charles Bronson; *Prudent:* Henry Hull; *Dorothy:* Mary Webster; *Philip:* David Frankham; *Alistair:* Richard Harrison; *Topage:* Vito Scotti: *Turner:* Wally Campo; *Weaver:* Steve Masino; *Shanks:* Ken Terrell; *Wilson:* Peter Besbas.

CREDITS
Executive Producer: Samuel Z. Arkoff; *Producer:* James H. Nicholson; *Director:* William Witney; *Assistant Director:* Robert Agnew; *Screenwriter:* Richard Matheson; *Based on the Novels* "Master of the World" *and* "Robur, the Conqueror" *by:* Jules Verne; *Cinematographer:* Gil Warrenton; *Aerial Photography:* Kay Norton; *Art Director:* Daniel Haller; *Set Decorator:* Harry Reif; *Special Effects:* Tim Barr, Wah Chang, Gene Warren, Ray Mercer; *Musical Score:* Les Baxter; *Editor:* Anthony Carras.
Running Time: 104 minutes.

THE FILM
Master of the World was based on a pair of Jules Verne novels, consolidated into one characteristically fantastic narrative. An ambitious and expensive production in 1961 from the modest exploitation-film company, American International, this colorful adventure yarn rode the crest of the Verne film wave that had turned out such audience favorites as *Journey to the Center of the Earth* and *20,000 Leagues Under the Sea* from more prestigious filmmakers than Samuel Z. Arkoff and James H. Nicholson.

Master of the World not only returned Bronson to leading-man status, but reunited him with *House of Wax's* Vincent Price, albeit, this time in a co-starring role with Price. Under William Witney's direction, this science-fiction tale centers on Robur (Price), a mad inventor who has built a strange aircraft, *The Albatross,* which he intends to use to destroy all the world's armaments, in the interests of lasting peace.

With David Frankham.

Bronson plays Strock, a government agent who, along with a munitions maker (Henry Hull), his daughter (Mary Webster) and her fiance (David Frankham), becomes a prisoner of Robur when their balloon is shot down. Kept prisoner aboard *The Albatross*, the foursome witnesses Robur's destruction of England's naval yards, as well as the armies of Egypt and Austria. Eventually, during a landing for repairs on a Mediterranean island, they escape. With explosives from the airship's armory, Strock manages to send Robur and his fantastic vehicle to the bottom of the ocean.

CRITICS' CORNER
"It is not so much the inevitable grotesquerie of the picture's mechanical marvels, but the drabness of characterization and dialogue that keeps it well below the level of interest adult moviegoers would expect."
    Paul V. Beckley, *The New York Herald Tribune*

"The hero, quietly acted by Charles Bronson, is a likeable type, homely, modest and altogether noble. Trapped with three helpless companions on an 1848 flying machine captained by a crazed inventor, he behaves with consistent calm sensibili-

With Henry Hull and David Frankham.

With David Frankham and Vincent Price.

ty. His friends misunderstand his motives, but he never complains and eventually saves the world and wins the girl away from her handsome, but irresolute, fiance.

"The villain, too, is the good old-fashioned kind, in the surprisingly restrained hands of Vincent Price."

Eugene Archer, *The New York Times*

"It is obvious that a great deal of care, expense and ingenuity went into the making of this picture, American International's most ambitious project to date. Therefore, it is doubly disheartening that the finished product emerges watered-down Jules Verne, diluted by modern dramatic agents foreign to the nature of the author's original fantasy."

"Tube.," *Variety*

With David Frankham, Mary Webster, and Henry Hull.

Richard Boone and George Hamilton.

A Thunder of Drums

A Metro-Goldwyn-Mayer Picture / 1961
In CinemaScope and Metrocolor

CAST
Capt. Stephen Maddocks: Richard Boone; *Lt. Curtis McQuade:* George Hamilton; *Tracey Hamilton:* Luana Patten; *Sgt. Rodermill:* Arthur O'Connell; *Trooper Hanna:* Charles Bronson; *Lt. Porter:* Richard Chamberlain; *Trooper Eddy:* Duane Eddy; *Lt. Gresham:* James Douglas; *Laurie:* Tammy Marihugh; *Camden Yates:* Carole Wells; *Trooper Erschick:* Slim Pickens; *Trooper Denton:* Clem Harvey; *Trooper Baker:* Casey Tibbs; *Mrs. Scarborough:* Irene Tedrow; *Mrs. Yates:* Marjorie Bennett; *Captain Scarborough:* J. Edward McKinley.

CREDITS
Producer: Robert J. Enders; *Associate Producer:* Stanley Bass; *Director:* Joseph M. Newman; *Assistant Director:* Hal Polaire; *Screenwriter:* James Warner Bellah; *Cinematographer:* William Spencer; *Art Directors:* George W. Davis, Gabriel Scognamillo; *Set Decorators:* Henry Grace, Jack Mills; *Musical Score:* Harry Sukman; *Songs* "Water from a Bad Well" and "Ballad of Camden Yates" *Composed and Sung by:* Duane Eddy; *Editor:* Ferris Webster.
Running Time: 97 minutes.

THE FILM
Bronson returned to the old West, to MGM—and to a nether section of the cast in this respectable outdoor action drama of the U.S. Cavalry Indian battles of the 1870s. As the film's fifth-billed actor, listed just above Richard Chamberlain (then learning his craft as TV's "Dr. Kildare"), Bronson portrayed Trooper Hanna, a veteran of Indian fighting who thrives on whiskey, women and

scraps with the Apaches. In one sequence, he engages in a knock-down-drag-out fight with the movie's young lieutenant juvenile lead (George Hamilton) over an illicit romance the youth has been carrying on with another Cavalry lieutenant's fiancee at Arizona's Fort Canby. With filming largely done on the story's actual locales in Arizona's desert plains, this James Warner Bellah screenplay spent its main focus on the turbulent relationship between green lieutenant Hamilton and the post's crusty old captain (Richard Boone), with Luana Patten as the distaff object of Hamilton's distractions—and Indians always waiting on the sidelines for the stars' personal problems to subside so that they can get back to the serious business of fighting.

CRITICS' CORNER
"*A Thunder of Drums* makes an effort to be a little more than just another Western, but if it succeeds in some respects, usually in the secondary characters and in the dialogue, it falls considerably short, especially in direction, which does not take full advantage of the script and tends toward over-emphasis of the obvious."
    Paul V. Beckley, *The New York Herald Tribune*

"Arthur O'Connell and Charles Bronson contribute valuable, colorful character work. Most of the other characters are two-dimensional.
    The recent furor over excessive violence on the screen should be soothed considerably by this film. The concept here is to 'look the other way' when the going gets too brutal and bloody."
    "Tube.," *Variety*

"Arthur O'Connell, as a wise, old topkick, and Charles Bronson as a ruffian of a trooper but an ace in battle are rough-hewn examples of the post-Civil War G.I.
    "Mr. Bellah has written excellent dialogue and Joseph Newman has directed this adventure, which catches the color of the lonely, arid Southwest in natural, vivid shades, with extreme diligence. But *A Thunder of Drums* is proof again that Cavalry and Indians and the passions, both grand and base, never do mix too well."
    A. H. Weiler, *The New York Times*

With George Hamilton.

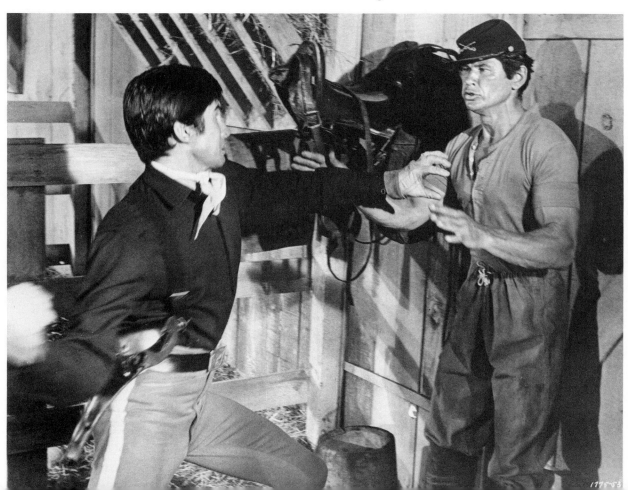

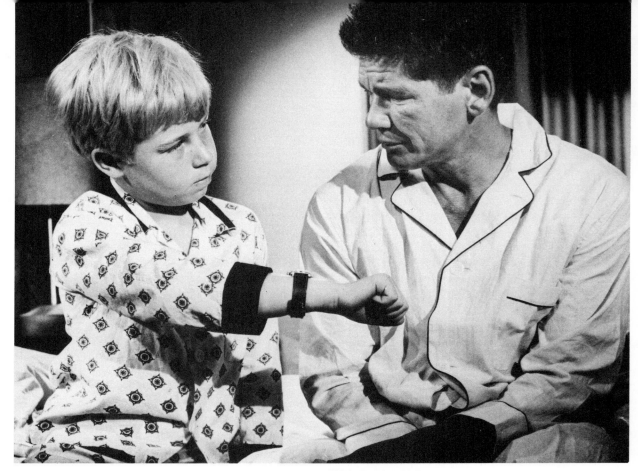

With Stanley Livingston.

X-15

An Essex Production / 1962
   for United Artists
In Panavision and Technicolor

CAST
Matt Powell: David McLean; *Lt. Col. Lee Brandon:* Charles Bronson; *Maj. Ernest Wilde:* Ralph Taeger; *Maj. Anthony Rinaldi:* Brad Dexter; *Col. Craig Brewster:* Kenneth Tobey; *Tom Deparma:* James Gregory; *Pamela Stewart:* Mary Tyler Moore; *Margaret Brandon:* Patricia Owens; *Diane Wilde:* Lisabeth Hush; *Mike Brandon:* Stanley Livingston; *Col. Jessup:* Lauren Gilbert; *Maj. McCully:* Phil Dean; *Lt. Comm. Joe Lacrosse:* Chuck Stanford; *Susan Brandon:* Patty McDonald; *B-52 Pilot:* Mike MacKane; *Test Engineer:* Robert Dornnam; *Security Policeman:* Frank Watkins; *Secretary:* Barbara Kelley; *Nurse:* Darlene Hendricks; *Themselves:* Ed Fleming, Lee Giroux, Grant Holcomb, Lew Erwin; *Engineers:* Ric Applewhite, Pat Renella; *Operators:* Jerry Lawrence, Richard Norris.

CREDITS
Executive Producer: Howard W. Koch; *Producers:* Henry Sanicola, Tony Lazzarino; *Director:* Richard D. Donner; *Assistant Directors:* Russ Haverick, Jay Sandrich; *Screenwriters:* Tony Lazzarino, James Warner Bellah; *Based on a Story by* Tony Lazzarino; *Cinematographer:* Carl Guthrie; *Art Director:* Rolland M. Brooks; *Set Decorator:* Kenneth Schwartz; *Special Effects:* Paul Pollard, Howard Anderson; *Musical Score:* Nathan Scott; *Editor:* Stanley Rabjohn; *Narrator:* James Stewart. *Running Time:* 107 minutes.

THE FILM
Bronson next appeared as one of three test pilots in this semi-documentary about those involved in the X-15 research work at California's Edwards Air

As Lee Brandon.

Force Base. The men are shown undergoing both mental and physical strain, while their wives do their share to lessen the pressure, during off-hours. Human drama mixes with technical footage and colorful aerial photography, to modestly exciting effect. Bronson plays the film's heroic fatality, killed while saving a fellow-pilot (David McLean), and after having set a world's speed record. Patricia Owens is his grieving widow, and young Stanley Livingston (of TV's *My Three Sons)* the son who shares an affecting key scene with Bronson.

X-15 marked the big-screen bow of TV director Richard Donner, who, in the 1970s, would go on to direct that chilling thriller *The Omen,* and the costly special-effects extravaganza, *Superman.*

CRITICS' CORNER

"A surprisingly appealing and sensible low-budget picture—a semi-documentary with some harmless fictional embroidery. Enhanced by some good color photography, a quick tone of steady purposefulness and some level-headed acting by a fairly unfamiliar cast, the picture sticks reasonably close to the business at hand.

"James Gregory is excellent throughout. So, for that matter, up or down, are David McLean and the always reliable Charles Bronson."
Howard Thompson, *The New York Times*

"Much too technically involved for the layman—at times it resembles a training film more than a popular entertainment.

"The screenplay is hackneyed and confusing and execution is awkward and frequently incoherent. None of the characters are endowed with any real identity or personality. Under the circumstances, the actors don't have much of a chance to put any sock into their performances. Charles Bronson and James Gregory seem to fare the best."

"Tube.," *Variety*

"David McLean, Charles Bronson and Ralph Taeger, as the astronauts, look the part and act commendably, especially Bronson, whose scene with his son is impressive."
Robert Salmaggi, *The New York Herald Tribune*

With David McLean.

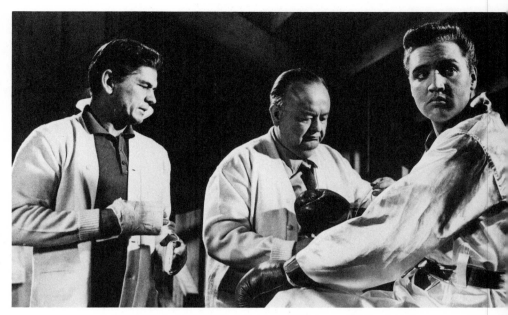

With Robert Emhardt and Elvis Presley.

Kid Galahad

A Mirisch Company Production / 1962
   for United Artists
In DeLuxe Color

CAST

Walter Gulick: Elvis Presley; *Willy Grogan:* Gig Young; *Dolly Fletcher:* Lola Albright; *Rose Grogan:* Joan Blackman; *Lew Nyack:* Charles Bronson; *Lieberman:* Ned Glass; *Maynard:* Robert Emhardt; *Otto Danzig:* David Lewis; *Joie Shakes:* Michael Dante; *Zimmerman:* Judson Pratt; *Sperling:* George Mitchell; *Marvin:* Richard Devon; *Ralphie:* Jeffrey Morris; *Father Higgins:* Liam Redmond.

CREDITS

Producer: David Weisbart; *Director:* Phil Karlson; *Assistant Director:* Jerome M. Siegel; *Screenwriter:* William Fay; *Based on a Story by:* Francis Wallace; *Cinematographer:* Burnett Guffey; *Art Director:* Cary Odell; *Set Decorator:* Edward G. Boyle; *Special Effects:* Milt Rice; *Musical Score:* Jeff Alexander; *The Songs:* "King of the Whole Wide World" by Ruth Batchelor and Bob Roberts; "This Is Living" and "Riding the Rainbow" by Fred Wise and Ben Wiesman; "Home Is Where the Heart Is" by Sherman Edwards and Hal David; "I Got Lucky" by Dee Fuller, Fred Wise and Ben Weisman; "A Whistling Tune" by Sherman Edwards and Hal David; "Love Is for Lovers" by Ruth Batchelor and Sharon Silbert; *Editor:* Stuart Gilmore.
Running Time: 95 minutes.

THE FILM

This Mirisch Company effort to stretch singer Elvis Presley's limited acting talents by presenting him as a pugilist-hopeful (albeit a *singing* one—with seven songs!) proved a somewhat uneasy comedy-drama-cum-music. Its hoary plot, based on a story by Francis Wallace, was updated rather well by scenarist William Fay. But there was no effort made to hide the fact that the movie was actually a remake of the 1937 Warner Bros. *Kid Galahad* that had featured Edward G. Robinson, Bette Davis and Wayne Morris—in the roles now taken by Gig Young, Lola Albright and Presley.

Again, Bronson impressed the film's critics in a supporting role, making an overweight Elvis seem

With Elvis Presley.

a better actor because of their scenes together (Bronson was his training-camp aide and sparring partner). Characteristic of Hollywood thinking, California locations were employed to represent New York State.

CRITICS' CORNER
"The last thing you might think Elvis Presley is qualified to do is act a diffident amateur boxer who turns out to be a tiger in the professional ring. And you might well persist in that opinion after seeing him in *King Galahad*. Charles Bronson, Ned Glass and Robert Emhardt make good training-camp characters.

"For a film about a singing prize-fighter (which is silly enough) it will do."
Bosley Crowther, *The New York Times*

"There are two strong principal performances. One is Lola Albright's (an accomplished actress who deserves bigger and better roles) as Young's unrequited torch-carrier, the other Charles Bronson's as an understanding trainer."
"Tube.," *Variety*

"If the wit and intelligence lavished on the excellent dialogue had also been used to give a shred of ingenuity to the plot or a momentary sparkle to the lyrics, this would have been a much more amusing comedy. As it is, however, the clever back-chat of William Fay's screenplay, the slick throwaway delivery of Charles Bronson, Gig Young and Lola Albright, and the charming woodland backgrounds of upstate New York (filmed at Idyllwild, California!) are wasted on a melange of folksiness, inanity and brutality."
Monthly Film Bulletin

With Gig Young and Jeffrey Morris.

This Rugged Land

A Wilrich Production / 1962
  for BLC/Columbia Pictures

CAST
Jim Redigo: Richard Egan; *Connie Garrett:* Terry Moore; *Paul Moreno:* Charles Bronson; *Lucia Garret:* Anne Seymour; *Tal Garret:* Ryan O'Neal; *Tom Rawlings:* Denver Pyle; *Harvey Welk:* Oliver McGowan; *Chuck:* Warren Vanders.

CREDITS
Producer: William Sackheim; *Director:* Arthur Hiller; *Assistant Director:* Herb Wallerstein; *Screenwriter:* Frank Nugent; *Based on a Story by:* Kathleen Hite; *Cinematographer:* Joseph Biroc; *Art Director:* Walter Holscher; *Set Decorator:* James N. Crowe; *Musical Score:* Johnny Green; *Editor:* Jack Ruggiero.
Running Time: 71 minutes

THE FILM
The *Empire* TV series, which ran from 1962 to 1964, was one of the many Westerns so popular with home audiences during the fifties and sixties. In this one, Richard Egan portrayed the central character of Jim Redigo, foreman of the half-million-acre Garret Ranch in Santa Fe, New Mexico, and Bronson had the running part of ranch-hand Paul Moreno.

In this television-derived feature, shown overseas as a *theatrical* film, Moreno is accused of murdering the foreman's daughter. He is tried and found innocent, a decision unacceptable to his fellow ranch-hands—until Redigo's trust and Moreno's subsequent behavior convince the men of their error in judgment.

This movie was an expanded version of the *Empire* debut episode of September 25, 1962. But it didn't reach British cinemas until 1965.

CRITICS' CORNER
"A solidly competent low-budget Western, whose main interest lies in its background picture of the workings of an enormous Texan ranch. Richard Egan and Charles Bronson are convincingly tough, and the story-line makes no concessions to romantic fiction."

Monthly Film Bulletin

As Paul Moreno.

With John Leyton.

The Great Escape

A Mirisch-Alpha Production   /   1963
  for United Artists
In Panavision and DeLuxe Color

CAST
Hilts: Steve McQueen; *Hendley:* James Garner; *Bartlett:* Richard Attenborough; *Ramsey:* James Donald; *Danny Velinski:* Charles Bronson; *Blythe:* Donald Pleasence; *Sedgwick:* James Coburn; *Ashley-Pitt:* David McCallum; *MacDonald:* Gordon Jackson; *Willie:* John Leyton; *Ives:* Angus Lennie; *Cavendish:* Nigel Stock; *Goff:* Jud Taylor; *Sorren:* William Russell; *Griffith:* Robert Desmond; *Nimmo:* Tom Adams; *Haynes;* Lawrence Montaigne; *Von Luger;* Hannes Messemer; *Werner:* Robert Graf; *Strachwitz:* Harry Riebauer; *Kugn:* Hans Reiser; *Posen:* Robert Freitag; *Kramer:* Heinz Weiss; *Frick:* Til Kiwe; *Preissen:* Ulrich Beiger; *Dietrich:* George Mikell; *Steinach:* Otto Alberty.

CREDITS
Producer-Director: John Sturges; *Assistant to Mr. Sturges:* Robert E. Relyea; *Assistant Director:* Jack Reddish; *Screenwriters:* James Clavell, W. R. Burnett; *Based on the Book by:* Paul Brickhill; *Cinematographer:* Daniel L. Fapp; *Art Director:* Fernando Carrere; *Musical Score:* Elmer Bernstein; *Editor:* Ferris Webster.
Running Time: 168 minutes.

THE FILM
It has been said that *The Great Escape* is a triumph of style over content. How else to explain the overwhelming popular success of this World War II prisoner-of-war yarn? Surely the starring team of up-and-coming Steve McQueen and James Garner, backed by a top-notch, all-male supporting cast, wasn't the only reason for making this engrossing adventure film such a box-office hit. But a fine script, adapted by James Clavell and W. R. Burnett, from Paul Brickhill's factual book, laid an excellent foundation for producer-director John Sturges, in his best form since *The Magnificent Seven.*

Humor, excitement and human drama are craftily blended in this amusing and exciting suspense tale, partly filmed on location in Bavaria. Expertly edited to just under three hours, *The Great Escape* proves too engrossing—even at that length—to lose its audience, a minor triumph in itself. And it's smartly underscored by Elmer Bernstein's memorable background music.

Billed fifth in the cast, Bronson plays "Danny Velinski," the Polish-American prisoner who supervises the digging of the three escape tunnels

111

by Allied prisoners, incarcerated in a Nazi stalag in 1942 Germany. At the film's close, though a claustrophobe, he is one of the few to have made a successful break to freedom. For, although seventy-six men escape from the prison camp, most are recaptured, and a full fifty are executed. The toll of freedom is dear, and the movie's ending provokes sober thoughts.

But what *The Great Escape* failed to garner in awards it more than compensated for in profits, becoming one of 1963's real box-office champions.

CRITICS' CORNER
"The most exhilarating and sobering adventure story of the year, *The Great Escape*, based on fact, is an ode to freedom, and to man's indomitable will to live free.

"It is taut, vibrant, tingling. And it soars exuberantly in great gusts of wild good humor. What gives the picture stature is the fact that, true to history, many of its protagonists are captured. For all its sobering finale, one leaves *The Great Escape* thoroughly entertained and spiritually enriched."

Arthur Knight, *Saturday Review*

"A motion picture that entertains, captivates, thrills and stirs, an experience rich in cinematic expression as well as dramatic impact. Since there are no marquee 'naturals' in the cast, this picture will illustrate how superior story and production

With Richard Attenborough.

With Lawrence Montaigne, Tom Adams, John Leyton,
and James Coburn.

Richard Attenborough, Gordon Jackson, and Steve McQueen.

values can carry a project to great success without the aid of prohibitively expensive souped-up stellar names.

"There are some exceptional performances. Probably the most provocative single impression is made by Steve McQueen. He is a throwback to the personalities of earlier screen eras. James Garner does his best screenwork to date as the compound's 'scrounger.' Charles Bronson and James Coburn do solid work, although the latter's character is anything but clearly defined."

"Tube.," *Variety*

"With accurate casting, a swift screenplay and authentic German settings, producer-director John Sturges has created classic cinema of action. There is no sermonizing, no soul probing, no sex. *The Great Escape* is simply great escapism."

Time

"A first-rate adventure film, fascinating in its plot, stirring in its climax, and excellent in performance. John Sturges has done a remarkable job in building from climax to climax. There is a driving force through the story and its development, with only moments out for a bit of humor, a broadened characterization, a hint of background. Slight as some of the portraits are, we are left with a gallery of men made memorable by their deeds. *The Great Escape* is one of those rare three-hour films that neither sag, lag nor allow, let alone inspire, watch-checking. It's out-and-out adventure, an absorbing story of very human heroes that is a top-notch entertainment."

Judith Crist, *The New York Herald Tribune*

With John Leyton, Richard Attenborough, and James Donald.

With James Coburn, director John Sturges, and Steve McQueen on location.

4 for Texas

A Sam Company Production / 1963
    for Warner Bros.
In Technicolor

CAST
Zack Thomas: Frank Sinatra; *Joe Jarrett:* Dean Martin; *Elya Carlson:* Anita Ekberg; *Maxine Richter:* Ursula Andress; *Matson:* Charles Bronson; *Harvey Burden:* Victor Buono; *Prince George:* Edric Connor; *Angel:* Nick Dennis; *Mancini:* Richard Jaeckel; *Chad:* Mike Mazurki; *Trowbridge:* Wesley Addy; *Miss Ermaline:* Marjorie Bennett; *Dobie:* Jack Elam; *Maitre D':* Fritz

Frank Sinatra, Anita Ekberg, Dean Martin, Ursula Andress, and Marjorie Bennett.

Feld; *Ansel:* Percy Helton; *Renee:* Jonathan Hole; *Monk:* Jack Lambert; *Beauregard:* Paul Langton; *Widow:* Jesslyn Fax; *Maid:* Allison Ames; *Guest Stars:* Arthur Godfrey; The Three Stooges; Teddy Bruckner & His All-Stars.

CREDITS
Producer-Director: Robert Aldrich; *Associate Producer:* Walter Blake; *2nd Unit Director:* Oscar Rudolph; *Assistant Directors:* Tom Connors, Dave Salven; *Screenwriters:* Teddi Sherman, Robert Aldrich; *Cinematographer:* Ernest Laszlo; *2nd Unit Photographers:* Carl Guthrie, Joseph Biroc, Burnett Guffey; *Art Director:* William Glasgow; *Set Decorator:* Raphael Bretton; *Musicial Score:* Nelson Riddle; *Editor:* Michael Luciano.
Running Time: 124 minutes.

THE FILM
Bronson was back in the saddle again in this supposed comedy-Western, as outlaw leader Matson who, in the employ of crooked Galveston banker Victor Buono, helps start the film off on a high note of action. He and his gang attack a desert stagecoach whose passengers include Dean Martin and Frank Sinatra (who manages to repulse them). Later, when Bronson tries to kill Sinatra, Martin wounds him.

Much of the plot, such as it is, is taken up with the comic rivalry between Martin and Sinatra, involved with gambling, boozing and womanizing. In the closing scenes, Bronson's gang is finally defeated, the bandit king is shot dead by Sinatra, and the movie's rival heroes wed their girlfriends, Ursula Andress and Anita Ekberg.

Bronson had his *Vera Cruz* producer-director, Robert Aldrich, to thank for this assignment, which may have provided a reasonable amount of amusement for its audiences. The critical fraternity, however, found little here to laugh about, and seemed agreed that the Sinatra-Martin "Clan," through sheer self-indulgence, had made a losing attempt to pull a fast one on the public.

CRITICS' CORNER
"If Robert Aldrich could have brought himself to

slash the script in half and jolt the camera, if not the actors, out of slow motion, there might have been fun afoot—but why daydream? As it stands, The Three Stooges doing one of their hoarier routines and an old lady falling out of her wheelchair provide the major laughs."

Judith Crist, *The New York Herald Tribune*

"It seems that when two or more of the 'Clan' get together, the last thing one should expect is a serious attempt at film-making. *4 For Texas* is a Western of sorts, where one suspects the most amusing antics were those that went on off-screen. Probably a good time was had by them all during production; unfortunately there is not very much on screen which will entertain the audience.

"Poor Charles Bronson, who introduces himself at the start with 'I'm the bad guy,' plays a most in-competent hired gunman. Shot up by Martin, he returns to have a bullet placed squarely in his forehead by Sinatra and be launched into the river by Ursula Andress."

Robin Bean, *Films and Filming*

"A Western too preoccupied with sex and romance to enthrall sagebrush-happy moppets and too unwilling to take itself seriously to sustain the attention of an adult. Sinatra and Martin carry on in accustomed manner, the latter getting most of what laughs there are. The film is loaded with distracting cleavage, thanks to the presence of Anita Ekberg and Ursula Andress. Buono and Bronson make an impression, but the editing tends to add to the confusion."

"Tube.," *Variety*

With Susan Oliver.

Guns of Diablo

A Metro-Goldwyn-Mayer Picture   /   1964
In Color

CAST

Linc Murdock: Charles Bronson; *Maria:* Susan Oliver; *Jaimie McPheeters:* Kurt Russell; *Rance Macklin:* Jan Merlin; *Ives:* John Fiedler; *Knudson:* Douglas Fowley; *Dan Macklin:* Rayford Barnes; *Mendez:* Robert Carricart; *Carey Macklin:* Ron Hagerthy; *Dr. McPheeters:* Russ Conway; *Hickey:* Byron Foulger; *Florrie:* Marguerita Cordova; *Bryce:* Mike de Anda.

CREDITS

Producer: Boris Ingster; *Assistant Producers:* Norman Siegel, Ardel Wray; *Director:* Boris Sagal; *Assistant Director:* Eddie Saeta; *Screenwriter:* Berne Giler; *Based on the Novel* "The Travels of Jaimie McPheeters" *by:* Robert Lewis Taylor; *Cinematographer:* John M. Nickolaus, Jr.; *Art Directors:* George W. Davis, Addison Hehr; *Set Decorators:* Henry Grace, Jack Mills; *Musical Score:* Walter Scharf, Harry Sukman, Leigh Harline; *Editor:* Harry Coswick.
Running Time: 79 minutes.

THE FILM

Like Bronson's 1962 TV-derived feature, *This Rugged Land, Guns of Diablo* represents an expansion from television, in this case the March 1964 "Day of Reckoning" episode from the Western series entitled *The Travels of Jaimie McPheeters.* Young Kurt Russell had the title role in these stories about wagon-train settlers' experiences in 1849, as seen through the eyes of a twelve-year-old passenger. Bronson portrayed the party's guide, Linc Murdock.

In this story, Linc and Jaimie tangle with outlaws who control the town into which they go for supplies—and where Linc encounters Maria (blonde Susan Oliver, with black wig and Spanish accent), an old flame of his, now married to gunman Rance Macklin (Jan Merlin), whose arm Linc had once shattered in a fight. Rance now sees his chance for revenge.

In the ensuing action, Linc is imprisoned by the Macklin gang, is freed by the still-ardent Maria, shoots it out with the outlaws and, aided by

With Jan Merlin.

With Kurt Russell, Susan Oliver, and Douglas Fowley.

Jaimie and an elderly townsman (Douglas Fowley), kills them. But the old man dies, claiming to be a millionaire and giving Jaimie the map to a California gold mine. Linc and Jaimie resume their westward journey with Maria.

In Great Britain, MGM "premiered" this movie-from-TV as a *theatrical* feature running a brief 56 minutes. In the 1970s, *Guns of Diablo* plays American TV once again—but this time as a *79-minute* movie, having come full-circle and then some!

CRITICS' CORNER

"Based—like the TV series, which uses some of the same actors—on an incident in the U.S. best-seller, *The Travels of Jaimie McPheeters,* this is a completely routine, small-scale horse opera. A great waste of Charles Bronson, as carved and weather-beaten a face as ever graced a totem-pole."

Monthly Film Bulletin

"Boris Sagal has concentrated a great deal on the small-town atmosphere. No traditional Western glamour here—it's all rather bare and empty. Once or twice I was reminded of *Shane*—perhaps that's inevitable with the small boy/idolised adult theme woven into the action. Goodie Linc Murdock is played somewhat stolidly by Charles Bronson with many meaningful stares."

David Rider, *Films and Filming*

With Susan Oliver.

121

As Cos Erickson.

With Elizabeth Taylor.

The Sandpiper

A Filmways Picture / 1965
   for Metro-Goldwyn-Mayer
In Panavision and Metrocolor

CAST

Laura Reynolds: Elizabeth Taylor; *Dr. Edward Hewitt:* Richard Burton; *Claire Hewitt:* Eva Marie Saint; *Cos Erickson:* Charles Bronson; *Ward Hendricks:* Robert Webber; *Larry Brant:* James Edwards; *Judge Thompson:* Torin Thatcher; *Walter Robinson:* Tom Drake; *Phil Sutcliff:* Doug Henderson; *Danny Reynolds:* Morgan Mason; *Troopers:* Dusty Cadis, John Hart; *First Trustee:* Jan Arvan; *Trustee's Wife:* Mary Benoit; *Second Trustee:* Tom Curtis; *Architect:* Paul Genge; *First Celebrant:* Rex Holman; *Second Celebrant:* Kelton Garwood; *Third Celebrant:* Jimmy Murphy; *Fourth Celebrant:* Mel Gallagher; *Poet Celebrant:* Ron Whelan; *Sixth Celebrant:* Diane Sayer; *Seventh Celebrant:* Joan Connors; *Eighth Celebrant:* Peggy Adams Laird; *Ninth Celebrant:* Shirley Bonne; *Voice:* Peter O'Toole.

CREDITS

Producer: Martin Ransohoff; *Associate Producer:* John Calley; *Director:* Vincente Minnelli; *Assistant Director:* William McGarry; *Screenwriters:* Dalton Trumbo, Michael Wilson; *Based on an Original Story by:* Martin Ransohoff; *Adaptors:* Irene and Louis Kamp; *Cinematographer:* Milton Krasner; *Wildlife Photographer:* Richard Borden; *Art Directors:* George W. Davis, Urie McCleary; *Set Decorators:* Henry Grace, Keogh Gleason; *Musical Score:* Johnny Mandel; *Song:* "The Shadow of Your Smile" *by:* Johnny Mandel and Paul Francis Webster; *Editor:* David Bretherton. *Running Time:* 116 minutes.

THE FILM

During 1965, Bronson appeared in the supporting casts of two big-budgeted films, *The Sandpiper* and *Battle of the Bulge*. The former, directed by Vincente Minnelli, was fashioned by screenwriters Dalton Trumbo and Michael Wilson as a vehicle for Richard Burton and Elizabeth Taylor, in the third of their eleven co-starring efforts. For tax reasons, the Burtons could only film on California's Big Sur coastal locations for two months, before moving on to a Paris studio for interior scenes.

In this sudsy love story about a married school-headmaster-minister's affair with a free-living, "widowed" artist (Taylor), Bronson portrayed her aging hippie friend. When he carves a naked wooden likeness of the film's star, as she poses for him semi-nude, Burton (understandably) misunderstands, and a fight ensues. After much

With Richard Burton and Elizabeth Taylor.

romantic soul-searching, Burton leaves his job and loving wife Eva Marie Saint to face a dubious future with Taylor.

CRITICS' CORNER
"There is no doubt, however, about the intentions behind the movie's selling points: the proper clergyman visits our heroine while she is posing nude (from the waist up) for a sculptor. She converses with him, demurely cupping her breasts with her hands—though they seem inadequate to the task.

"The director, Vincente Minnelli, a man with a sophisticated, charming talent, who has in the past made movies about the Hollywood juggernaut, is here crushed under it."

Pauline Kael, *The New Yorker*

"Doubtless as an exploitation gimmick, Elizabeth Taylor, who co-stars with Richard Burton, is frequently overexposed via lowcut sweaters and tops, and there is one scene where she is completely nude to the waist except for her hands barely covering focal points. Since there is no definite story point to be established by such cleavage, many unquestionably will be offended by the poor taste evidenced by the star.

"Burton probably comes off best with a more restrained performance, although Miss Taylor plays well enough a role without any great acting demands. Charles Bronson also scores as a beatnik sculptor."

"Whit.," *Variety*

With Elizabeth Taylor and Richard Burton.

With Henry Fonda.

Battle of the Bulge

A Co-production of Sidney Harmon and
  United States Pictures / 1965
  for Warner Bros.
In Ultra-Panavision Cinerama and Technicolor

CAST
Lt. Col. Kiley: Henry Fonda; *Col. Hessler:* Robert Shaw; *Gen. Grey:* Robert Ryan; *Col. Pritchard:* Dana Andrews; *Sgt. Duquesne:* George Montgomery; *Schumacher:* Ty Hardin; *Louise:* Pier Angeli; *Elena:* Barbara Werle; *Wolenski:* Charles Bronson; *Gen. Kohler:* Werner Peters; *Conrad:* Hans Christian Blech; *Lt. Weaver:* James MacArthur; *Guffy:* Telly Savalas; *Bits:* Steve Rowland, Karl Alberty.

CREDITS
Producers: Milton Sperling, Philip Yordan; *Director:* Ken Annakin; *Assistant Directors:* Jose Lopez Rodero, Martin Sacristan, Luis Garcia; *Screenwriters:* Philip Yordan, Milton Sperling, John Melson; *Cinematographer:* Jack Hildyard; *2nd Unit Photographer:* John Cabrera; *Aerial Photographer:* Jack Willoughby; *Art Director:* Eugene Lourie; *Special Effects:* Alex Weldon; *Musical Score:* Benjamin Frankel; *Editor:* Derek Parsons; *Technical Advisers:* Gen. Meinrad von Lauchert, Col. Sherman Joffe, Maj. Edward King.
Running Time: 167 minutes.

THE FILM
The huge, tri-part Cinerama screen had its first combat film in this World War II adventure spectacle purporting to tell the story of that epic 1944 battle in Belgium's Ardennes sector, during which the German effort to break through Allied lines was brought to a halt.

This Milton Sperling-Philip Yordan production for Warner Bros. was filmed in Spain under the direction of British-born Ken Annakin, who had gained similar experience on 20th Century-Fox's far superior *The Longest Day*. But the script Sperling and Yordan developed with John Melson took so liberal a view of the events here depicted that they fully earned the film's many critical brickbats, chiefly hurled by those who resented fact distortions committed in the name of spectacle.

Released for Christmas audiences in 1965, *Battle of the Bulge* opened originally as a "roadshow," which meant reserved seats at "advanced" prices. This showmanship paid off. The movie proved a popular box-office attraction and earned a tidy profit.

Cast as a Polish-American named "Wolenski," Bronson joined a starry cast, and was well paid for a reasonably brief role which introduced him some thirty minutes into the story, then killed him off soon after the intermission (then a standard practice with lengthy, reserved-seat movies).

As Wolenski.

With Robert Shaw.

CRITICS' CORNER

"What John Wayne did for victory in The Pacific, Henry Fonda now does in the Belgian Bulge in this landlocked super-cliche-ridden version of *In Harm's Way* that will do little but irritate World War II veterans or buffs by what the producers politely term the "synthesizing" of details of this one phase of the war.

"This nonsense goes on amid panoramic vistas and ferocious battle scenes in the snow and greenery that seem to co-exist in Spain and spectaculars, but somehow don't carry the aura of Belgium in December.

"The genius of Messrs. Fonda and Shaw is evidenced by the ability to play along with their roles. Hans Christian Blech, as Shaw's batman, and Charles Bronson, as an American major, have moments of excellence."

Judith Crist, *The New York Herald Tribune*

"Since movie audiences have always been notoriously bad historians, seeming to prefer the Hollywood version to the truth, this bit of wartime fiction should be as readily acceptable and as marketable as most of the past World War II melodramas.

"Henry Fonda and Robert Shaw are best in the large cast, both playing opponents in a simplified test of wills, representing the U.S. and German sides, respectively. George Montgomery, Telly Savalas, Pier Angeli, Ty Hardin, Charles Bronson and James MacArthur tend to be at a disadvantage with rather ill-defined stock sketches."

The Independent Film Journal

"Doubtless the Ardennes offensive never happened like this at all. But what matters about *Battle of the Bulge* is that it is a rattling good war story, told with admirable clarity and plenty of panache.

"There are a number of solid performances, and two outstanding ones from George Montgomery and Charles Bronson as battlewise old soldiers, but the tanks have the starring role."

Monthly Film Bulletin

"Charles Bronson impresses as the up-front infantry officer who must be sacrificed to the advancing Germans as cover for the retreating Yanks."

"Murf.," *Variety*

As J.J. Nichols in *This Property Is Condemned* (1966).

With Natalie Wood.

This Property Is Condemned

A Seven Arts-Ray Stark Production / 1966
    for Paramount Pictures
In Technicolor

CAST
Alva Starr: Natalie Wood; *Owen Legate:* Robert Redford; *J. J. Nichols:* Charles Bronson; *Hazel Starr:* Kate Reid; *Willie Starr:* Mary Badham; *Knopke:* Alan Baxter; *Sidney:* Robert Blake; *Johnson:* John Harding; *Salesman:* Dabney Coleman; *Jimmy Bell:* Ray Hemphill; *Charlie Steinkamp:* Brett Pearson; *Tom:* Jon Provost; *Hank:* Quentin Sondergaard; *Max:* Michael Steen; *Lindsay Tate:* Bruce Watson; *Tiny:* Bob Random; *Railroad Conductor:* Nick Stuart.

CREDITS
Producer: John Houseman; *Director:* Sydney Pollack; *Assistant Director:* Eddie Saeta; *Screenwriters:* Francis Ford Coppola, Fred Coe, Edith Sommer; *Based on the One-Act Play by:* Tennessee Williams; *Cinematographer:* James Wong Howe; *Art Director:* Phil Jeffries; *Set Decorator:* William Kiernan; *Special Effects:* Paul Lerpae; *Musical Score:* Kenyon Hopkins; *Song "Wish Me a Rainbow" by* Jay Livingston, Ray Evans; *Editor:* Adrienne Fazan.
Running Time: 110 minutes.

THE FILM
Of all the fifteen motion pictures based to date on the writings of Tennessee Williams, *This Property is Condemned* represents the greatest expansion and the most "creative" effort. For the original one-act Williams play of this title has only two characters, children whose conversation sketches the bizarre story of a wanton sister, now deceased.

Although this screenplay is credited to only three writers, Francis Ford Coppola, Fred Coe and Edith Sommer, no less than sixteen hands are reported to have toiled on a script that might have passed, if uncredited, for one of Tennessee's own various self-derivative plays. For the film of *This Property Is Condemned* is alive with echoes of other voices in the Williams general canon. Indeed, Charles Bronson's brutish skirt-chaser here contains sufficient reminders of *A Streetcar Named Desire's* Stanley Kowalski to make the open-minded viewer consider how Bronson might have handled that role, so closely associated with the early Marlon Brando.

This Property Is Condemned opens, as it closes,

129

With Natalie Wood.

on the railroad tracks of a small 1930s Mississippi community, where thirteen-year-old Willie Starr (Mary Badham) tells her young companion Tom (Jon Provost) about her now-departed older sister Alva (Natalie Wood), who was once "the main attraction" at her mother's near-by, now-abandoned boarding house.

Most of the film is a lengthy flashback in which we are witness to the heavily sexual undercurrents of life at this dwelling, where Willie's mother (Kate Reid) attempts to marry off the flirtatious Alva to an older man of reputed wealth. Into this world of railroad men and their women comes Owen Legate (Robert Redford), a handsome stranger whose duty it is to close down the town's station and fire the men. He and Alva are drawn to one another, although he soon sees her for the loose-moraled girl her mother has made of her. In defiance, Alva hosts a noctural, nude swimming party, at which she arouses the lust of her mother's boyfriend, J. J. Nichols (Bronson), whom she eventually marries, in reckless haste, after her serious relationship with Owen has exploded in a quarrel. Alva leaves J. J. before their marriage bed has cooled, running off to New Orleans in Owen's wake. When her vengeful mother publicly reveals the details of Alva's marriage to J. J., Alva is too hurt to remain with Owen, and she runs off to a certain doomed future of life in the streets. But to Willie, the idealized Alva remains a queen.

Bronson was not too happy with his lot on location in the Mississippi town of Bay St. Louis, and

With Kate Reid.

according to director Sydney Pollack, the actor tried to get Pollack to make something more of the film's incipient love-triangle involving himself, Wood and Redford. But more concerned (on only his second movie) with Natalie Wood's considerable responsibility to the screenplay, Pollack now reports, "I couldn't deal with it. I couldn't re-write the part and make it bigger. And the least of my worries at this point was Charlie Bronson's character."

CRITICS' CORNER
"Miss Wood turns in her best acting since the memorable *Splendor in the Grass.* Director Sydney Pollack successfully captures the spirit

and feel of the South during the thirties, as does Kenyon Hopkins' fine musical score."
The Independent Film Journal

"Charles Bronson is excellent as the earthy boarder. Kate Reid is outstanding in her projection of brittle warmth and calculating cruelty. Mary Badham is the younger daughter who sets the stage for the plot unfoldment in excellent fashion, giving warmth, dimension and appeal throughout."
"Murf.," *Variety*

"What condemns *This Property* is a plot tacked on by three zealous screenwriters, to whom the

Williams original 'suggested' a long, lurid flashback starring Natalie Wood.

"Aiming for bold, big-screen entertainment, director Sydney Pollack emphasizes rowdy period flavor and gives his cast leeway for showy performances. The movie, as a whole, is too bright and vulgar to be dull, but expensive talent has been squandered on every chore except the crucial one of keeping a small, evanescent tragedy in focus."
Time

"Camille in Dixieland. The environment itself passes muster, even though the people in it do not. It is sodden, tacky and tinseled, in the fashion of an ugly southern town. But the people, beginning with Mama, the boarding-house keeper whom Kate Reid makes monstrously meaty and maudlin, are clearly theatrical, and this includes Charles Bronson as a lecher and John Harding as an older, lonely man. Under Sidney Pollack's direction, they are all acting seamy stereotypes."
Bosley Crowther, *The New York Times*

With director Sydney Pollack on the set of *This Property Is Condemned.*

As J.J. Nichols.

With Telly Savalas.

The Dirty Dozen

A Metro-Goldwyn-Mayer Picture / 1967
In 70mm. and Metrocolor

CAST

Maj. Reisman: Lee Marvin; *Gen. Worden:* Ernest Borgnine; *Joseph Wladislaw:* Charles Bronson; *Robert Jefferson:* Jim Brown; *Victor Franko:* John Cassavetes; *Sgt. Bowren:* Richard Jaeckel; *Maj. Max Armbruster:* George Kennedy; *Pedro Jiminez:* Trini Lopez; *Capt. Stuart Kinder:* Ralph Meeker; *Col. Everett Dasher Breed:* Robert Ryan; *Archer Maggott:* Telly Savalas; *Vernon Pinkley:* Donald Sutherland; *Samson Posey:* Clint Walker; *Gen. Denton:* Robert Webber; *Milo Vladek:* Tom Busby; *Glenn Gilpin:* Ben Carruthers; *Roscoe Lever:* Stuart Cooper; *Corp. Morgan:* Robert Phillips; *Seth Sawyer:* Colin Maitland; *Tassos Bravos:* Al Mancini; *Pvt. Arthur James Gardner:* George Roubicek; *Gen. Worden's Aide:* Thick Wilson; *German Officer's Girl:* Dora Reisser.

CREDITS

Producer: Kenneth Hyman; *Associate Producer:* Raymond Anzarut; *Director:* Robert Aldrich; *Assistant Director:* Bert Batt; *Screenwriters:* Nunnally Johnson, Lukas Heller; *Based on the Novel by:* E. M. Nathanson; *Cinematographer:* Edward

As Joseph Wladislaw.

With Jim Brown and George Kennedy.

Scaife; *Art Director:* W. E. Hutchinson; *Special Effects:* Cliff Richardson; *Musical Score:* Frank De Vol; *Songs:* "The Bramble Bush" by Frank De Vol, Mack David; "Einsam" by Frank De Vol, Sibylle Siegfried; *Editor:* Michael Luciano. *Running Time:* 149 minutes.

THE FILM

In *Variety's* annual update of the "All-Time Film Rental Champs" (covering only the U.S.-Canada market), *The Dirty Dozen,* as of January 1979, was the highest-grossing movie in which Charles Bronson had yet appeared, stateside. At a reported box-office take of $20,300,000, this hardly seems impressive in the light of present-day cinema prices. However, for a twelve-year-old movie, initially released at a time when moviegoing was far more financially accessible than in the late seventies, this Robert Aldrich war film can still be considered a powerful box-office champ whose money-making days may not yet be over, despite its many airings on television.

World War II action is the film's keynote. The story begins in England a few months before D-Day. Iconoclastic U.S. Army Major Reisman (Lee Marvin) has been given a tough order. In

With Clint Walker, Al Mancini, Jim Brown, Stuart Cooper, Trini Lopez, Ben Carruthers, Tom Busby, Colin Maitland, Telly Savalas, Donald Sutherland, and John Cassavetes.

record time, he must whip into shape no less than twelve hardened criminals—rapists, killers and thieves—serving sentences in the post's stockade. Under Reisman's command, they are to parachute into Nazi-occupied France on a suicidal mission to destroy a chateau housing German brass. Although the "Dozen" view Reisman either with contempt or mere indifference, each agrees to the mission with the understanding that, if he survives, he'll be granted a pardon.

After Lee Marvin and Ernest Borgnine, Bronson comes third in a cast that, lucky for him, appears to be largely alphabetical. The script that veteran screenwriters Nunnally Johnson and Lukas Heller derived from E. M. Nathanson's novel does not attempt to avoid the usual allotment of ethnic types customarily involved in stories of men at war. And so we have Slavic-featured Charles Bronson as the Slavic-named "Wladislaw," one of the only three of the Dozen to survive the film's explosive finale. After winding up a casualty on so many such previous occasions, Bronson here seemed to have a role prophetic of his movie future: in his late forties, the actor had become a full-fledged survivor, in more ways than one.

The third of Bronson's male-oriented blockbuster movies, The Dirty Dozen, like The Magnificent Seven and The Great Escape, gains remarkable verisimilitude from its location filming in Britain. Henceforth, Bronson would see

With Stuart Cooper and Telly Savalas.

little of the Hollywood soundstages in the years to follow, and his career would benefit accordingly. For him, the roads to super-stardom lay on foreign soil. To date, this was the last of Bronson's four films with director Robert Aldrich.

CRITICS' CORNER
"Taking the premise that war is a sport for murderers, criminals and near madmen, Robert Aldrich has turned *The Dirty Dozen* into one of the best and least compromising he-man adventure films. It's superbly cast. Everyone is excellent from Lee Marvin down. And thanks to

Aldrich, it will keep you on the edge of your seat for about two-and-a-half hours. It's a slam-bang, grown-up adventure story, thumbing its nose at authority and morality and at the compromise that is Hollywood's war cliche. It is cruel and unpleasant on an intellectual level but that, of course, is war."
Judith Crist, The NBC-TV "Today" Show

"The viewer who settles for sheer action-adventure entertainment will be rewarded in spades. Entertaining it is, in the complete Hollywood tradition of tough, he-man, ribald, no-quarters-a few of the dozen, Charles Bronson, ex-foot-

As Joseph Wladislaw.

THE NAZIS NEVER BARGAINED FOR THE DIRTY DOZEN!

METRO-GOLDWYN-MAYER presents A KENNETH HYMAN PRODUCTION

The Dirty Dozen

Starring LEE MARVIN · ERNEST BORGNINE · CHARLES BRONSON · JIM BROWN · JOHN CASSAVETES · RICHARD JAECKEL · GEORGE KENNEDY · TRINI LOPEZ · RALPH MEEKER · ROBERT RYAN · TELLY SAVALAS · CLINT WALKER · ROBERT WEBBER

screenplay by NUNNALLY JOHNSON and LUKAS HELLER · From the novel by E M NATHANSON · Produced by KENNETH HYMAN · Directed by ROBERT ALDRICH · IN METROCOLOR · MGM

Copyright ©1967 Metro-Goldwyn-Mayer Inc. Country of Origin U. S. A. Property of National Screen Service Corp. Licensed for display only in connection with the exhibition of this picture at your theatre. Must be returned immediately thereafter. 67/176

baller Jim Brown, John Cassavetes, Telly Savalas and Trini Lopez."

Jesse Zunser, *Cue*

"A raw and preposterous glorification of a group of criminal soldiers who are trained to kill and who then go about this brutal business with hot, sadistic zeal is advanced in *The Dirty Dozen,* an astonishingly wanton war film. It is clear that the intent of this loud picture is just to delight and stimulate the easily moved."

Bosley Crowther, *The New York Times*

"The game of death is played by *The Dirty Dozen* in a unique, powerfully executed war tale that will rank easily among the top adventure-thrillers of the year. First-rate performances and superb production values combine with a novel twist in storyline to transform the ordinary situations of Army life and war into an audience-gripping study of twelve condemned soldier-criminals.

"The high climax, of course, is the seizure of the Nazi chateau, where the suspense and action is big league, with Charles Bronson distinguishing himself as a German linguist."

The Independent Film Journal

"*The Dirty Dozen* is the definitive enlisted man's picture. Director Robert Aldrich gets convincingly raw, tough performances in even the smallest roles."

Time

"E.M. Nathanson's novel was careful to disclaim any truth to the basic plot, for, if ever

140

With Lee Marvin.

pressed, the U.S. Army apparently can claim no records exist on the subject. Still, Nathanson's book, as well as the very good Nunnally Johnson-Lukas Heller screenplay, has a ring of authenticity to it.

"Marvin again delivers a top performance, probably because he seems at his best in a role as a sardonic authoritarian. Charles Bronson, a very capable actor, stands out as a Polish-American who, once affixing his loyalty, does not shift under even physical brutality."

"Murf.," *Variety*

With Al Mancini,
Stuart Cooper, Trini Lopez, Clint
Walker, Jim Brown, John Cassavetes,
Telly Savalas, and George Kennedy.

As Teclo.

With Anthony Quinn.

La Bataille de San Sebastian

(Guns for San Sebastian)

A Co-production of CIPRA Films (Paris), / 1967
    Pelliculas Ernesto
    Enriquez (Mexico) and Filmes
    Cinematografica (Rome)
U.S. Distributor: Metro-Goldwyn-Mayer
In Franscope and Eastman Color

CAST
Leon Alastray: Anthony Quinn; *Kinita:* Anjanette Comer; *Teclo:* Charles Bronson; *Father Joseph:* Sam Jaffe; *Felicia:* Silvia Pinal; *Cayetano:* Jorge Martinez De Hoyos; *Golden Lance:* Jaime Fernandez; *Agueda:* Rosa Furman; *Pedro:* Jorge Russek; *Vicar General:* Leon Askin; *Antonito:* Jose Chavez; *Col. Calleja:* Ivan Desny; *Governor:* Fernand Gravey; *Father Lucas:* Pedro Armendariz, Jr., *Magdalena:* Aurora Clavel; *Diego:* Julio Aldama; *Luis;* Ferrusquilla; *Kino:* Pancho Cordova; *Renaldo:* Enrique Lucero; *Miguel:* Chano Urueta; *Capt. Lopez:* Noe Murayama; *Timoteo:* Guillermo Hernandez; *Bishop:* Francisco Reiguera; *Pablo:* Carlos Berriochea; *Pascual:* Armando Acosta; *Villagers:* Guy Fox, Rico Lopez.

CREDITS
Producer: Jacques Bar; *Associate Producer:* Ernesto Enriquez; *Director:* Henri Verneuil; *Assistant Directors:* Claude Pinoteau, Juan Luis Bunuel; *Screenwriters (European Version):* Serge Ganz, Miguel Morayta, Ennio de Concini; *Screenwriter (English Version):* James R. Webb; *Based on the Novel "A Wall for San Sebastian" by:* William Barby Faherty, S.J.; *Cinematographer:* Armand Thirard; *Art Directors:* Robert Clavel, Roberto Silva; *Special Effects:* J. McMillan Johnson, Lee Zavits; *Musical Score:* Ennio Morricone; *Editor:* Francoise Bonnot.
Running Time: 111 minutes.

THE FILM
Not a few of *Guns for San Sebastian's* critics found comparisons between its plot and *The Seven Samurai/The Magnificent Seven's* tale of gunmen saving a beleaguered village from

1854-67E

periodic ravishment. And with good reason, for this French-Mexican-Italian co-production, directed by Henri Verneuil (best known in the U.S. for the Jean Gabin-Alain Delon heist thriller *Any Number Can Win)* had Anthony Quinn as Leon Alastray, the legendary rebel-bandit-patriot, helping Mexican mountain villagers fight off marauding Yaqui Indians in the mid-18th century. The picture was photographed in some beautiful Mexican desert locations, and that, plus its action scenes, is *Guns for San Sebastian's* chief attribute. MGM, its American distributor, gave the movie a fast play-off; in Europe, its popularity was greater.

In this outdoor adventure yarn, Bronson, billed third after Quinn and the movie's ''love interest,'' Anjanette Comer, is back in Indian garb as ''Teclo,'' a half-breed vaquero who rides for the Yaquis, demanding that the Christian peasant residents of San Sebastian revert to paganism or face further Indian raids. Before the film's close, Alastray manages to kill Teclo in hand-to-hand combat.

CRITICS' CORNER
''Despite the vigor of the action scenes and all the color of the vividly photographed Mexican locales, the end effect is numbingly bland. This may be because the film, another example of one of those international co-production projects, is so completely de-nationalized. It was produced and directed by Frenchmen, written by Americans, scored by an Italian and played by Amer-icans and Mexicans. No one wins.''
Vincent Canby, *The New York Times*

''As a sort of Mexican version of *The Seven Samurai,* the film never really comes to life until the end, when Verneuil pulls out all the stops for a splendidly, if conventionally, staged battle. For the rest, the Mexican desert locations make attractive backgrounds, the color is uniformly good, and the performances are competent but quite unremarkable—though Sam Jaffe provides a few moments of light relief as the old priest with a twinkle in his eye. Ennio Morricone's music score (all heavenly choirs and stridently dramatic chords) is irritatingly obtrusive.''
Monthly Film Bulletin

''*Guns for San Sebastian,* a plodding mix of religious-themed action comedy-romance, has some good direction and battle scenes, but the very poor dubbing (in the dramatic sense) is hard going. As far as plot structuring is concerned, it takes too long to develop its points. But the direction, by Henri Verneuil, and editing, to a tedious 100 minutes plus, also is blame-worthy in this regard. Some directorial life is evident, and some good exterior lensing.

''Anthony Quinn, despite the story, remains a likeable, gutsy and virile actor. Anjanette Comer is very poor, Charles Bronson only a shade better.''
''Murf.,'' *Variety*

With Anjanette Comer,
Jorge Russak, and Anthony Quinn.

As Fierro.

Villa Rides

A Paramount Picture / 1968
In Panavision and Technicolor

CAST
Pancho Villa: Yul Brynner; *Lee Arnold:* Robert Mitchum; *Fina Gonzalez:* Grazia Buccella; *Fierro:* Charles Bronson; *Urbina:* Robert Viharo; *Capt. Ramirez:* Frank Wolff; *Gen. Huerta:* Herbert Lom; *President Madero:* Alexander Knox; *Emilita:* Diana Lorys; *Luis Gonzalez:* Robert Carricart; *Fuentes:* Fernando Rey: *Lupita Gonzalez:* Regina de Julian; *Herrera:* Andres Monreal; *Juan Gonzalez:* Antonio Ruiz; *Man in Barber Shop:* John Ireland; *Girl in Restaurant:* Jill Ireland.

CREDITS
Producer: Ted Richmond; *Director:* Buzz Kulik; *Assistant Director:* Tony Fuentes; *Screenwriters:* Robert Towne, Sam Peckinpah; *Based on the Novel "Pancho Villa' by:* William Douglas Lansford; *Cinematographer:* Jack Hildyard; *2nd Unit Photographer:* John Cabrera; *Production Designer:* Ted Haworth; *Art Director:* Jose Alguero; *Set Decorator:* Roman Calatayud; *Special Effects:* Milt Rice; *Musical Score:* Maurice Jarre; *Editor:* David Bretherton. *Running Time:* 125 minutes.

THE FILM
Bronson continued his Latin globe-hopping odyssey with a trip to Spain for this romanticized film about a portion of the much-dramatized career of Mexican revolutionary Pancho Villa (1877-1923). Starting with MGM's famed *Viva Villa!* of 1934, in which Wallace Beery had portrayed the man, he has been vivified on the English-speaking screen by Maurice Black (Under *Strange Flags,* 1937; Leo Carrillo (*Pancho Villa Returns,* 1950); Alan Reed (*Viva Zapata!,* 1952); and Rodolfo Hoyos (*Villa!,* 1958). In *Villa Rides,* reckless casting offers no less than the exotic Yul Brynner (in one of his few bewigged roles) as Mexico's folk hero.

Not uncharacteristically, screenwriters Robert Towne and Sam Peckinpah were more concerned with violence than accuracy, and TV veteran Buzz Kulik's direction followed through in full accord.

Bronson played another in his tough-visaged gallery of ruthless villains, as "Fierro," Villa's sadistic sidekick. In a cast headed by Brynner and Robert Mitchum, Bronson nevertheless was given considerable footage by script and

With Robert Viharo, Yul Brynner, and Robert Mitchum.

direction. His performance here reflects the burgeoning impact of his screen image upon a public whose fascination is destined, in the not-too-distant future, to push Bronson up, finally, into the superstar category. For this film, he adopted the thin, slightly drooping mustache that would so frequently adorn his features in the era of his greatest screen fame. And, for the first time, the name of Jill Ireland, here cast in a bit role, was featured in the cast list of a Bronson film. Before 1968 was over, they would be off-screen husband and wife.

CRITICS' CORNER

"Has there been in the past few years such a surfeit of violence on the screen that people have become numbed to pain and suffering? I had a sobering experience the other evening, at a preview of a film called *Villa Rides*. In the course of the picture, Charles Bronson, playing one of Villa's lieutenants, lines up three of the captured enemy 'Colorados,' one behind the other. He then steps behind them and shoots all three through the heart with a single bullet. The audience, primarily adult, howled as if it

With Robert Carricart and Yul Brynner.

With Robert Carricart.

With Yul Brynner.

were a scene out of Laurel and Hardy! Presumably, people still laugh when, in a comedy, someone slips on a banana peel, or receives a custard pie full in the face. *Villa Rides,* however, is not a comedy; its people and places are real. But it quickly becomes evident that the film's historicity is merely a pretext, an excuse to douse the screen with one bloodbath after another. But more profoundly disturbing is the filmmakers' obvious and implicit belief that their sadistic catalogue of gory death can be turned out in today's market in the name of entertainment. And what is still worse, as the laughter the other evening indicated, they may be right.''

Arthur Knight, *Saturday Review*

"Ted Richmond's handsome exterior production, filmed last year in Spain, is competently, if leisurely and routinely, directed by Buzz Kulik, with the accent on violent death. The script fails to establish clearly the precise political framework, while overdeveloping some lesser details. This, plus overlength, adds up to dramatic tedium. With a relatively brief depiction of those military forces being opposed by Villa, the film concerns itself with Villa's own aggressive acts. Thus there is an imbalance of violence on one side. With the aid of Charles Bronson and Robert Viharo, Yul Brynner is responsible for the on-screen deaths of literally dozens of men, by diverse means, most explicitly detailed.

"Brynner makes Villa sympathetic at times, as a man fighting for human rights, though that's a bit hard to swallow since his philosophy does not get spelled out for 105 minutes into the film. Mitchum, still a gutsy actor who commands attention just by being seen, takes the curse off some of the script by reacting in bewilderment to events. Bronson delights a trifle too much in murder. Jill Ireland, with a phony south-western accent, is okay as a girl whose prettiness helps Mitchum reach his final decision to rejoin Brynner in another revolution.''

"Murf.,'' *Variety*

"Yul Brynner, Robert Mitchum, cavalry, politicos and even the faint strains of 'La Cucaracha' fail to disguise the fact that *Villa Rides* is simply a sprawling Western and not history. As such, it incessantly fills the screen with the din of pistols and rifles, and assorted warfare and wenching, shot in sharp color on rugged Spanish sites that strikingly simulate Mexico. And neither the imperturbable Mr. Mitchum, nor Mr. Brynner, as the stoically tough Villa, nor Charles Bronson and Robert Viharo as Villa's rough lieutenants, try to dig beneath the surface of the characters involved.''

A.H. Weiler, *The New York Times*

VR-1035-4-18

As Fierro.

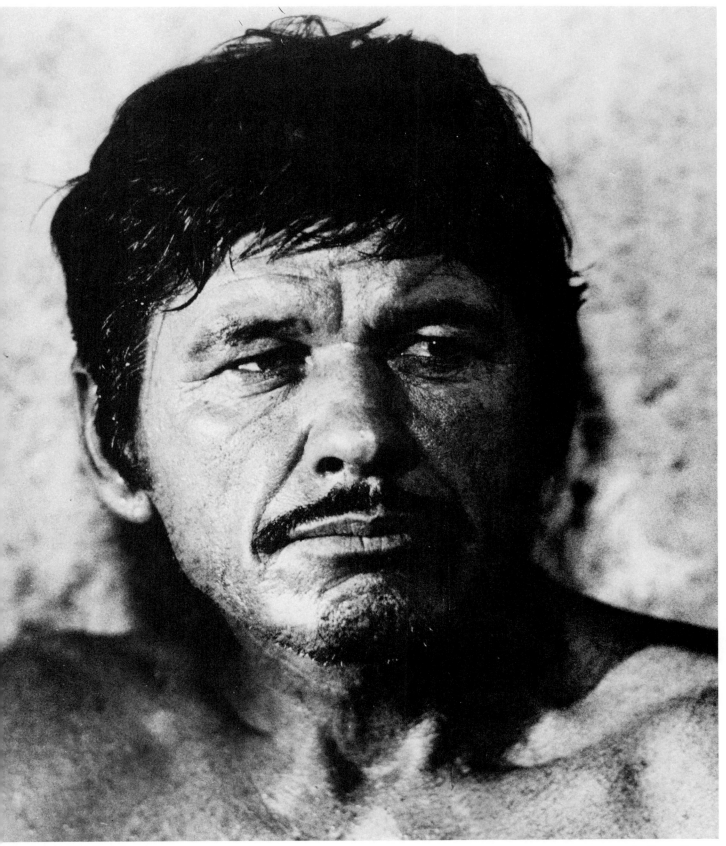

As Franz Propp.

Adieu L'Ami (Farewell, Friend)

A Co-production of Greenwich
   Film Productions (Paris)
   and Medusa Distribuzione (Rome) / 1968
In Eastman Color

CAST
Dino Barran: Alain Delon; *Franz Propp:* Charles Bronson; *Isabelle Manue:* Olga Georges-Picot; *Dominique "Waterloo" Austerlitz:* Brigitte Fossey; *Inspector Antoine Meloutis:* Bernard Fresson; *Inspector Muratti:* Michel Barcet; *Catherine:* Marianna Falk; *Personnel Director:* Andre Dumas; *Martha:* Ellen Bahl; *Gilberte:* Lisette Lebon; *Nurse:* Catherine Sola; *Big Man:* Steve Eckardt; *Man from Neuilly:* Guy Delorme.

CREDITS
Producer: Serge Silberman; *Associate Producer:* Ulrich Picard; *Director:* Jean Herman; *Assistant Directors:* Pierre Lary, Pierre Grunstein; *Screenwriter:* Sebastien Japrisot; *Cinematographer:* Jean-Jacques Tarbes; *Art Director:* Jacques Dugied; *Set Decorator:* Tanine Autre; *Musical Score:* Francoise de Roubaix; *Editor:* Helene Plemiannikov.
Running Time: 115 minutes.

THE FILM
In 1968, Alain Delon was the most popular of French male movie stars, thanks largely to the impact made by his roles in Rene Clement's 1960 thriller *Purple Noon* and Mark Robson's Algerian War adventure *Lost Command* (1966), with Anthony Quinn and Claudia Cardinale. Delon's name on a film practically guaranteed its European success. When he signed to star in director Jean Herman's *Adieu L'Ami,* Serge Silberman, producer of this Franco-Italian co-production, tried to get Richard Widmark as Delon's co-star, hoping for an American "name" that would insure international interest in the movie. But Widmark was otherwise engaged, and Delon then thought of Charles Bronson, from whom he had once purchased a painting. He and Silberman subsequently screened some of Bronson's films, including *Machine Gun Kelly,* a performance with which they were especially impressed. Silberman met with a reluctant Bronson in Spain, and talked him into it.

Adieu L'Ami made a European star of Bronson. In France, it proved a financial blockbuster and 1968's greatest box-office hit. Somehow, the Bronson and Delon personalities blended well; their chemistry produced an extraordinary ensemble performance, and a European public that already adored Delon-the-beautiful now expressed equal appreciation of Bronson-the-homely. And, as *Adieu L'Ami's* success spread through Continental Europe, so did the macho charisma of Charles Bronson, putting him up into the popularity league of that ugly-sexy French favorite, Jean-Paul Belmondo. It also raised him into the $100,000 salary bracket!

Bronson's reluctance in becoming a *European* star—when he would have preferred to be an *American* one—is understandable, in the light of *Adieu L'Ami's* Continental box-office impact. For although Paramount acquired the movie for U.S. and Canadian distribution, they relegated it to the proverbial "shelf," apparently dismayed by the poorly dubbed English-language version made simultaneously with the original French one. In addition to which, neither the Bronson nor Delon "names" was then considered sufficiently sure-fire to assure an American theatrical success. And so *Farewell, Friend,* as the film was called in English, was not seen in North America—until its eventual appearance years later, on television.

The movie's complex plot offers Bronson as an American mercenary who forms an uneasy friendship in Marseilles with doctor Delon when both are discharged from the French Army at the close of the Algerian War. After variously indulging in minor criminal activities, the two men eventually join forces in the attempted robbery of two hundred million francs from a large business firm. In doing so, they are trapped for three days in underground vaults, where they find the company safe empty. They have been duped by two attractive young women (Olga Georges-Picot and Brigitte Fossey) looking for someone to frame for *their* major

With Michel Barcet, Bernard Fresson, and Alain Delon.

theft of bonds and francs. Finally, in a violent shoot-out, both women are killed, and Delon is cleared. But Bronson is taken into custody for an earlier crime and, as he's led away, the two honor an earlier agreement: neither acknowledges knowing the other.

CRITICS' CORNER
"Fairly slickly made film about virile friendship of two anti-heroes gives this pic the air of being influenced by American themes. But the cursory characterization and routine psychological aspects make it primarily an acceptable actioner for fast playoff and dualers, with the Bronson and Delon names as added assets.

"Bronson plays it in his usual brutish and laconic way but indicating a sort of grudging acceptance of the ritual of friendship, and Delon plays with dash and dedication, with most of the others fairly stereotyped in their roles.

"Director Jean Herman has given this a glossy surface and okay action segs, but not the sharp pitch and suspense it needed. Script is a bit too labored with gimmicks and character tics to overcome the shortcomings. It is technically good and with fine tints and production dress."
"Mosk," *Variety*

"*Farewell, Friend* is a stylish thriller, marred by a glib and overly busy plot which, like others in the genre, appears to have been worked out backwards. Coincidences of relationship, place and chance meeting abound. But there is sufficient bedrock in the film to support the Bronson-Delon confrontation and partnership, as the two men overcome their initial hostility to extend a respectful distance to each other's heroic isolation: Bronson is the more evidently shady of the two, accepting the criminal life as a corollary to survival and delighting in a thuggish animalism; Delon is the epitome of detached elegance, with a spoilt, sulky cool, unruffled in his undertaker's black tie and white shirt. Interestingly, it is Delon who is motivated by guilt, or at least remorse, but the amoral Bronson who takes the rap to preserve the honor which has developed between thieves."
Monthly Film Bulletin
"The best part of the film is the fact that the actors correspond perfectly to the characters they play. Delon and Bronson, the taciturn and the boor, form a remarkable pair."
Le Figaro

With Henry Fonda.

C'era Una Volta Il West (Once Upon a Time in the West)

A Co-production of Rafran
   Cinematografica and
   San Marco Films   /   1969
   for Paramount Pictures
In Techniscope and Technicolor

CAST

Frank: Henry Fonda; *Jill McBain:* Claudia Cardinale; *Cheyenne:* Jason Robards; *The Man (Harmonica):* Charles Bronson; *Brett McBain:* Frank Wolff; *Morton:* Gabriele Ferzetti; *Sheriff of Flagstone:* Keenan Wynn; *Sam:* Paolo Stoppa; *Wobbles:* Marco Zuanelli; *Barman:* Lionel Stander; *Knuckles:* Jack Elam; *Frank's Henchman:* John Frederick; *Stony:* Woody Strode; *Timmy McBain:* Enzo Santianello; *Harmonica as a Boy:* Dino Mele; *Man from Cheyenne:* Aldo Sambrell; *Station Manager:* Benito Stefanelli; *Maureen McBain:* Marilu Carteny; *Frank's Aide:* Michael Harvey.

CREDITS

Executive Producer: Bino Cicogna; *Producer:* Fulvio Morsella; *Director:* Sergio Leone; *Assistant Director:* Giancarlo Santi; *Screenwriters:* Sergio Leone, Sergio Donati; *Based on a Story by:* Dario Argento, Bernardo Bertolucci, Sergio Leone; *Cinematographer:* Tonino delli Colli; *Art Director:* Carlo Simi; *Set Decorator:* Carlo Leva; *Musical Score:* Ennio Morricone; *Editor:* Nino Baragli.
Running Time: 165 minutes.

THE FILM

Sergio Leone, that Cecil B. DeMille of Italian so-called "Spaghetti Westerns," might have made an international superstar of Charles Bronson in the early 1960s, had the actor accepted one of Leone's various offers to star in his European horse operas. But Bronson successively rejected contracts for *A Fistful of Dollars, For a Few Dollars More* and *The Good, the Bad and the Ugly*—to the good fortune of actors Clint Eastwood, Lee Van Cleef and Eli Wallach, who respectively accepted the roles Bronson had rejected.

When the persistent Leone subsequently

offered Bronson *Once Upon a Time in the West,* he was finally wise enough to accept. With co-stars like Henry Fonda, Jason Robards and Claudia Cardinale, Bronson had every reason to envision an international box-office block-buster. But such was not quite the case. Faced with a 165-minute super-Western, Paramount, the film's co-financier and U.S. distributor, was at a loss, and virtually kept the film's *American* release a secret. Its New York City run was brief, with Paramount trimming the movie by a half-hour before booking it elsewhere. But this indiscriminate re-editing only rendered the story confusing, and U.S. moviegoers were apathetic. In France, however, Leone's epic oater was a great success, playing continuously for *four years* and setting a record as that country's all-time box-office champion.

Leone's casting is rather unique here, present-ing that all-American-hero Henry Fonda as not only the story's "heavy," but also as perhaps the most dastardly villain in cinema history. And with Bronson as the movie's true hero, a rugged and quietly enigmatic fellow, for whom death is a natural part of life. This film and his role in it quite sealed Bronson's European status as a superstar. Ironically, this wasn't duplicated in the land of his birth, where Bronson remained thought of merely as a good character actor, expert at the delineation of certain tough he-man types.

In the Seventies, *Once Upon a Time in the West* has become a minority favorite in the U.S., a sort of "cult classic" among those who appreciate Leone's inimitable cinematic excesses. For this violent tale of vengeance is a sprawl-ing tribute to Hollywood Westerns by an Italian who grew up in reverence of the genre. In

154

this lengthy homage, Leone employs Arizona, Utah and Spanish locations, artily captured by cinematographer Tonino Delli Colli to reflect the classic Western locales of John Ford, director of so many outdoor film classics.

Once Upon a Time in the West has become Leone's masterpiece—a triumph of style and flair over banal content. Its plot centers on a vicious rivalry over a parcel of land in the un-specified 1870s American West. The railroad wants the property for its water well, but it belongs to the newly widowed Jill McBain (Claudia Cardinale), a New Orleans fancy lady new to the area. In the crooked employ of a railroad magnate, Frank (Henry Fonda), is the hired gun who killed her husband and will proceed until he gets her land. The outlaw Cheyenne (Jason Robards) is determined to help Jill, as well as clear his name. And Harmonica (Bronson) is a mysterious stranger out to settle an old personal score—against Frank (when Harmonica was fifteen, Frank had forced him to play the harmonica while watching the torture and hanging of his older brother). In one of the film's most effective final scenes, Harmonica shoots down Frank before the killer can draw his gun. And while Frank lies dying, the stranger reveals why he has hunted him down, stuffing his ever-

With Claudia Cardinale.

present musical instrument into Frank's mouth, as an epitaph.

CRITICS' CORNER

"It's debatable as to whether Paramount's *Once Upon a Time in the West,* with its extremely long running-time, can capture and sustain the wider audience which attended the director's first three European hayburners. The previous 'camp' element grafted a uniquely comic and very Italian style onto the U.S. Western genre. This time, with Henry Fonda and Jason Robards relishing each screen minute as the heavies, and Charles Bronson in Clint Eastwood's 'man with no name' role (from the early *Dollar* pix), Leone has pulled a basic switch. The impression develops that the film's thematic content is being played completely 'straight.' This is not to be confused with Leone's exaggerated visual style, which remains as baroquely appealing and easy to watch as it was in his first Italian fun-and-games workouts."

"Tarb.," *Variety*

"*Once Upon a Time in the West* is the biggest, longest, most expensive Leone Western to date, and, in many ways, the most absurd. Granting the fact that it is quite bad, the film is almost always interesting, wobbling, as it does, between being an epic lampoon and a serious homage to the men who created the dreams of Leone's childhood. Charles Bronson plays Leone's favorite Western character, the enigmatic Man With No Name, en route from nowhere to nowhere, a kind of Flying Dutchman of the plains.

"*Once Upon a Time in the West* is a movie either for the undiscriminating patron or for the buff. If you fall somewhere in between these categories, you had better stay home."

Vincent Canby, *The New York Times*

With Claudia Cardinale and Lionel Stander.

"Leone spends most of his time focusing on the actors' eyes squinting tensely in the camera lens. The intent is operatic, but the effect is soporific.

"The picture, such as it is, belongs to Charles Bronson. A flinty character actor who has appeared in everything from *The Great Escape* to *The Dirty Dozen,* he plays his first important lead with commendable skill. Unfortunately, such an overblown and overbearing film as this is too great a weight for any one man. The only thing capable of carrying *Once Upon a Time in the West* is a stagecoach—the one headed out of town."

Time

"The score by Ennio Morricone suggests how Puccini would have written his Western, *La Fanciulla del West,* if he had done it about 1935. This Western has the first shootout in which I expected the deullists to burst into *bel canto.*

The story could have been told, as it often has, in 80 minutes, or so."

Stanley Kauffmann, *New Republic*

"Leone has some interesting ideas about casting: Henry Fonda is made uncharacteristically evil, Robards' ambiguous style of playing is well exploited. Most striking of all is Charles Bronson (who is made to slide panther-like into the frame each time he appears), working another variation on the cool, laconic avenger theme."

John Gillett, *Monthly Film Bulletin*

"A simple-minded, blood-spattered amorality tale. The Italian moviemakers have hired a half-dozen good American actors and then failed to utilize these men's talents in respectable fashion."

Judith Crist, *New York*

With Susan George.

Twinky (Lola)

A World Film Services Production / 1970
   for The Rank Organisation (Great Britain)
U.S. Distributor (1971): American International
Pictures

CAST

Scott Wardman: Charles Bronson; *Sybil "Twinky" Londonderry:* Susan George; *Daddy:* Michael Craig; *Mummy:* Honor Blackman; *Hal:* Orson Bean; *Scott's Father:* Paul Ford; *Scott's Mother:* Kay Medford, *Judge Millington-Draper:* Jack Hawkins; *Grandfather:* Trevor Howard; *Mr. Creighton:* Lionel Jeffries; *Judge Roxburgh:* Robert Morley; *Secretary:* Elspeth March; *Client:* Eric Chitty; *Felicity:* Cathy Jose; *1st Policeman:* Leslie Schofield; *2nd Policeman:* Derek Steen; *Marty:* Gordon Waller; *1st TV Comic:* Jimmy Tarbuck; *2nd TV Comic:* Norman Vaughan; *Old Gentleman:* Reg Lever; *New York Judge:* Tony Arpino; *Marriage Clerk:* Eric Barker; *Hotel Receptionist:* John Rae; *Hotel Waiter:* John Wright.

CREDITS

Executive Producers: John Heyman, Bino Cicogna: *Producer:* Clive Sharp; *Associate* *Producers:* Norman Thaddeus Vane, Ralph Serpe; *Director:* Richard Donner; *Assistant Director:* Richard Dalton; *Screenwriter:* Norman Thaddeus Vane; *Cinematographer:* Walter Lassally; *Art Director:* Michael Wield; *Musical Score:* John Scott; *Songs:* "Twinky," "The Lonely Years," "Go Where the Sun Goes" *written and sung by:* Jim Dale; *Editor:* Norman Wanstall. *Running Time:* 98 minutes,

THE FILM

Bronson now radically changed his pace and returned to the contemporary milieu for *Twinky,* a slight British-Italian production, shown fleetingly in the U.S. as *Lola.* Much of the film was shot in New York but, ironically, that city never witnessed a formal opening of *Lola.* Its American distributor, American International Pictures, held screenings for the trade, then swept it

With Trevor Howard.

away under a carpet with some fast playoffs on double-bill bookings. Originally, A.I.P. had named their import *Child Bride,* but must have sensed, in *Lola* (the closest they could have legally approached *Lolita* without risking legal action on that title), a more exploitable one, despite the movie's nominal nymphet (already named "Twinky," and not "Lola" at all!). Such minor problems seldom give distributors pause; a little tampering with the soundtrack could suffice.

But *Twinky/Lola* seems an odd and offbeat motion picture for Bronson, at this stage of his

burgeoning career. Quite likely, he mistakenly thought it might help his U.S. screen image. It did reunite him with Richard Donner, who had directed the actor eight years earlier in *X-15.*

Twinky is the somewhat credulity-straining account of a 38-year-old American novelist's romantic involvement with a 16-year-old English schoolgirl (Susan George) in London. When they marry, problems with her family drive them to relocate in New York City, where *his* family only adds to their worries, and where the twenty-two-year age gap eventually splits them permanently apart.

With Paul Ford and Kay Medford.

161

With Susan George and extras.

As Scott Wardman.

CRITICS' CORNER

"Pix about nymphets are liable to totter just over the edge into near-grimness. The John Heyman-Bino Cicogna production avoids this pitfall, though its theme is wide open to problems. Much of the credit for this must be pinned on Charles Bronson, whose rugged, almost earthy charm—with no hint of the 'smart-aleck' gigolo-boy—keeps much of the film on a wayout, but acceptable basis. The film primarily is a duo between Bronson (surprising but effective casting) and lively Susan George, in the title role."

"Rich.," *Variety*

"Initially promising, but too quickly both the girl and the movie prove exasperating. There is some slick and pretty photography by Walter Lassally, but Charles Bronson is too dominating or rough-hewn to be convincing as a male counterpart to Simone Signoret, which is what his role calls for. Some viewers will probably want to shake some sense into him, or better, shake Susan George, who makes Lola a pouty, exasperating child indeed."

The Independent Film Journal

"But it is the casting that is truly superb, full of character jewels throughout, and if one must criticize here, it is only to say that Honor Blackman is not seen enough. Her unflappable Mummy is a joy of comic originality.

"And so are they all, but the film finally makes it on the two leads, and whoever came up with the idea of pairing off Charles Bronson with Susan George deserves some kind of prize. Bronson, with his beautiful-ugly, crisscrossed face and hulky animal frame, perfectly catches the confusion, frustration, happiness and, finally, despair of a man in love with a child. Susan George is simply marvelous as the girl halfway into womanhood but never out of childhood. She never takes the easy way out of being just cute or gooey, but remains warmly natural, true, and beautifully believeable. Between the two of them, they make a little something special out of *Twinky*—an unpretentious, bittersweet, simple film that is finished off with style, that might make you cry, is guaranteed to make you laugh, and is sure to charm you."

Peter Buckley, *Films and Filming*

With Susan George.

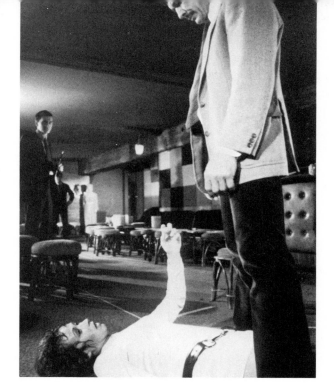

With Marlene Jobert.

Le Passager De La Pluie (Rider on the Rain)

A Co-production of Greenwich Productions
(Paris) and Medusa Distribuzione
(Rome) / 1970
U.S. Distributor: Avco Embassy Pictures
In Eastmancolor

CAST
Melancolie "Mellie" Mau: Marlene Jobert; *Col. Harry Dobbs:* Charles Bronson; *Juliette:* Annie Cordy; *Nicole:* Jill Ireland; *Tony:* Gabriele Tinti; *Toussaint:* Jean Gaven; *The Stranger (Bruno Sakki, alias McGuffin):* Marc Manza; *Tania:* Corinne Marchand; *M. Armand:* Jean Piat; *Hostess at Tania's:* Marika Green; *Madeleine Legauff:* Ellen Bahl; *Station Manager:* Marcel Peres.

CREDITS
Producer: Serge Silberman; *Director:* Rene Clement; *Assistant Directors:* Georges Grodzenczyk, Jacques Bourdon; *Screenwriters:* Sebastien Japrisot, Lorenzo Ventavoli; *Cinematographer:* Andreas Winding; *Art Director:* Pierre Guffroy; *Musical Score:* Francis Lai; *Editor:* Francoise Javet.
Running Time: 119 minutes.

THE FILM
In France, Charles Bronson continued on his incredible winning streak with *Rider on the Rain.* During the period of little over a year, *Rider* and two others *(Once Upon a Time in the West* and *Farewell, Friend)* were among the four films that had broken all French box-office records (the other one: *Borsalino,* a nostalgic gangster yarn teaming Alain Delon and Jean-Paul Belmondo).

In *Rider on the Rain,* Bronson appears at his best-groomed—short of hair, shorn of mustache and smartly attired—as Harry Dobbs, a mysterious American (actually, an Army colonel) who, in his hunt for an escaped sex maniac with stolen Army funds, stumbles across a mystery that appears to connect with his mission. In the south of France, he is caught up in a puzzling case of murder in which, in the temporary absence of her husband, a well-to-do

With Marlene Jobert.

young Frenchwoman (Marlene Jobert) kills her rapist and disposes of the body (thought to be that of the fugitive American sex offender).

But nothing is quite what it seems in this slick and stylish thriller, cleverly written by Sebastien Japrisot and Lorenzo Ventavoli, and directed in the Hitchcock tradition by Rene Clement *(Purple Noon)*. And the battle of wits, fired by sexual undercurrents, that ensues between Bronson and Jobert (a particularly felicitous pairing) elevates the yarn's more ordinary moments.

With brilliant Eastmancolor photography by Andreas Winding, the movie's intriguing location backgrounds of Paris and Cap des Pins help immensely to heighten the script's atmospheric tensions. Again, Jill Ireland appeared in a brief supporting role, as she frequently did at this juncture of the Bronson career, before graduating to become his regular leading lady in film after film of the Seventies.

Following close on the heels of its Paris success, *Rider on the Rain* reached the U.S. in a well-dubbed version that, while not receiving praise from every critic, nevertheless created sufficient initial notice to intrigue a public more geared to sophisticated filmgoing than those previously drawn to Bronson films. Word-of-mouth took it from there, making of the film a quite popular 1970 foreign import. Some who had never done so before began to consider Charles Bronson in a new and more respectful light. Unfortunately, for this portion of the moviegoing public, there would be no follow-ups: the remainder of 1970 would produce only the prophetically titled *You Can't Win 'Em All*, a mindless mercenary-adventure flick with Tony Curtis.

CRITICS' CORNER
"A tantalizing suspense picture by the distinguished French director, Rene Clement. His stars, Marlene Jobert and Charles Bronson, sharpen interest in the mystery that calls for two exciting portrayals of a man and a woman pitted against each other in the intrigues of a murder case. Marlene, a very appealing actress, illuminates the screen by a diversified characteriza-

With Marlene Jobert.

Bronson and his wife, Jill Ireland, clowning on the
location for *Rider on the Rain* (1969).

With Marlene Jobert.

With Corinne Marchand.

tion of a young woman who goes through a horrendous experience. Bronson, with a sarcastic smile on his rough, manly face, is marvelous as the tough American colonel investigating the whereabout of an insane military prisoner who escaped with $60,000 in American bills."

Wanda Hale, *The New York Daily News*

"The customary dislocation-effect of English dialogue in a French ambiance is less irritating than usual, partly because one of the two central characters is American anyway—and Charles Bronson plays him delightfully, in perfect balance between menace and charm."

Gordon Gow, *Films and Filming*

"Rene Clement is one of the top film craftsmen on the scene. He has fashioned a sleek thriller that has too many red herrings and psychological sidelights, but fine playing, crafty direction and underlying menace and twists keep it moving, despite loose ends. Bronson is effective as the good-bad guy."

"Mosk.," *Variety*

"*Rider on the Rain* is one of the current major box-office hits in Paris. The success, I'm told, is attributed in part to the tremendous popularity of Charles Bronson, the 50-year-old American television *(Meet McGraw)* and film *(Once Upon a Time in the West)* actor who had to go to Europe to attain stardom.

"In *Rider on the Rain,* as in so many of his other films, Bronson spends most of the time acting like a villain—seemingly insensitive, short-sighted, arrogant and cruel—before being revealed as the hero who is suddenly, almost foolishly generous. It's one of the ironies of national taste that the very qualities that the French pretend to find so abhorrent in American foreign policy become so beloved in an American savior-figure."

Vincent Canby, *The New York Times*

"As a mysterious sleuth *qui s'appelle* Harry Dobbs, Charles Bronson, who has been knocking around for years in American movies, turns in a fine, sturdy performance and, as the housewife with never a dull moment, an outstanding young actress named Marlene Jobert is a kind of gutsy, French Shirley MacLaine."

Rex Reed

As Harry Dobbs.

With Tony Curtis.

You Can't Win 'Em All

An S.R.O. Company Production / 1970
  for Columbia Pictures
In Panavision and Technicolor

CAST
Adam Dyer: Tony Curtis; *Josh Corey:* Charles Bronson; *Aila:* Michele Mercier; *The General:* Patrick Magee; *Osman Bey:* Gregoire Aslan; *Col. Elci:* Fikret Hakan; *Capt. Enver:* Salih Guney: *Reese:* Tony Bonner; *Davis:* John Acheson; *U.S. Major:* John Alderson; *Woller:* Horst Jansen; *Bolek:* Leo Gordon; *U.S. Chief Petty Officer:* Reed De Ruen; *Gunner Major:* Paul Stassino; *Girl in Cafe:* Suna Keskin; *Papadopoulos:* Yuksel Gozen; *Madam:* Jenia Halil.

CREDITS
Producer: Gene Corman; *Associate Producer:* Harold Buck; *Director:* Peter Collinson; *2nd*

Unit Director: Skeets Kelly; *Assistant Director:* Scott Wodehouse; *Screenwriter:* Leo V. Gordon; *Cinematographer:* Kenneth Higgins; *Art Director:* Seamus Flannery; *Musical Score:* Bert Kaempfert; *Editor:* Ray Poulton.
Running Time: 99 minutes.

THE FILM
Dubious Patriots was this rambunctious adventure's title when it began filming in Turkey during the summer of 1969. Despite its exotic locale, this marked a return to American moviemaking for Bronson, cast opposite Tony Curtis in this Gene Corman-Harold Buck production

168

As Josh Corey.

for Columbia Pictures. Leo V. Gordon, a character actor in the film's cast, wrote this negligible picture's screenplay, with the stars playing reluctant sidekicks, soldiers of fortune amid a band of mercenaries caught up in the Turkish civil war of 1922. Such bunglers are they that they manage to mess up an ambush they had arranged, ruin a mutiny, lose some of their loot, and get robbed of the rest. Neither wins the girl (sultry Michele Mercier), and no one steals the picture, inadvisedly retitled, prior to its mid-1970 release, *You Can't Win 'Em All.*

Bronson and Curtis play well together, and the film's initial half-hour offers some promise, but their luck soon runs out. In the late Seventies, *You Can't Win 'em All* is most often shown as a late-night TV offering. As such, it's a sure cure for insomnia.

CRITICS' CORNER
"Had Howard Hawks made this film, as originally planned, it might conceivably have amounted to something—if only a mildly enjoyable adventure-with-wisecracks. As directed by Peter Collinson, all muddle and flurry, the script (such as it is) is well and truly sabotaged and only amiable performances by Charles Bronson and Tony Curtis survive the wreckage."

Tom Milne, *Monthly Film Bulletin*
"You Can't Win 'Em All is both a title and a kind of dismissal to this Gene Corman potboiler.

With Tony Curtis.

With Tony Curtis and Michele Mercier.

As Josh Corey.

Poorly directed by Peter Collinson from a programmer script by Leo V. Gordon, the film wastes the authentic locale and large cast in dull derring-do.

"Curtis and Bronson, who laugh at each other's forced gags (with Curtis pouring on the Cary Grant imitation) are variously at loose odds in uneasy alliance as they search for gold and for the affections of Michele Mercier. Collinson's direction attempts to hype interest by camera movement, but the device only serves to emphasize the artistic vapidity."

"Murf.," *Variety*

"The tortuous plot is hard to follow, but the film derives its main motivation from the relationship between Curtis and Bronson as they alternately collaborate and double cross each other in a spontaneous and off-hand manner. Tony Curtis stars as the mercenary with some vestiges of conscience, but Charles Bronson as the engaging, amoral scoundrel takes most of the honors in a rather dull film."

Margaret Tarratt, *Films and Filming*

With Tony Curtis and Leo Gordon.

172

With Jill Ireland.

Citta Violenta (The Family or Violent City)

A Co-production of Fono Roma/Unidis (Rome) and Universal France (Paris) / 1970
U.S. Distributor (1974): International Co-productions & EDP Films Inc.
In Techniscope and Technicolor

CAST
Jeff: Charles Bronson; *Vanessa:* Jill Ireland; *Killain:* Michel Constantin; *Weber:* Telly Savalas; *Steve:* Umberto Orsini; *Shapiro:* George Savalas; *Balck Prisoner:* Ray Sanders; *Young Prisoner:* Benjamin Lev; *Television M.C.:* Peter Dane.

CREDITS
Producers: Arrigo Colombo, Giorgio Papi; *Associate Producer:* Solly Bianco; *Director:* Sergio Sollima; *Assistant Director:* Fabrizio Gianni; *Screenwriters:* Sauro Scavolini, Gianfranco Calligarich, Lina Wertmuller, Sergio Sollima; *Based on a Story by:* Dino Maiuri, Massimo De Rita; *Cinematographer:* Aldo Tonti; *Art Director:* Francesco Bronzi; *Musical Score:* Ennio Morricone; *Editor:* Nino Baragli.
Running Time: 109 minutes.

THE FILM
In this 1970 Franco-Italian crime melodrama, shown in the United Kingdom as *Violent City* and in the U.S. (but not until 1974) as *The Family,* Jill Ireland finally reached co-starring status with, and got very much manhandled by, her more celebrated husband. But neither his name nor the film's importance were deemed quite sufficient in 1970 to secure an American release for the movie. In 1974, when it his U.S. cinemas as half of a double-bill with an Angie Dickinson crime drama, *Big Bad Mama,* the distributor's effort at commercialism was all too obvious: Dickinson was a hit as television's *Police Woman;* Bronson was an important box-office draw in the wake of *Death Wish;* and Telly Savalas, a major supporting actor in *The Family,* had subsequently become a major TV star as *Kojak.*

The Family has violence (each of its leading players dies by gunfire), sex and a lot of confusion. At least in its English-dubbed edition, The Family proved almost hopelessly confusing to critics and public alike. Later, edited of its nudity and a bit of its gore for television, it proved even more confusing to home audiences.

CRITICS' CORNER

"Sergio Sollima prepared Violent City scrupulously and the intensive effort pays off handsomely in this violent spectacle pitting a lone hired-gun against the modern crime machine.

"Largely contributing is a first-rate cast, dominated by Charles Bronson in rare form, a

With Jill Ireland.

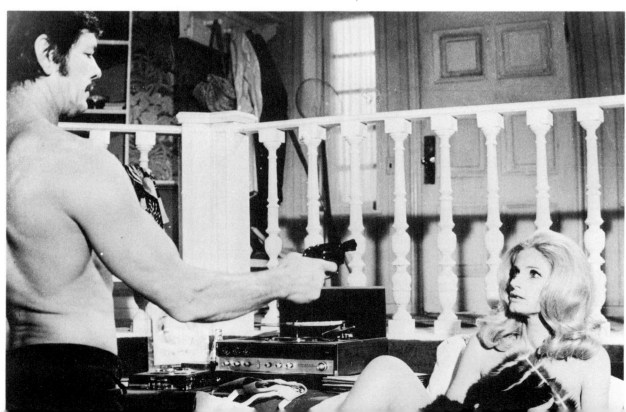

With Jill Ireland.

surprisingly effective performance by Jill Ireland of femme fatale betrayal, supported by Telly Savalas (but with star billing) as the crime lord.
"Werb.," *Variety*

"While the two principals perform with an almost stoical lack of expression, the camera zooms in and out with unflagging energy, and the flashy editing seems more appropriate to a trailer than to a feature film. Yet though the European taking a black, depressed look at the anarchic violence of American life is fast in danger of becoming a cliche, there are times here when the convoluted stream of ideas sud-

With Telly Savalas.

denly strikes the right images, notably in the climax, with two victims (Jill Ireland and Umberto Orsini) trapped in a lift, soundlessly mouthing their despair as avenging bullets (Bronson's) smack through their glass cage."

James D. White, *Monthly Film Bulletin*

"This sluggish Italian-made Mafioso melodrama was filmed four years ago in Rome with some location work in New Orleans, and were it not for the success subsequently achieved by its stars, Charles Bronson in *Death Wish* and Telly Savalas in *Kojak*, it's doubtful that *The Family* would ever have gotten wide U.S. release.

"Bronson, walking stolidly through the role of a hit man betrayed by girlfriend Jill Ireland, wears a single expression throughout the film— his patently pained stare—and appears to be stifling a yawn. In a relatively brief role consuming no more than twenty minutes, Savalas has no chance to make an impact. Ireland, Bronson's real-life wife, is a talented actress whose physical endowments are exploited for a couple of nude scenes."

The Independent Film Journal

"An Italian-French overdubbed concoction of violence, called *Violent City* (would you believe New Orleans?) in 1970 but fashionably (and irrelevantly) retitled *The Family*. It stars murders, car chases and thuggery as well as Charles Bronson, Jill Ireland and Telly Savalas."

Judith Crist, *TV Guide*

With Jill Ireland.

With Liv Ullmann.

De La Part Des Copains (Cold Sweat)

A co-production of Les Films Corona (Paris)
   and Fair Film (Rome) / 1971
U.S. Distributor (1974): Emerson Film Ent. Inc.
In Eastmancolor

CAST
Joe Martin: Charles Bronson; *Fabienne Martin:* Liv Ullmann; *Ross:* James Mason; *Moira:* Jill Ireland; *Whitey:* Michel Constantin; *Katanga:* Jean Topart; *Michele Martin:* Yannick Delulle; *Fausto:* Luigi Pistilli; *Bit Players:* Gabriele Ferzetti, Nathalie Varallo.

CREDITS
Executive Producer: Serge Lebeau; *Producer:* Robert Dorfmann; *Associate Producer:* Maurice Jacquin; *Director:* Terence Young; *Assistant Director:* Daniel Wronecki; *Screenwriters:* Shimon Wincelberg, Albert Simonin; *Based on the Novel* "Ride the Nightmare" *by:* Richard Matheson; *Cinematographer:* Jean Rabier; *Art Director:* Tony Roman; *Musical Score:* Michel Magne; *Editor:* Johnny Dwyre.
Running Time: 94 minutes.

THE FILM
By 1971, Bronson's "expatriate" film career patterns appeared well established. As his *Cold Sweat* colleague James Mason has said, "The Bronson public proliferates in Italy, Japan, South America and, above all, in France, where, the year in which we shot this film, he was voted the world's most attractive human male."

Theoretically, a crime-adventure film boasting a cast topped by Bronson, Liv Ullmann and James Mason would carry sufficient box-office power to interest major U.S. distributors. But such did not appear to be the case with this co-produced Franco-Italian melodrama, even though it was simultaneously shot in an English version. Like *The Family,* its Bronson predecessor, *Cold Sweat* took several years to reach American audiences (courtesy of Emerson, a small-time distributor) on its equally rapid journey to tele-

With Liv Ullmann.

vision.

Once more, Bronson's vehicle involved him with intrigue, guns and violence, as a reformed criminal leading a temporarily serene life on France's Cote d'Azur (Villefranche locations were employed). Married, with a wife (Ullmann) and daughter (Yannick Delulle), he now makes his living by servicing wealthy tourists, who hire out his fishing boat. But into this quiet setting intrude drug smugglers from his secret past. Headed by James Mason, they take Ullmann and Delulle hostage, forcing Bronson to help them make an illegal trip.

The complex plot now moves into side-paths of murder, treachery and turnabout loyalities. Bronson tricks Mason's mistress (Jill Ireland) and kidnaps her and the money she's carrying to help the crooks with their caper. Action sequences consume much of the film's latter footage, in which both Mason and henchman Jean Topart are killed off. As the movie ends, the reunited Bronson and family are joining in a Bastille Day celebration.

By now, Charles Bronson had become the movies' macho-superstar hero of Europe and the Orient, and his salary was commensurate

With Jill Ireland.

With Liv Ullmann and Yannick Delulle.

with his drawing power.

In *Cold Sweat,* there appears to have been little money left for wardrobe: Bronson goes through the film in jeans, sneakers and a black tee-shirt. The women are only slightly more decoratively attired.

CRITICS' CORNER
"A flabbily effete thriller with none of the un-selfconscious polish of Terence Young's Bond films and which, unlike them, pays a queasy lip-service to moral awareness. Charles Bronson, still flashing his aging whipcord muscle, bounds woodenly through his ordeal, expressing little beyond a certain satisfaction with his prowess in neck-breaking and dangerous driving."
Sylvia Millar, *Monthly Film Bulletin*

"Terence Young directs competently, but has a tale oft seen from Hollywood, with overtones of *The Killers* and others. The shrewd and rugged Bronson plays with ease, but still with his disturbing underlying violence. James Mason, with a strange Yankee accent, is the gangleader. Liv Ullmann, noted for her striking dramatic roles in several Ingmar Bergman pix, is the wife in distress. She acquits herself well, but is wasted in a fairly rote role. Bronson's real-life spouse, Jill Ireland, is fetching as a hippie moll friend of Mason.

"But it has a breakneck car chase, good fights and is passable action fare without that needed extra fillip of character delineation which its Yank counterparts usually had."
"Mosk.," *Variety*

"To watch Liv Ullmann, the queen of Ingmar Bergman's fine arts stable, making soft puppy eyes at Bronson, the God of Grunts, is an experience I had never hoped to enjoy.

"Abysmally written, harshly overdubbed, and with photographic development that would flunk the film out of a Kiwanis home-movie contest, *Cold Sweat* is almost beyond belief."
David Elliot, *The Chicago Daily News*

With Jill Ireland.

Quelqu'un Derriere La Porte
(Someone Behind the Door)

A Lira Film / 1971
U.S. Distributor: GSF Productions Inc.
In Eastmancolor

CAST
The Stranger: Charles Bronson; *Laurence Jeffries:* Anthony Perkins; *Frances Jeffries:* Jill Ireland; *Paul Damien:* Henri Garcin; *Andrew:* Adriano Magestretti; *Lucy:* Agathe Natanson; *Young Girl on Beach:* Viviane Everly; *Intern:* Andre Penvern.

CREDITS
Producer: Raymond Danon; *Associate Producer:* Maurice Jacquin; *Director:* Nicolas Gessner; *Assistant Directors:* Michel Lang, Guy Sauteret; *Screenwriters:* Jacques Robert, Marc Behm, Nicolas Gessner, Lorenzo Ventavoli; *Based on the Novel by:* Jacques Robert; *Cinematographer:* Pierre Lhomme; *Art Director:* Marc Frederix; *Musical Score:* Georges Garvarentz; *Editor:* Victoria Mercanton.
Running Time: 97 minutes.

THE FILM
Another French-made suspense melodrama occupied Charles Bronson and Jill Ireland during 1971. Co-starring Tony Perkins, this one offered Bronson in the initially mute role of a stranger suffering from amnesia. When he's brought into an English hospital, this mystery man comes under the care of a neuro-psychiatrist (Perkins), who uncovers evidence that

180

With Anthony Perkins.

Bronson has committed a brutal rape-murder. Perkins subsequently formulates a plan to make Bronson kill the Parisian lover (Henri Garcin) of his adulterous wife (Jill Ireland), via mind control and clever manipulation. Confusion abounds as identities are mixed and motivations are clouded—but Bronson does indeed kill Garcin, and nearly murders Ireland, as well, before Perkins saves her. As Bronson wanders, bewildered, off into a police dragnet, Perkins confesses all to Ireland.

As with many of his starring roles, Bronson apparently found the better part of characterization, when faced with an enigmatic screenplay, was plain lack-of-expression, with that ubiquitous gun serving as a virtual security-blanket. In view of co-star Perkins' quirky role (and peculiar acting mannerisms), perhaps this was Bronson's best resort. Obviously, there was little help to be had from Nicolas Gessner, the

With Jill Ireland.

181

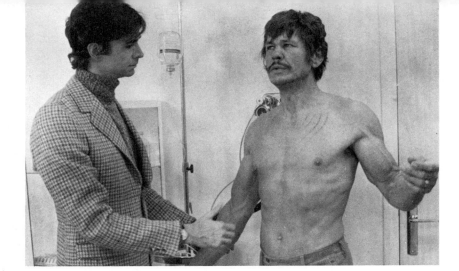

With Anthony Perkins.

film's director.

CRITICS' CORNER
"There exists in Europe, probably under some neutral Swiss Alp, a giant, fully-equipped computer-controlled movie studio from which French and Italian producers can obtain their co-productions by mail-order catalogue. That, at least, is the suspicion when I see a film as impersonal and anational as *Someone Behind the Door,* a perfunctory sort of suspense melo-drama, supposedly set in England, but photo-graphed in a recognizable France, where almost everyone speaks American English.

"The movie opened yesterday at the New Amsterdam on 42nd Street, where, at the lunch-time performance anyway, a lot of people napped."

Vincent Canby, *The New York Times*

"Director Nicolas Gessner gives the pic too straightforward a mounting without the deeper characterization which is necessary to make its motives more potent. It thus remains a surface affair as the neurologist, played with boyish charm by Perkins, takes home an amnesia victim brought to his hospital. This man is played with bearish charm by Bronson. Jill Ireland gets little chance to do much with her part."

"Mosk.," *Variety*

"The trouble with *Someone Behind the Door* is that the plot is too incredible. A brain surgeon takes an amnesiac into his home and proceeds to feed him false memories to stimulate him into committing murder. It's a toss-up as to who is in more need of psychiatric help, the doctor or the patient.

"Charles Bronson struggles with his amnesiac role, but it's a losing proposition. This may be due more to script failure than interpretation. Three writers helped Jacques Robert adapt his novel, and that could have been three too many. The reactions of the patient are not believ-able. Anthony Perkins as the surgeon and Jill Ireland as his wife come across more realistically."

Ann Guarino, *The New York Daily News*

With Henri Garcin.

With Toshiro Mifune.

Soleil Rouge (Red Sun)

A Co-production of Corona Films (Paris)
  Oceania Films (Rome) and Balcazar Films
  (Madrid) / 1971
  U.S. Distributor (1972);
National General Pictures In Eastmancolor

CAST
Link: Charles Bronson; *Christina:* Ursula Andress; *Kuroda:* Toshiro Mifune; *Gauche:* Alain Delon; *Pepita:* Capucine; *Ambassador:* Satoshi Naka-moura; *Sheriff:* Bart Barry; *and:* Lee Burton, Anthony Dawson, John Hamilton, George W. Lycan, Luc Merenda, Jose Nieto, Julio Pena, Monica Randall, Hiroshi Tanaka, John Vermont.

CREDITS
Executive Producer: Robert Dorfmann; *Producer:* Ted Richmond; *Director:* Terence Young; *2nd Unit Director:* Bernard Farrel; *Assistant Directors:* Christian Raoux, Ricardo Huerta; *Screenwriters:* Laird Koenig, Denne Bart Petit-clerc, William Roberts, Lawrence Roman; *Based on a Story by:* Laird Koenig, *Cinematographer:* Henri Alekan; *2nd Unit Photographer:* Raymond Picon-Borel; *Art Director:* Enrique Alarcon; *Set Decorator:* Rafael Salazar; *Special Effects:* Karl Baumgartner; *Musical Score:* Maurice Jarre; *Editor:* Johnny Dwyre.
Running Time: 112 minutes.

THE FILM
With its hand-picked collection of international stars *Red Sun* bears all the earmarks of a well-

With Capucine, Toshiro Mifune, and Monica Randall.

calculated (almost computerized) bid for world-wide box-office success. In Europe and the Far East, this canny Robert Dorfmann-Ted Richmond production, utilizing finances from France, Italy and Spain, broke many an attendance record and banked a mint of money.

Lack of critical enthusiasm hardly proved a deterrent to European and Oriental audiences, who wanted only to see their favorites, Charles Bronson, Toshiro Mifune and Alain Delon. In the U.S., where this trio's drawing power was infinitely less influential, *Red Sun* failed to catch fire with the public. The film's reviewers were apathetic to its charms, and those that did see it—mainly action fans—found little to provoke word-of-mouth excitement.

With Capucine.

With Toshiro Mifune.

The film's genesis derives from 1966, when the American producer Ted Richmond was informed of a little-known factual event by a student of Japanese history. In the late nineteenth-century Arizona Territory, a band of outlaws had attacked and pillaged a cross-country train, one of whose passengers was the Japanese Ambassador to Washington. The desperadoes not only killed one of his Japanese aides, but also made off with the Ambassador's jeweled Samurai sword, thus provoking a justifiable Nipponese vendetta.

With only a brief draft of his idea, Richmond went to Japan and signed Toshiro Mifune to star. But it was several years before he was able to secure the necessary financing, in the person of French executive-producer Robert Dorfmann. With the expensive addition of Bronson and Delon, plus the distaff presence of those ripely mature sex symbols, Capucine and Ursula Andress, the production began filming in Spain. There, the outdoor expanses of Almeria doubled for frontier America, under the direction of James Bond-film veteran Terence Young, who had recently guided Bronson through *Cold Sweat*.

With Ursula Andress.

CRITICS' CORNER

"Samurai movies have been compared to Westerns for so long that it's surprising that the two genres weren't somehow combined before the amiable but hokey and uneven *Red Sun,* which teams Charles Bronson, the current chief anti-hero of Italian Westerns, and Toshiro Mifune, Japan's longtime top screen swordsman.

"This release is at its best in its humorous, affectionate treatment of the uneasy truce between Bronson and Mifune that develops into friendship when these two proud, strong men realize that they are going to have to depend upon each other. Unfortunately, the various incidents and characters they encounter along the way have not been handled with the same kind of care, and therefore undermine the film's credibility.

"Mifune is the same appealing and dignified figure that he has been in countless Samurai movies, but *Red Sun* does not begin to suggest what a great actor he can be in his native language. Like Alain Delon, also a fine actor, Mifune is handicapped by his sometimes unintelligible postsynched English. Bronson is staunch and likable, but that voluptous nonactress, Ursula Andress, cast as a treacherous prostitute, is strident and ludicrous. The elegant Capucine is woefully miscast as Miss Andress's hearty frontier madam."

Kevin Thomas, *Los Angeles Times*

"Charles Bronson is really in charge, full of evil warmth, well-oiled muscles, smiling crinkling eyes, and a few flat pithy remarks. But then even his makeup is pretty terrific, and how he

With Capucine.

As Link.

manages to keep those suede jeans in such remarkably trim snappy condition, I'll never know. It would all be laughable, if it wasn't for the dubious morality preached."

Peter Buckley, *Films and Filming*

"The pity about *Red Sun* is that opportunities offered by an excellent story (based on a true incident) are invariably muffed. A certain level of watchability is maintained by Bronson and Mifune, striking up an excellent partnership with their monosyllabic personalities matching perfectly; but Alain Delon is completely colorless, and Ursula Andress is outshone by Capucine in an almost nonexistent part."

Tom Milne, *Monthly Film Bulletin*

"The ladies talk dirty, Bronson talks tough and Mifune grunts. They do this through lips clenched for dubbing. Laird Koenig wrote the stupid story and Terence Young directed the mindless movie and I am sure that all concerned will continue to make a mint—thanks to equally mindless moviegoers the wide world over."

Judith Crist, *New York*

"Though Charles Bronson is nominally the star of the picture, Mifune is its heart and soul, and audiences will probably respond best to the scenes in which Bronson is constantly attacking Mifune and just as constantly getting thrown on his ass.

"Terence Young's direction is pedestrian, but at least he knows when to keep the cameras trained on Mifune and Bronson. These two are virtual legends, Mifune in Japan, Bronson in Europe, and this film gives a pretty good idea why."

The Independent Film Journal

With Alain Delon and Bart Barry.

With Ursula Andress and Toshiro Mifune.

Chato's Land

A Scimitar Films Production / 1972
  for United Artists
In Technicolor

CAST
Pardon Chato: Charles Bronson; *Quincey Whitmore:* Jack Palance; *Nye Buell:* Richard Basehart; *Joshua Everette:* James Whitmore; *Jubal Hooker:* Simon Oakland; *Elias Hooker:* Ralph Waite; *Earl Hooker:* Richard Jordan; *Martin Hall:* Victor French; *Harvey Lansing:* William Watson: *Gavin Malechie:* Roddy McMillan; *Brady Logan:* Paul Young; *George Dunn:* Lee Patterson; *Will Coop:* Rudy Ugland; *Mexican Scout:* Raul Castro; *Chato's Woman:* Sonia Rangan; *Jacob Meade:* Clive Endersby; *Edna Malechie:* Rebecca Wilson; *Shelby Hooker:* Verna Harvey; *Moira Logan:* Sally Adez; *Ezra:* Peter Dyneley; *Bartender:* Hugh McDermott.

CREDITS

Producer-Director: Michael Winner; *2nd Unit Director:* Raul Perez Cubero; *Assistant Directors:* Peter Price, Antonio Tarruella, Stefano Capriati; *Screenwriter:* Gerald Wilson; *Cinematographer:* Robert Paynter, *Art Director:* Manolo Manpaso; *Special Effects:* Antonio Parra; *Musical Score:* Jerry Fielding; *Editor:* Freddie Wilson.
Running Time: 100 minutes.

THE FILM

Before teaming with Charles Bronson on a succession of the Seventies' more violent melodramas, British director Michael Winner had paid his filmmaking dues with everything from youth-oriented musicals (*The Cool Mikado*) to crime dramas (*The System*) to popular Terry-Thomas comedies (*You Must Be Joking!*). Following his great success with *The Jokers,* Winner turned producer-director, unsuccessfully, with *I'll Never Forget What's 'Isname* and *Hannibal Brooks,* before turning out *The Nightcomers,* an atmospheric prequel to Henry James' *Turn of the Screw,* that repelled while it fascinated. Featuring a heavy, Irish-accented Marlon Brando, this beautifully photographed blend of bucolic serenity, perversity and violence foretokened the path of Winner's greatest successes. With Bronson as his starring symbol of violent impassivity, Winner would enjoy a prolific period of moviemaking that, while

With Sonia Rangan.

As Pardon Chato.

satisfying the fans of explosive action, would earn little but disdain from the critical fraternity. But, in league with Bronson (at the height of his money-making powers), their lucrative collaborations would finally result in an *American* blockbuster, the 1974 *Death Wish*.

Winner's first Bronson film, *Chato's Land,* was written by Gerald Wilson, author of the director's previous film (and *first* Western), the Burt Lancaster vehicle *Lawman*. This Wilson screenplay was well tailored to Bronson's evolutionary screen persona, that of the strong, relatively silent avenger—a hardened figure of definite intent but few words. As Pardon Chato, the vengeful Apache half-breed of this rugged 1972 Western, Bronson enjoyed the most vocally reticent role of his starring career, speaking but fifteen lines—and thirteen of those in Apache!

Again, Spanish locations represented the American frontier West for this post-Civil War tale about a makeshift posse's search for Chato, who, in self-defense, had killed the white sheriff of a small New Mexico town. As the pursuers forge deeper into Apache country, the situation shifts around, with hunters becoming the hunted. Falling out among themselves, the posse

CL-6

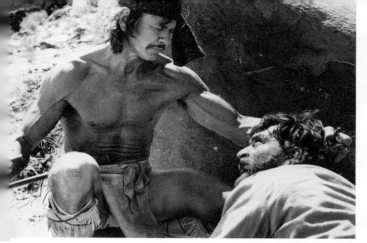

With Victor French.   With Hugh McDermott and Peter Dyneley.

members gradually become victim either to each other's violence or to Chato's well-justified vengeance, after they rape his woman.

In the non-U.S. countries where Bronson enjoyed his greatest popularity, *Chato's Land* was well met and highly successful. But its American distributor, United Artists, showed so little faith in the movie that they packaged it in tandem with a trivial Sophia Loren comedy, *Lady Liberty,* and left it to flounder, before selling it to television.

CRITICS' CORNER
"The almost completely male cast has been very carefully chosen, with especially good work coming from James Whitmore as a hunched-up sheriff, Richard Jordan as the young pup and a very toned-down Jack Palance as a seasoned veteran in Indian matters. As Chato, Charles Bronson has little to do but look stoical and physically fit, at which, especially the latter, he is unexcelled."
The Independent Film Journal

"Charles Bronson, as a half-breed Apache, is perhaps the mutest hero ever. He mumbles only a few words in Apache during the film, but his silences are eloquent enough."
Archer Winsten, *The New York Post*
"Michael Winner takes a hard look at the early American West and comes up with a violence-drenched meller which should do well enough in its intended market. Lensed in Spain and cast mostly with Hollywood principals, the film carries certain suspense, drive and grim realism, but lacks story development that would have made this a real winner. Only during the actual business of tracking down Chato and his leading them into waterless country does the script build.

"Bronson is a standout as he picks off posse-men one by one, delivering forcefully in a role requiring a minimum of dialog but dripping with menace."
"Whit.," *Variety*

"The screenplay is truthful, the direction understanding, and the performances are unnerving. No one is the hero. Chato himself is more a symbol of conscience. Bronson in fact dominates the film by a mystic presence, rather than actually being on screen for any length of time."
Robin Bean, *Films and Filming*

"For those who enjoy blood sports, *Chato's Land* makes you devote 100 minutes to watching a dozen men die as Charles Bronson knocks off an entire posse of pursuers with such savvy that you wonder how the white man ever retained a foothold in the picturesque old Southwest. Your cup of violence will overflow."
Judith Crist, *TV Guide*

"Bronson alone, freed from the script's inane repartee, succeeds in bringing shape and some element of conviction to a film which, for most of its length, seems determined to remain formless. Winner's incessant use of the zoom, the hideously photographed day-for-night sequences, Jerry Fielding's lacklustre score and the phoney, gratuitous violence are constant irritations. The only truly magical scene is of Bronson's return to his woman and child, shot in bright sunlight and without dialogue."
Derek Elley, *Monthly Film Bulletin*

193

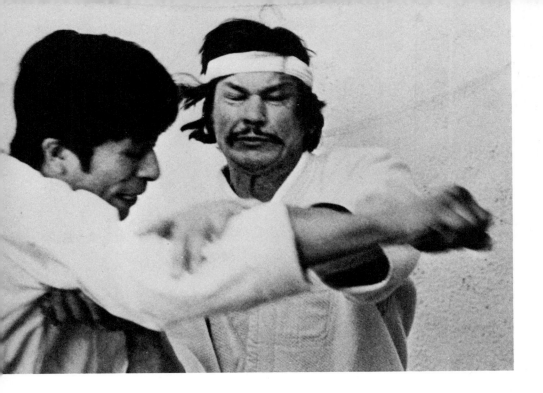

The Mechanic

A United Artists Picture / 1972
In DeLuxe Color

CAST

Arthur Bishop: Charles Bronson; *Steve McKenna:* Jan-Michael Vincent; *Harry McKenna:* Keenan Wynn; *Prostitute:* Jill Ireland; *Louise:* Linda Ridgeway; *Syndicate Head:* Frank de Kova: *Policeman:* Lindsay H. Crosby; *Karate Master:* Takayuki Kubota; *American Tourist:* Martin Gordon; *Intern:* James Davidson; *Messenger:* Steve Cory; *Old Man:* Patrick O'Moore; *Cam:* Kevin O'Neal; *Bathtub Girl:* Linda Grant; *Librarian:* Louise Fitch; *Kori:* Hank Hamilton; *Aikido Master:* Hiroyasu Fujishima; *Rifle Range Attendant:* Michael Hinn; *Bikini Waitress:* Christine Forbes; *Priest:* Father Amando de Vincenzo; *Butler:* Gerald Saunderson Peters; *Chickin Lickin Driver:* Ernie Orsatti; *Gang Leader:* J.N. Roberts; *Garden Party Woman:* Sara Taft; *Garden Party Man:* John Barclay; *Bodyguards:* Alan Gibbs, Frank Orsatti; *The Mark's Girl:* Celeste Yarnall; *Old Woman:* Athena Lorde; *Car Polish Man:* Howard Morton; *1st Hippie:* Ken Wolger; *Young Girl:* Alison Rose; *The Mark:* Enzo Fiermonte; *5th Hippie:* Stephen Vinovich; *3rd Hippie:* Trina Mitchum.

CREDITS

Producers: Robert Chartoff, Irwin Winkler, Lewis John Carlino; *Associate Producer:* Henry Gellis; *Director:* Michael Winner; *2nd Unit Director:* Antonio Tarruella *(Europe); Assistant Directors:* Jerome M. Siegel *(USA),* Peter Price and Francesco Cinieri *(Europe); Screenwriter:* Lewis John Carlino; *Cinematographers:* Richard Kline *(USA),* Robert Paynter *(Europe); Art Directors:* Roger E. Maus *(USA),* Herbert Westbrook *(Europe); Special Effects:* Richard F. Albain; *Musical Score:* Jerry Fielding; *Editor:* Freddie Wilson.
Running Time: 100 minutes.

THE FILM

Bronson followed his return to U.S. filmmaking in *Chato's Land* with another male-dominated script, *The Mechanic,* well tailored to the actor's violent screen image by Lewis John Carlino. And again Michael Winner was producer-director on the project. Winner had enjoyed the experience of *Chato's Land,* while finding his star's remoteness puzzling. "I thought he was excellent," says Winner. "But there was a funny thing. Normally, you have a very close rapport with your leading actor. But when we finished *Chato's Land,* although I admire Bronson tremendously, I would have been very careful about saying whether I'd gotten close to him. I was surprised when he phoned me up to ask me to direct *The Mechanic.* He'd asked for me." And Winner concludes, "On that picture, I got to know him much better, although, apart from his family, he *is* a very private man."

The Mechanic is a thoroughly antisocial and rather complex contemporary action melodrama, murkily and episodically plotted. Bronson plays Arthur Bishop, a coldly efficient professional hit man—or "mechanic"—whose philosophy is summed up by "Murder is only killing without a license, and everybody kills—the Army, the police. . ." In this one, sniper killings, explosions and vehicular destruction abound, interspersed with some beautifully photographed views of California and Italy's Amalfi coast, highlighted by Ravello, Positano and the Bay of Naples. Aside from Bronson's high fee, *The Mechanic* represents costly moviemaking— well calculated to earn back its investment many times over. The film was nearly as popular in America as, expectedly, it was with the multitude of worldwide Bronson buffs. And, more so than any of his previous films, it cemented the fifty-two-year-old actor's reputation as a larger-than-life image of late-twentieth-century *violence.*

In *The Mechanic,* Bronson was curiously, but effectively, paired with young Jan-Michael Vincent, an equally sinewy, muscular actor given, like his co-star, to equally smouldering on-screen moodiness, uncannily reflecting Bronson's eternal promise of pressure-cooker explosiveness. Together, as seasoned professional killer and cocky protege, Bronson and Vincent were almost a love team, and certain of the film's critics took note of that impression. Indeed, when Jill Ireland is brought in for one brief sequence, as Bronson's call-girlfriend, it appears included merely to prove that Arthur Bishop (Bronson) has a normal sex life.

The Mechanic sometimes approaches the heights of James Bondian ingenuity in a slick and entertaining motion picture that, nonetheless, fails to engage our concern for any of its

With Jan-Michael Vincent.

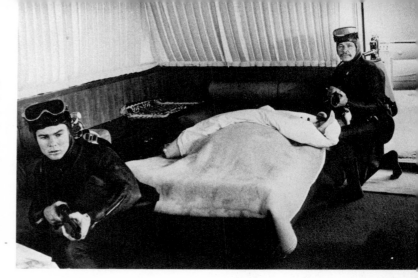

With Jan-Michael Vincent and Keenan Wynn.

dubious protagonists. The movie opens with a clever contract killing and closes with a double-twist of cheating-cheaters retribution—a tough, heartless crime fantasy affording its audiences a sublimated crack at antisocial vengeance. But the movie bears about as much relation to actuality as do the escapades of Ian Fleming's *007*.

CRITICS' CORNER
"A neat, crisp piece of mayhem, done with a dash. Charles Bronson plays the assassin with just the right pitch of bland, don't-give-a-damn disinterest."

David Castell, *Films Illustrated*

As Arthur Bishop.

With Jan-Michael Vincent.

"A tricky melodrama of professional killers with international connections, this movie verges on the grotesque, as far as the surface plot is concerned. But there is an engrossingly homosexual sub-text in the peculiar master-apprentice relationship between Bronson and Vincent."

Andrew Sarris, *The Village Voice*

"For my money, it's one of the best thrillers of the year—thanks largely to Winner's crisp Warner-1940s direction and to the acting of Charles Bronson, who grows less and less scrutable with each picture he makes. Looking now like a samurai on western leave, he inches his way through the picture, doling out death with all the remorse of a computer. Jill Ireland is wildly miscast as a call-girl."

Sheridan Morley, *Films and Filming*

"A dubious achievement is reached with *The Mechanic* in that it's hard to see how much more casually vicious, lifeless and mechanical this sort of super-cool gangster film can become.

There isn't any acting. Bronson seems to have eschewed it in favor of keeping a straight face, while Vincent covers everything up with as bad a display of The Smirks as any pretty boy climbing the ladder in Hollywood has ever had."

The Independent Film Journal

"Like its protagonist, Michael Winner's latest excursion into the improbable is cold, calculating, efficient, flashy and—despite its cultural and philosophical pretentions—vacuous. There are some occasional gestures towards an analysis of Bishop and McKenna's ambiguous relationship and the nature of callousness, but these are rapidly eclipsed by the next explosion or car-wrecking.

"Despite all Bronson's efforts, the character of Bishop himself—one moment puffing away at his pipe and philosophizing against a background of classical music in his tasteful, antique-strewn Beverly Hills home, and at the next rushing out to bump off total strangers—imposes a tremendous strain on the credulity."

Clyde Jeavons, *Monthly Film Bulletin*

With Jill Ireland.

Joe Valachi: I Segreti Di Cosa Nostra
(The Valachi Papers or Cosa Nostra)

A Co-production of Euro France Films (Paris)
  and De Laurentiis Intermarco (Rome) / 1972
U.S. Distributor: Columbia Pictures
In Technicolor

CAST
Joseph Valachi: Charles Bronson; *Don Vito Genovese:* Lino Ventura; *Maria Reina:* Jill Ireland; *Dominick "The Gap" Petrilli:* Walter Chiari; *Salvatore Maranzano:* Joseph Wiseman; *Federal Agent Ryan:* Gerald S. O'Loughlin; *Gaetano Reina:* Amedeo Nazzari; *Charles "Lucky" Luciano:* Angelo Infanti; *Albert Anastasia:* Fausto Tozzi; *Tony Bender:* Guido Leontini; *Salerno:* Mario Pilar; *Johnny Beck:* Fred Valleca; *Little Augie:* Giacomino De Michelis; *Warden, Atlanta Penitentiary:* Arny Freeman; *Commander, Fort Monmouth:* Sylvester Lamont; *Buster from Chicago:* Franco Borelli; *Giuseppe "Joe the Boss" Masseria:* Allessandro Sperli; *Ferrigno:* John Alarimo; *Rosanna Reina:* Pupella Maggio; *Jane:* Sabine Sun; *Mary Lou:* Isabelle Marchal; *Donna Petrillo:* Maria Baxa; *Donna's Girlfriend:* Imelde Marani; *Donald Valachi:* Jason McCallum; *Federal Investigators:* Anthony Dawson, Gianni Medici; *Masseria:* Saro Urzi; *Frank:* Frank Gio; *Vinnie:* Steve Belouise.

CREDITS
Executive Producer: Nino E. Krisman; *Producer:* Dino De Laurentiis; *Director:* Terence Young; *Assistant Directors:* Christian Raoux, Giorgio Gentili, Gianni Cozo; *Screenwriter:* Stephen Geller; *Based on the Book by:* Peter Maas; *Cinematographer:* Aldo Tonti; *Art Director:* Mario Carbuglia; *Set Decorator:* John Godfrey; *Special Effects:* Eros Baciucchi; *Musical Score:* Riz Ortolani; *Editor:* John Dwyre.
Running Time: 125 minutes.

THE FILM
Released in the same year as, but in the wake of, Francis Ford Coppola's *The Godfather,* Italian super-producer Dino De Laurentiis's *The Valachi Papers* came in for a great deal of critical comparison—and was rather unanimously found wanting. Ironically, its fictional predecessor, although bearing some resemblance to certain real-life figures in and around the fringes of organized crime, sidestepped actuality to tell a long but fascinating story that, nevertheless, bore the ring of truth. *The Valachi Papers,* based on the life of a minor mobster, Brooklyn-born Joseph Valachi, opted to name the notorious

As Joseph Valachi.

Mafia names and present a goodly measure of factual revelations. Strangely, these truths, often more crudely presented than in Coppola's popular blockbuster, held less interest for intelligent moviegoers, appealing chiefly to

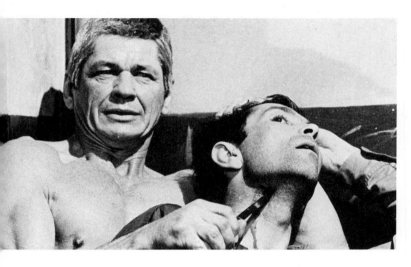

With Guido Leontini, Walter Chiari, and Joseph Wiseman.

action fans (and Bronson buffs), whose support made a great success of *The Valachi Papers* for its distributor, Columbia Pictures—much to the dismay of Paramount (which had been all set to add the film to its 1972 release schedule, until there was a major falling-out with De Laurentiis over distribution details).

The Valachi Papers, written for the screen by Stephen Geller, derives from the factual Peter Maas book covering over three decades of American underworld activity, as revealed by Valachi himself. While serving a life sentence for his criminal activities, Valachi was induced by a Federal agent to testify before the McClellan U.S. Senate investigating committee. Because Valachi talked freely about the Cosa Nostra's inner workings, his ex-boss, Mafia kingpin Vito Genovese (incarcerated in the same facility as Valachi), put out a $100,000 contract on this formerly unimportant (but now heavily guarded) crime family "soldier."

The moviemakers *also* needed "protection" during *The Valachi Papers* filming, for the disapproving New York Mafia saw to it that a series of incidents plagued the Manhattan-based production—until De Laurentiis wisely retreated to Rome, where the picture was completed.

Prior to *The Valachi Papers* release, Manhattan "godfathers" made another effort to sabotage the film, emptying the critics' screening room with a bomb threat. But such scare tactics did little to impede this movie's progress—or keep it from blasting U.S. box-office records ($9,400,000 in domestic rentals for the first eight months of its distribution).

Charles Bronson was initially reluctant to star in this project. But Dino De Laurentiis wanted him badly enough to make a special deal with the actor: Bronson signed a three-picture contract, each film of which would pay him a million dollars, plus a percentage of the gross—and a generous expense account to accommodate Bronson's family and entourage. An incredible contract indeed—putting Bronson into the top echelon of movie wage-earners. And insuring that this investment would be backed by a hard-sell advertising campaign.

The Valachi Papers marked Bronson's third collaborative effort with director Terence Young (*Cold Sweat, Red Sun*). And again the film's nominal female lead went to Jill Ireland—in a black wig that made her resemble Carol Lawrence.

CRITICS' CORNER
"Whether or not *The Valachi Papers* boosts

Charles Bronson to superstar status in America, his performance is honest, affecting and strangely poignant. The role offers little of the machismo associated with Bronson's established image, but the story is compelling and carries the sting of truth. Bronson's unsentimentalized yet human portrayal sets the tone for an atmospheric gangland drama in which cowardice, treachery and cruelty are shown to be precisely that—without redeeming virtues."

Bruce Williamson, *Playboy*

"Valachi is played by Charles Bronson, who, believe it or not, is reportedly the most popular actor in the world. Bronson's resemblance to the gangsters of the '30s movies and his ability to effect an expression of constant bewilderment have made him a natural for the uncomprehending mobster roles, although he is capable of much more. Unfortunately, because Valachi never attempts to understand his own role, other than that he is a protector of 'The Family's' interests, he is virtually an undefined character, leaving little for Bronson to do."

Michael Kerbel, *The Village Voice*

"Bronson is impressive as Valachi, delivering a powerful performance which should put him in the Oscar sweepstakes. His aging from 30 to 62 is done smoothly, both in appearance and movement, and he seems to display a rare understanding of the character. As Genovese, Lino Ventura shares prominence with Bronson and seems ideally cast in a strong role to which he contributes menacing power. In an international cast, British Jill Ireland portrays Bronson's wife, daughter of a gangster, in intelligent fashion and with charm."

"Whit.," *Variety*

The Valachi Papers is a stiff. It may be possible to make a duller gangster melodrama, but I would hate to sit through the attempt.

"Not that it matters, but Charles Bronson isn't bad as the older Valachi. He isn't ethnically right, but he tries to do right by the character, and one is impressed by his sincerity."

Gary Arnold, *Washington Post*

"In recent years the career of Charles Bronson has skyrocketed. From being cast as a heavy in Westerns, prison films and detective movies, Bronson emerged in Europe as a star. He is an accomplished actor with depth and great range to his craft. In fact, he is such an accomplished

actor and so conscious of the subtle nuances of the part he portrays, he helps make *The Valachi Papers* one of the most accurate, no-nonsense gangster films in years."

Jeffrey Lyons, *WPIX-TV, New York*

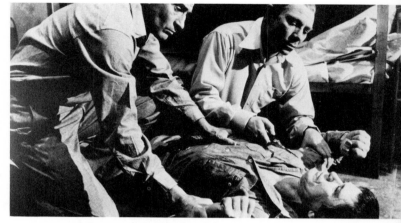

With Walter Chiari and Guido Leontini.

With Joseph Wiseman and Amedeo Nazzari.

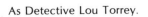
As Detective Lou Torrey.

The Stone Killer

A Dino De Laurentiis Production / 1973
 for Columbia Pictures
In Technicolor

CAST
Detective Lou Torrey: Charles Bronson; *Vescari:*
Martin Balsam; *Guido Lorenz:* David Sheiner;
Les Daniels: Norman Fell; *Mathews:* Ralph
Waite; *George Armitage:* Eddie Forestone; *J.D.:*
Walter Burke; *Gus Lipper:* David Moody; *Psychiatrist:* Charles Tyner; *Al Langley:* Paul Koslo;
Lawrence: Stuart Margolin; *Hart:* John Ritter;
L.A. Police Chief: Byron Morrow; *Lionel Jumper:*
Jack Colvin; *Calabriese:* Frank Campanella;
Tony Champion: Alfred Ryder; *Paul Long:* Gene
Woodbury: *Mossman:* Harry Basch; *Vechetti:*
Jan Arvan; *Helen:* Lisabeth Hush; *Waitress:* Mary
Cross; *Gerry Wexton:* Kelly Miles; *Mathews'*
Daughter: Cristina Raines; *Fussy Man:* Robert
Emhardt; *Sergeant:* Tom Falk; *Drug Pusher:*
Frenchia Guizon.

CREDITS
Executive Producer: Dino De Laurentiis; *Producer-Director:* Michael Winner; *Assistant Directors:* Joe Ellis, Mel Efros; *Screenwriter:* Gerald
Wilson; *Based on the Novel "A Complete*
State of Death" by: John Gardner; *Cinematographer:* Richard Moore; *Art Director:* Ward
Preston; *Set Decorator:* Norman Rockett; *Musical*
Score: Roy Budd; *Editor:* Frederick Wilson.
Running Time: 95 minutes.

THE FILM
The Stone Killer, Bronson's only film released
during 1973, provided for its audiences an
understandable sense of *deja vu,* what with its
car-crashing chase scenes, Mafioso in-fighting,
violent shoot-outs and confused, locale-jump-

ing plotting. Since this action-oriented melodrama marked a reunion of executive-producer Dino De Laurentiis, director Michael Winner, screenwriter Gerald Wilson and gun-toting actor Bronson, the feeling is understandable. The machismo was as thick as ever, but this time the film was totally filmed in the U.S., where De Laurentiis's production company had now relocated. And Bronson's rock-hard detective role put him back on the side of the law — although the character's work methods were indeed questionable.

In short, *The Stone Killer* is a cunning bundle of all the ingredients that De Laurentiis realized the Bronson public wanted and expected of their superhero. And this time there was even less purpose than ever for women on the scene, with the plot's few relegated to virtual bits —with not even so much as a *cameo* role for Jill Ireland. The inhumanity of Bronson's flint-eyed screen image had reached its zenith. And, while the Bronson buffs ate it up, the critical consensus remained, unsurprisingly, negative.

With Norman Fell and Ralph Waite.

With director Michael Winner and
producer Dino De Laurentiis.

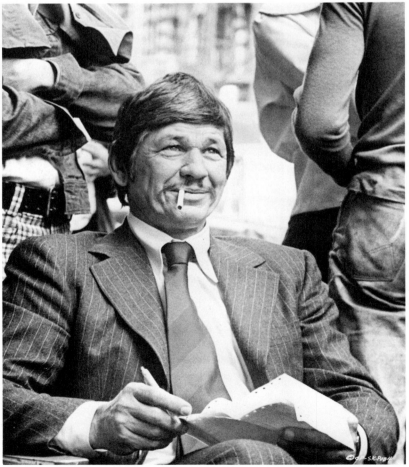

Relaxing on the set of *The Stone Killer*.

With Ralph Waite.

With Ralph Waite and Frenchia Guizon.

why he killed a fleeing suspect who was only seventeen, Bronson replies, 'His gun made him older.' And for this he gets suspended from the New York police force and immediately hired by the L.A. police force, a progression realistic enough to give us all the shivers.

"Bronson is as usual capable, quick and slightly dull. He never forces things in these films, which is good, but his dry, withdrawn style of acting reveals only so much."

The Independent Film Journal

"*The Stone Killer* lacks the dignity of *Scorpio* and the sheer gritty excitement of *The Mechanic,* Winner's last two and, I believe, most successful films. It is, in fact, a routine *policier,* distinguished only by Winner's usual unerring eye for character actors who tell it all in their faces, and by the steely presence of Mr. Bronson. This time rather surprisingly on the side of the police, not that the changeover makes any difference to his death rate, which must be somewhere in the high twenties by the end. In the end it becomes as ritualized a performance as Kabuki drama. There, as here, the coldness is all, and it is surely no coincidence that Bronson is getting increasingly Oriental around the eyes."

Sheridan Morley, *Films and Filming*

With Kelly Miles.

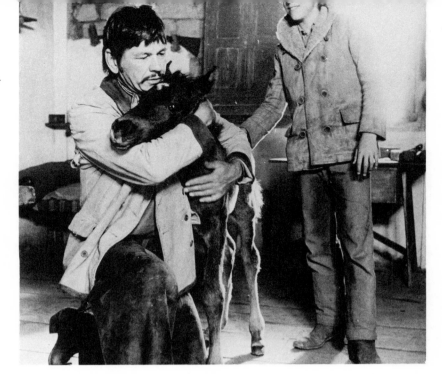

With Vincent Van Patten.

Valdez Il Mezzosangue

(Chino or Valdez, the Halfbreed)

A Co-production of De Laurentiis Intermaco
(Rome), Coral Film (Madrid) and
Universal Production France (Paris) / 1974
U.S. Distributor (1977): Intercontinental
Releasing Corp.

CAST
Chino Valdez: Charles Bronson; *Louise:* Jill Ireland;
Jamie Wagner: Vincent Van Patten; *Maral:*
Marcel Bozzuffi; *Indian Girl:* Melissa Chimenti;
Cruz: Fausto Tozzi; *Sheriff:* Ettore Manni; *Cayote:*
Adolfo Thous; *Little Bear:* Florencio Amarilla;
Indians: Corrado Gaida, Diana Lorys.

CREDITS
Executive Producer: Alfredo De Laurentiis;
Producer: Duilio Coletti; *Director:* John Sturges;
Screenwriters: Dino Maiuri, Massimo De Rita,
Clair Huffaker; *Based on the Novel* "The Valdez
Horses" *by:* Lee Hoffman; *Cinematographer:*
Armando Nannuzzi; *Art Director:* Mario Garbuglia;
Set Decorator: Boris Juraga; *Musical Score:*
Guido De Angelis, Maurizio De Angelis; *Editors:*
Vanio Amici, Peter Zinner.
Running Time: 97 minutes.

THE FILM
This Italian-Spanish-French co-production (only
partially produced by Dino De Laurentiis, this
time) was filmed just *prior* to *The Stone Killer,*
though released afterwards. In the U.S., the
film, then called *The Wild Horses,* was acquired
for distribution in late 1972 by Paramount,
which kept it "on the shelf." Subsequently,
the movie was picked up by a small independent
distributor, Intercontinental Releasing Corp.,
which accorded it a double-bill, action-house
release in 1977, under the title *Chino.*

For this Western, directed by Bronson's re-
nowned *Magnificent Seven/Great Escape* mentor,
John Sturges, Bronson packed up Jill, their six
collective offspring and three tutors and returned to Almeria, Spain, for exterior locations
(interiors were shot in Rome).

As the American ads for the movie pro-

claimed: "They took his land, his horses, his woman, but they couldn't take Chino." Nor, apparently could even a director of Sturges's stature make anything noteworthy of this script. Lino Ventura, Bronson's Mafioso nemesis from *The Valachi Papers,* was hired to portray this film's "heavy," but walked out when he discovered how brief his role actually was. Marcel Bozzuffi, an actor nearly unknown in the U.S., replaced him, adding little to Chino's potential North American sales value—except a nearly impenetrable foreign accent.

The story's setting is a crude New Mexico stud farm run by the halfbreed Chino Valdez (Bronson), who reluctantly grants shelter to Jamie Wagner (Vincent Van Patten), a teen-age runaway. Chino then comes into conflict with a wealthy ranch owner named Maral (Bozzuffi), whose sister Louise (Jill Ireland) tries to effect a truce by purchasing one of Chino's horses. She and Chino fall in love, while Jamie has a brief romantic interlude with a young Arapahoe squaw. The prospect of his sister's marrying Chino inspires Maral to have Chino beaten up, jailed and whipped. After recuperating with his Indian friends, Chino returns to his ranch to find a favorite horse killed. In submission, he turns loose his herd, incinerates his farm and sends Jamie on his way before riding off to start anew elsewhere. Admittedly, *Chino* does *not* adhere to the established Bronson image— which might account for Paramount's failure to market it stateside.

On television, *Chino* has, of course, been relieved of all its sexual content, thus rendering it more acceptable for "family" viewing, if less explicable in its already-episodic storyline.

CRITICS' CORNER
"Superstar Charles Bronson appears in this unusual Western, playing a strong, sensitive, quiet hero who decides to quit the fight at the climax, rather than risk his horses. He burns his home and stampedes the horses. This twist gives the film a different dimension from the usual Italian or Spanish oaters."

Boxoffice

"Merely by lending his presence to them, the ubiquitous and director-proof Charles Bronson manages to dictate the style of his lightweight star vehicles. Chino Valdez alias The Mechanic alias Pardon Chato is a morose loner of uncertain origins, who loves simple things but is dangerous when riled. Any other details seem to fall into inevitable place around this obdurate image. Certainly, in this case, John Sturges appears to have been content to supply the requisite framework and then relax. He and his cameramen do produce some rather grand action scenes that occur along the very bottom of the frame line, while the glory of the New Mexican landscape towers above, and a mood of rustic tranquility is helped by pleasantly muted color. But otherwise it is the Bronson charisma that calls the tune. Amid the standard one-man-against-many conflicts, there is some amusement to be had from the earnest talks Chino has with Jamie about the parts of high-born Eastern ladies that mustn't be discussed (their legs), and there is also an odd, pulp romance quality about the way pouting Jill Ireland is suddenly ravished in the dust by her hero, after they have observed two horses mating."

David McGillivray, *Monthly Film Bulletin*

With Jill Ireland.

Mr. Majestyk

A Mirisch Corp. Production
    for United Artists   /   1974
In DeLuxe Color

CAST

Vince Majestyk: Charles Bronson; *Frank Renda:* Al Lettieri; *Nancy Chavez:* Linda Cristal; *Wiley:* Lee Purcell; *Bobby Kopas:* Paul Koslo; *Gene Lundy:* Taylor Lacher; *Det. Lt. McAllen:* Frank Maxwell; *Larry Mendoza:* Alejandro Rey; *Deputy Sheriff Harold Ritchie:* Jordan Rhodes; *Julio Tamaz:* Bert Santos; *Gas Station Attendant:* Vern Porter; *Kopas Muscle Men:* Allan Pinson, Robert Templeton; *Police Officer:* Bill Morris; *Black Prisoner:* Jim Reynolds; *Chicano Prisoners:* Eddy Reyes, Larry Cortinez; *TV Reporter Ron Malone:* Howard Beasley; *TV Camera Crew:* Bus Gindhart, Tom Hickman; *Press Photographers:* Kenny Bell, Max Reed; *Laber Contractor:* Luis Ramirez; *Mrs. Mendoza:* Alma Lawrentz.

CREDITS

Producer: Walter Mirisch; *Director:* Richard Fleischer; *Assistant Director:* Buck Hall; *Screenwriter:* Elmore Leonard; *Cinematographer:* Richard H. Kline; *Art Director:* Cary Odell; *Special Effects:* Robert N. Dawson; *Musical Score:* Charles Bernstein; *Editor:* Ralph E. Winters. *Running Time:* 103 minutes.

THE FILM

Social themes were not the usual stuff of Bronson films, but in *Mr. Majestyk,* directed by the prolific Richard Fleischer for producer Walter Mirisch and United Artists, Elmore Leonard's screenplay dealt with the exploitation of Chicano migrant workers by an unscrupulous union. A basically good idea this, but it was compromised for commerce, tailored to the melodramatic image its makers divined would please and appease the Bronson grandstandees, with their bloodlust for action and, of course, violence. *Mr. Majestyk*'s initial promise, then, of social responsibility and concern for an abused contemporary minority, is a false beacon indeed. The proverbial ships are still, inevitably, rock-bound, with the resultant crash certain to be spectacular.

In short, *Mr. Majestyk* is a "formula" Bronson picture, with its indomitable star again a fighting loner who solves his problems with muscle and firearms — this time a formidable shotgun.

Producer Mirisch obviously considered Bronson worth his by-now considerable salary, admitting that for *Mr. Majestyk,* he was paying

As Vince Majestyk.

the actor twenty thousand dollars a day for a six-day week, plus ten percent of the gross, as well as twenty five hundred a week "walking-around" money. For his fans (as well as some of his producers), Charles Bronson had become a veritable twentieth-century Robin Hood.

CRITICS' CORNER

"Mr. Majestyk is a competently standard showcase for Charles Bronson's superhero cool. This time, as a Colorado melon farmer, he jostles an obsessive killer with syndicate backing. Guess who wins.

"The picture might have amounted to more, originally, with sharper use of its migrant-worker background, instead of sloping off to the usual showdown. Bronson addicts, here he is, at it again."

Howard Thompson, *The New York Times*

"Since actors, we're told, must eat (and Bronson is the money-makingest actor around today), you'll find him amid the bloody moronic mayhem and murder of *Mr. Majestyk,* a certainly 'original' concoction by Elmore Leonard, directed with a total lack of taste by Richard Fleischer. It is all mindless violence, with a score of men being

slaughtered and a dozen automobiles crashing and exploding to incinerate the occupants. But the only time there's emotional impact is when a couple of hoods machine-gun Bronson's stack of watermelons."

Judith Crist, *New York*

"Mr. Majestyk makes a first-reel pretense of dealing with the thorny subject of migrant Chicano farm laborers, but its heart really lies in cramming the maximal amount of violence into a PG-rated melodrama. Social relevance is soon clobbered by the usual Charles Bronson heroics, here mechanically navigated by director Richard Fleischer."

"Beau.," *Variety*

"Director Richard Fleischer has not only carried it off, but makes you believe it. One must also give some of the credit to Charles Bronson whose erect, muscular body and hard face gives some credence to the heroics. Hard-face Bronson has done it again for his immense world-wide following."

Archer Winsten, *The New York Post*

With Jordan Rhodes.   With Linda Cristal and Alejandro Ray.

Death Wish

A Dino De Laurentiis Production
for Paramount Pictures / 1974
In Technicolor

CAST

Paul Kersey: Charles Bronson; *Joanna Kersey:* Hope Lange; *Inspector Frank Ochoa:* Vincent Gardenia; *Jack Toby:* Steven Keats; *Sam Kreutzer:* William Redfield; *Aimes Jainchill:* Stuart Margolin; *Police Commissioner:* Stephen Elliott; *Carol Toby:* Kathleen Tolan; *Hank:* Jack Wallace; *District Attorney:* Fred Scollay; *Ives:* Chris Gampel; *Joe Charles:* Robert Kya-Hill; *Lt. Briggs:* Ed Grover; *1st Freak:* Jeff Goldberg; *2nd Freak:* Christopher Logan; *Spraycan:* Gregory Rozakis; *Desk Sergeant:* Floyd Levine; *Alma Lee Brown:* Helen Martin; *Andrew McCabe:* Hank Garrett; *Patrolman Reilly:* Christopher Guest.

CREDITS

Producers: Hal Landers, Bobby Roberts, Michael Winner; *Director:* Michael Winner; *Assistant Directors:* Charles Okun, Larry Albucher, Ralph Singleton; *Screenwriter:* Wendell Mayes; *Based on the Novel by:* Brian Garfield; *Cinematographer:* Arthur J. Ornitz; *Production Designer:* Robert Gundlach; *Scenic Artist:* Sante Fiore; *Set Decorator:* George De Titta; *Musical Score:* Herbie Hancock; *Editor:* Bernard Gribble.
Running Time: 93 minutes.

THE FILM

Death Wish presents the oppressed underdog's

As Paul Kersey.

ultimate fantasy—of becoming suddenly, miraculously, empowered to rise up, track down and destroy all those who have persecuted him (and/or those he cares most about). In the case of *Death Wish*'s hero, a Manhattan architect, it's a matter of vengeance, after three spaced-out muggers have, in his absence, invaded the man's home in an incident which leaves his wife dead and his married daughter raped and traumatized into a near-vegetable state. Presented with a gun by a business associate, he eventually turns vigilante, decimating New York City's street-and-subway criminal element. This makes him a veritable phantom folk-hero in the eyes of the general populace.

The provocative movie, adapted from Brian Garfield's novel by screenwriter Wendell Mayes, reunited executive-producer Dino De Laurentiis, director Michael Winner and superstar Bronson on what would prove their greatest joint success —and their most controversial. The film's content, understandably, fomented a storm of conflicting opinion, sharply dividing the critical fraternity, outraging a great many liberals, but pleasing the common denominator of filmgoer.

Word-of-mouth built fast on *Death Wish,* and the picture quickly found its audience, not only from the established pro-Bronson violence buffs, but from a steadily building, increasingly vocal faction, whose dollars now made Paramount Pictures' cash registers ring loudly.

In a *New York Times* Sunday essay, appearing some five weeks after the film's Manhattan opening, Judy Klemesrud interviewed departing moviegoers for their views on *Death Wish.* A forty-seven-year-old New Yorker expressed his satisfaction, adding, "I don't necessarily agree with the vigilante philosophy, but the movie is so entertaining that I don't bother with the morality." While a Californian of thirty-six admitted to a mere liking for the movie's star: "I go to a movie to see Bronson, and not so much for the story. His movies are pretty much the same, but what I like to watch is how he portrays his character. He's kind of tough and rugged, an individualist. He does things *his* way."

Brian Garfield, the story's original author, had some reservations about the changes made in his story enroute to the screen, deploring the movie's advocacy (unlike his book) of outright vigilantism. Later, Garfield also appealed (in vain) to the CBS television network, requesting that they not air the film during "prime time" hours, when it might impress immature minds and inspire imitation.

But a psychologist interviewed by Klemesrud for her *Times* article, refuted that possibility: "This movie plays out the fantasy of getting even. It's not dangerous: it's the kind of thing people cheer when the bad guy gets his come-uppance. It's a fantasy release, something we all want to do. For most people, it's the equivalent of a very satisfying dream."

Bronson himself replied, briefly and succinctly to the critical charges of irresponsible exploitation of fear: "We don't make movies for critics, since they don't pay to see them anyhow."

CRITICS' CORNER
"Death Wish is a movie that takes a very dim view of New York City, particularly of its muggers who, according to this film, could be easily eliminated if every upright, middle-class, middle-aged citizen got himself a gun and used it at least three times a week. The movie seems to have been made for no reason except to exploit its audience's urban paranoia and vestigial fascination with violence for its own sake."

Vincent Canby, *The New York Times*

"In terms of movie-making, this is a gripping, absorbing job, even it you reject the outlook. Charles Bronson is superb in a tension-filled performance."

William Wolf, *Cue*

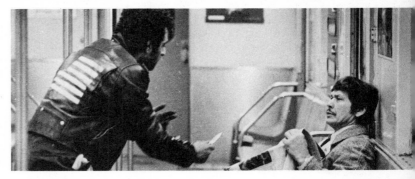

"Bronson, who looks older than usual in keeping with his character of the father of an adult daughter, has here a role of greater depth than heretofore. To be sure, he mechanically guns down the heavies when the story gets rolling, but at least the script lets him manifest a third dimension.

"Winner exhibits a far better control and economy than heretofore. Another meritorious achievement here is the relative discretion in the violent episodes. The early rape sequence is powerful, well staged and not at all over-done; the periodic Bronson killings are swift and devoid of slow-motion bleeding and other choreography endemic to most such action highlights."

"Murf.," *Variety*

"By touching an exposed nerve in fearful contemporary America, director Winner has handed granite-faced Bronson the role most likely to show moviegoers at home what European audiences saw in him ages ago—a rough-cut superstar and folk-hero par excellence!"

Bruce Williamson, *Playboy*

"A first-rate suspenser. What makes this fantasy work is the superb performance of Charles Bronson as the protagonist, complemented by Vincent Gardenia as the detective, and the entire cast. Bronson gives credibility to even the bits of illogic on hand, with Winner's fast-

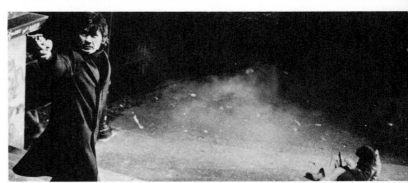

Jeff Goldberg, Hope Lange, Kathleen Tolan, and
Christopher Logan.

With Steven Keats.

paced, exquisitely detailed direction supplementing the authenticity of Bronson's creation.''

Judith Crist, *New York*

''Rarely in movie history has a movie caused so much violent and controversial reaction from both audiences and critics. And rarely have I found myself so caught between my own gut reactions and intellectual reservations. *Death Wish* is so cleverly constructed as entertainment that it bounces liberal challenges off its political back like a duck shaking raindrops. Even the most militant liberals are applauding like kids at a Saturday afternoon Punch and Judy show.

"*Death Wish* is a powerful, explosive audience-identification movie that is probably going to make millions because it stimulates our latent sadism with some truly spectacular moments of voyeurism. People who are tired of being frightened, endangered and ripped-off daily in New York City are going to love Charles Bronson in *Death Wish* as much as I do.

"*Death Wish* is a complex and startlingly original film that will anger and provoke, but its most important questions are the ones it raises about ourselves.''

Rex Reed, *The New York Daily News*

With Hope Lange.

Breakout

A Columbia Picture / 1975
In Panavision and Eastmancolor

CAST
Nick Colton: Charles Bronson; *Jay Wagner:* Robert Duvall; *Ann Wagner:* Jill Ireland; *Hawk Hawkins:* Randy Quaid; *Myrna:* Sheree North; *Harris Wagner:* John Huston; *Sanchez:* Alejandro Rey; *Cable:* Paul Mantee; *Spencer:* Roy Jenson; *Helicopter Pilot:* Alan Vint; *Soza:* Jorge Moreno; *Henderson:* Sidney Klute; *Warden:* Emilio Fernandez.

CREDITS
Executive Producer: Ron Buck; *Producers:* Robert Chartoff, Irwin Winkler; *Director:* Tom Gries; *Assistant Director:* Ronald L. Schwary; *Screenwriters:* Howard B. Kreitsek, Marc Norman, Elliott Baker; *Based on the Novel "Ten-Second Jailbreak" by:* Warren Hinckle, William Turner, Eliot Asinof; *Cinematographer:* Lucien Ballard; *Art Director:* Alfred Sweeney, Jr.; *Set Decorator:* Ira Bates; *Special Effects:* Augie Lohman; *Musical Score:* Jerry Goldsmith; *Editor:* Bud Isaacs.
Running Time: 96 minutes.

THE FILM
Death Wish, Bronson's greatest box-office hit as a superstar, ironically marked the end of his multi-picture association with Dino De Laurentiis. But the actor's so-called "bankability" was, in the wake of his celluloid vigilante activities, responsible for a flood of offers from various independent producers willing to meet his by-now considerable price. Bronson had his choice of vehicles, and it would be hard to blame him, in his early fifties, for selecting roles suited to his established screen image.

Breakout, the first of his two 1975 movies, is a disjointed tale of adventure, rescue, double-dealing and, of course, occasional violence. Again, the actor's mustachioed, macho persona held sway over a somewhat unraveled plot. But this time his independent, enterprising character—small-plane pilot Nick Colton— evidences a gentle tongue-in-cheek humor that is as disarming as it is unexpected. A certain wry levity had occasionally bubbled behind Bronson's movie tough-guys, but now it appeared

that his screen future might, under the right circumstances, be capable of showing his public a few surprises.

Columbia Pictures fully realized that they had no *Death Wish* on their hands here, so they cunningly devised a heavy "saturation" campaign, bombarding the media with hard-sell tactics to make the public want to see *Breakout* during its "special limited engagements." ("The greatest escape film ever!" as one of their less modest ads put it.) *Variety* reported a Columbia expenditure of $3,600,000 on this campaign—and a gross of $12,711,224, during its first two weeks of nationwide bookings!

CRITICS' CORNER

"Charles Bronson fans will find him as squinting, sun-tanned and gung-ho as ever as a free-lance pilot in *Breakout,* which boasts as absolutely incomprehensible and unmotivated plot via its screenplay by Howard B. Kreitsek, Marc Norman and Elliott Baker, based on a book by Warren Hinckle, William Turner and Eliot Asinof. Whatever broth the sextet horsed around with emerges, under Tom Gries' direction, as a plodding tale of attempts by Texas-based Bronson to rescue Robert Duvall from a Mexican prison where he's in for life as the result of a frame-up sponsored by his American-mogul grandfather (John Huston) and the CIA, for no apparent reason.

"Bronson co-stars with a helicopter in the derring-do; Duvall looks sulky; Randy Quaid acts dopey as Bronson's partner; Sheree North is likeable as a former flame of Bronson; and Jill Ireland, as Duvall's wife, shows that she has big blue eyes and a British accent. The CIA man is, of course, top villain, but not to worry: he gets chopped to pieces in a plane propeller."
Judith Crist, *New York*

"*Breakout* keeps grinning throughout its potentially gruesome moments, and never does it descend to the blood-and-guts level promised by the uncharacteristically bloodthirsty opening. This is due entirely to Bronson's rakish performance, which displays a talent for humor that he too rarely lets surface nowadays. Bronson gently satirizes both himself and the set-up, while still maintaining the muscular pose for which he is famed. He receives devoted support from Sheree North, who shows a nice line in desperate humor ('Rape? I should be so lucky.') while maintaining an intensely physical presence."
Derek Elley, *Films and Filming*

"With Charles Bronson playing a more amicably fallible hero than his usual superman, the script even manages to incorporate an element of self-mockery, and the supporting players supply cheerfully engaging characterizations to match. Lucien Ballard's fine unshowy camerawork is also a joy to watch."

Tom Milne, *Monthly Film Bulletin*

"Although the action is mapped out on a more modest scale than might be expected, the plot has a direct, assertive appeal that grabs the attention and stirs up a rooting interest in the outcome.

Less expected is Bronson's ingratiatingly comic performance. Encouraged by the self-deprecating humor marking his role, Bronson does a series of 'you've got to be kidding' double takes when confronted with danger, and playfully lampoons his image as the screen's clenched, squinty-eyed Mr. Macho."

The Independent Film Journal

With Sheree North, Randy Quaid, and Robert Duvall.

With Jill Ireland, Roy Jenson, and Randy Quaid.

With Sheree North.

With Jill Ireland.

Hard Times (The Streetfighter)

A Columbia Picture / 1975
In Panavision and Metrocolor

CAST
Chaney: Charles Bronson; *Spencer "Speed" Weed:* James Coburn; *Luby Simpson:* Jill Ireland; *Poe:* Strother Martin; *Gayleen Schoonover:* Maggie Blye; *Gandil:* Michael McGuire; *Jim Henry:* Robert Tessier; *Street:* Nick Dimitri; *Le Beau:* Felice Orlandi; *Doty:* Bruce Glover; *Pettibon:* Edward Walsh; *Hammerman:* Frank McRae; *Caesare:* Maurice Kowalewski; *Madam:* Naomi Stevens; *Counterman:* Robert Castleberry; *Peo's Date:* Becky Allen; *Carol:* Joan Kleven; *Secretary:* Anne Welsch; *Diner Waitress:* Lyla Hay Owen; *Barge Fighter:* Jim Nickerson; *Apartment Manager:* John Creamer; *Caesare's Hitter;* Fred Lerner; *Speed's Hitter:* Chuck Hicks; *Poolplayers:* Walter Scott, Max Kleven; *Handler:* Valerian Smith; *Zack:* Bob Minor; *Driver:* Larry Martindale; *Card Players:* Charles W. Schaeffer, Jr., Leslie Bonano; *Cajun Fighter:* Ronnie Philips; with the Greater Liberty Baptist Church Choir and Congregation.

CREDITS
Executive Producer: Paul Maslansky; *Producer:* Lawrence Gordon; *Associate Producer:* Fred Lemoine; *Director:* Walter Hill; *Assistant Director:* Michael Daves; *Screenwriters:* Walter Hill, Bryan Gindorff, Bruce Henstell; *From a Story by:* Gindorff and Henstell; *Cinematographer:* Philip Lathrop; *Art Director:* Trevor Williams; *Set Decorator:* Dennis Peeples; *Musical Score:* Barry DeVorzon; *Editor:* Roger Spottiswoode. *Running Time:* 97 minutes.

THE FILM
The early pugilistic years of prizefighter Jack Dempsey are said to have loosely inspired this rather offbeat little yarn, an original devised by Bryan Gindorff and Bruce Henstell, who made the screen adaptation in collaboration with Walter Hill. Hill was then best known for having written the screenplay of *The Getaway,* a violent 1972 vehicle for Steve McQueen,

directed characteristically by Sam Peckinpah.

Producer Larry Gordon financed *Hard Times* with tax shelter dollars, enabling him to sign Charles Bronson as his star, as well as give writer Hill a crack at directing his first movie. Interviewed on location for the TV show *Weekend*, Gordon readily admitted, "If it wasn't for tax shelter dollars, I don't think I'd be in New Orleans [scene of the story]; I don't think this film would be financed."

Like any film star, Bronson has his champions, as well as his detractors, and there were those among the latter faction who took new notice of the actor, after seeing his performance as Chaney, the itinerant 1930s street fighter of *Hard Times*. Some chose to give credit for this achievement to Walter Hill, while a majority found cause to admire in Bronson a talent they had previously overlooked. Director Hill *did* evidence skill and promise with this movie, but his subsequent pictures, *The Driver* and *The Warriors*, have been greeted with an almost consistently negative press.

Some consider *Hard Times'* Chaney to be Bronson's best performance to date, while others have found him offering nothing he had not previously done on screen. But, for the most part, *Hard Times* brought new attention to Bronson and brought him respect from unexpected quarters. It also brought back Jill Ireland, as his romantic vis-a-vis, and witnessed, in Bronson, a decided physical alteration appropriate to the film's time and place: gone were the drooping mustache and the ear-covering locks. Instead, the actor's somewhat graying hair was cut quite short. And, of course, his well-toned musculature was, at fifty-four, still carefully enough maintained to go on public display, for the role.

CRITICS' CORNER
"We could be anywhere. A man with a past and a future we'll never know or understand emerges from the shadows of the night. An hour-and-a-half of movie time later, he'll fade back into the shadows without explaining himself—without even saying goodbye. But in between he'll have proven himself in a tough arena where men can prove their manhood, he'll have earned the respect of strangers and he'll have loved a woman.

"Working from this plain story, screenwriter Walter Hill has made an enviable directorial debut and given Charles Bronson the best starring vehicle he's ever had.

As Chaney.

With James Coburn.

"The film is mainly set in New Orleans, and in part it works because Hill has evocatively re-created the dark green gloom of the dingy saloons, boarding houses and cafes of the city's under-belly. He is equally precise in his staging of the action sequences, which are the bread and butter of *Hard Times,* as they are of every Bronson movie.

"Still, this picture might not be nearly as effec-tive as it is, were it not for Bronson himself. This star's granite presence is properly exploited for its resonant possibilities for the first time in *Hard Times.* The tension hidden in the actor's body and the secrets locked behind his cold, sad eyes link Chaney to our most romantic image of the woeful hard-times hobo — the man who proverbially 'built a railroad and made it run' before the bottom dropped out."

Frank Rich, *New York Post*

"*Hard Times* turns out to be Charles Bronson's most effective vehicle since Sergio Leone's *Once Upon a Time in the West.* Interesting touch: Bronson is greeted skeptically at first because of his apparent age. Are there signals being flashed out to Hollywood that audiences are beginning to notice the wrinkles on fortyish and fiftyish 'action' types?"

Andrew Sarris, *The Village Voice*

"*Hard Times* is to be admired as a sincere attempt to broaden Charles Bronson's role spectrum. The Lawrence Gordon production has a very handsome mid-Thirties New Orleans period flavor, but there is a fatal lack of 'center' in the story of vagabond Bronson coming to the aid of small-time gambler James Coburn. Walter Hill directed a very good cast, which can't lick the script. Jill Ireland is excellent in a touching

With Bruce Glover, Felice Orlandi, and Nick Dimitri.

With Jill Ireland.

performance as a down-and-out girl who has a brief affair with Bronson, only to break it off for a more stable liaison elsewhere."

"Murf.," *Variety*

"A gritty and surprisingly effective combination of mood and action that makes *Hard Times* a standout example of its genre. As the ruggedly individualistic streetfighter who won't let his invincible fists richen or corrupt him, Bronson finds himself in an ideal vehicle. Relying on his scarred, glinting presence, he manages to work negligible dialogue and crinkled looks into a viable substitute for emoting. Along with his strong character and excellent support from James Coburn as Bronson's likeable weasel of a promoter, *Hard Times* is liberally laden with action and relies more on atmosphere and tip-top pacing than on outright violence."

The Independent Film Journal

"The film is hardly a triumph, but it is so well suited to Bronson's low-key intensity, his stubborn silences and icy aloofness, that it becomes easily the best thing he's ever done."

Kathleen Carroll, *The New York Daily News*

"Surprise: a good Charles Bronson movie. *Hard Times* is unassuming, tough and spare, a tidy little parable about strength and honor. Against current Hollywood competition, which lately seems underthought and overextended, *Hard Times* is especially welcome.

"Perhaps Bronson-vehicle and quality are no longer a contradition in terms. This summer's *Breakout,* a diverting prison-break yarn, showed the usually saturnine star cracking jokes, playing big, generally and infectiously enjoying himself. This time, the stolid performer manages to achieve an authentic, scruffy street dignity. *Hard Times* is the best script Bronson has enjoyed since he became box office.

"Walter Hill' directorial debut is controlled and fairly confident; working at his peak, he gives a strong taste of the heel-end poverty of the times. Hill is also responsible for Charles Bronson's finest performance to date. If this seems a modest compliment, *Hard Times* is evidence that there may be larger ones on the way."

Jay Cocks, *Time*

With James Coburn.

With James Coburn, Maggie Blye, and Strother Martin.

With Strother Martin and James Coburn.

As John Deakin.

Breakheart Pass

An Elliott Kastner Corp. Production
  for United Artists / 1976
in DeLuxe Color

CAST
John Deakin: Charles Bronson; *Nathan Pearce:* Ben Johnson; *Governor Fairchild:* Richard Crenna; *Marica Scoville:* Jill Ireland; *Frank O'Brien;* Charles Durning; *Maj. Claremont:* Ed Lauter; *Dr. Edward Molyneux:* David Huddleston; *Banlon:* Roy Jenson; *Jackson:* Casey Tibbs; *Carlos, the Cook:* Archie Moore; *Henry:* Joe Kapp; *Capt. Oakland:* Read Morgan; *Lt. Newell:* Robert Rothwell; *Bellew:* Rayford Barnes; *Rafferty:* Scott Newman; *Ferguson:* Eldon Burke; *Rev. Theodore Peabody:* William McKinney; *White Hand:* Eddie Little Sky; *Sepp Calhoun:* Robert Tessier; *Jane Marie:* Sally Kirkland; *Jebbo:* Doug Atkins; *Prostitute:* Sally Kemp; *Col. Scoville:* Irv Faling; *Seamon Devlin:* Bill Klem; *Red Beard:* John Mitchum; *Gabriel:* Keith McConnell.

CREDITS
Executive Producer: Elliott Kastner; *Producer:* Jerry Gershwin; *Director:* Tom Gries; *Action Sequences Directed by:* Yakima Canutt; *Assistant Directors:* Ronald L. Schwary, Ron Wright, Peter Gries, Lorin Salob, Tony Brand; *Screenwriter:* Alistair MacLean, *Based on His Novel; Cinematographer:* Lucien Ballard; *2nd Unit Photographer:* Robert McBride; *Production Designer:* Johannes Larsen; *Art Directors:* Herbert S. Deverill, Richard Gilbert Clayton; *Set Decorator:* Darrell Silvera; *Special Effects:* A. D.

Flowers, Gerald Endler, Logan Frazee, Jr.;
Musical Score: Jerry Goldsmith; *Editor:* Byron
"Buzz" Brandt.
Running Time: 95 minutes.

THE FILM

Bronson's familiar, shaggy-haired and mustachioed image returned with this rather unusual
mixture of murder and mystery set in an 1870s
Western milieu and based on a novel by Alistair
MacLean, who also wrote the screenplay. With
unexpected twists and tricks that not a few
critics likened to Agatha Christie's, MacLean
put most of the plot's action aboard a train
bound for an Army fort. Enroute, a succession
of unexplained deaths occur, with few of the
passengers proving to be quite what they seem.

With Jill Ireland in her tenth role opposite
her husband, *Showdown at Breakheart Pass* (its
in-production title) went on location in Idaho's
wintry Bitterroot Mountains, under the direction
of Tom Gries who, in 1968, had made a minor
classic of the Charlton Heston Western *Will
Penny.* The train used consisted of an actual
wood-burning locomotive and a museum-piece
private car that had once carried 19th-century
politicians. Surprisingly enough, no miniatures
were employed for the train-dynamiting scenes
handled by the veteran stunt director Yakima
Canutt, still active in his eighties.

So-called "saturation" engagements continued
to prove lucrative for the distributor of a Bronson
movie: United Artists booked *Breakheart Pass*
into two-hundred-and-fifty-four U.S. theatres
which, in the first two weeks alone, grossed
over a million dollars.

CRITICS' CORNER

"For Bronson addicts, *Breakheart Pass* offers a
dandy suspense melodrama—fast-paced and
breath-bating, with a slam-bang conclusion."
Judith Crist, *American Way*

"Unsuccessful cross between a conventional
whodunit and a conventional Western. Bronson
glides through the nonsensical action with a
serene, dignified air of purposefulness that is
both attractive and professional."
Gary Arnold, *The Washington Post*

"*Breakheart Pass* is a cheating mystery that
could break a Bronson fan's heart. To win over
an audience, just about all Bronson has to do
is appear on screen. His presence is so galvanic,
he dominates every frame he's in. When Bronson

With Jill Ireland, Richard Crenna, Joe Kapp, Ed Lauter, Ben Johnson, Roy Jenson, and Charles Durning.

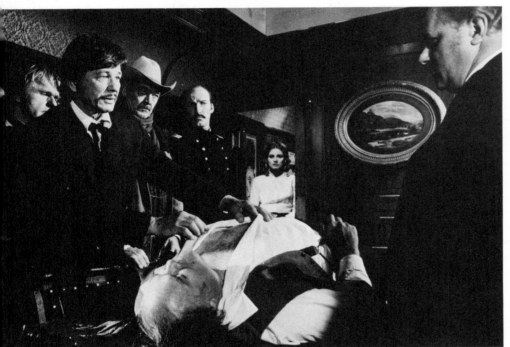

With Roy Jenson, Ben Johnson, Ed Lauter, Jill Ireland, David Huddleston, and Charles Durning.

With Ben Johnson, Richard Crenna, and Ed Lauter.

is on, you simply can't watch anyone else. Yet, with all this, he isn't much of an actor. He is incapable of lending nuance to a line. They all slide out in that same low, raspy monotone. If dead men could talk, I suspect they would sound like Charles Bronson. What he needs is a script that's heavy on action and the strong hand of a director who understands Bronson's limitations and can work a movie around his menacing, anti-hero mystique—keeping him front and center while covering his verbal inadequacies by making him ominously silent. This is what he got from Walter Hill, who wrote and directed *Hard Times* and what made it one of Bronson's best pictures. And it's precisely what he doesn't get in *Breakheart Pass.*"

Carol White, *The Chicago Sun-Times*

"Unfairly synopsized by some critics as *Ten Little Indians on the Orient Express in the West,* it boasts a pragmatic script by Alistair MacLean, performances entirely in tune with the nefarious goings-on, and a sheer pace which harks back thirty years. *Breakheart Pass* makes no attempt to rival the intricacies of Agatha Christie, but it keeps one guessing quite reasonably for most of the time.

"Securely in charge of the second-unit work is Yakima Canutt: him I hold responsible for the superb train-top fight through snowy landscapes. One cheers (silently) at the sheer enjoyment of it all, and Charles Bronson, who by now is making a genuine virtue out of acting by numbers, must be laughing all the way to the bank."

Derek Elley, *Films and Filming*

"With *Breakheart Pass,* Charles Bronson seems to have settled into a comfortable new persona —the temperate man of action who doesn't particularly enjoy violence but sure knows how to lay it on when it's necessary—that first surfaced in *Hard Times* and continues here with especially fine results.

"Old-guard Bronson fans expecting the gut-crunching pace or pyrotechnics of a comic-book entry like *Breakout* may be surprised to find a lot more attention devoted to clever plot logistics than to the amount of potential gore in the story line.

"Romantic interest gets only lip service in the form of Jill Ireland, as the Governor's unofficial companion, but Bronson ultimately wanders off into the sunset without her."

The Independent Film Journal

With Jill Ireland.

With Jill Ireland on location.

With Jerry Brutsche.

St. Ives

A Kohner-Beckerman-Canter Production
    for Warner Bros. / 1976
In Technicolor

CAST

Raymond St. Ives: Charles Bronson; *Abner Procane:* John Houseman; *Janet Whistler:* Jacqueline Bisset; *Dr. John Constable:* Maximilian Schell; *Detective Deal:* Harry Guardino; *Detective Oller:* Harris Yulin; *Charlie Blunt:* Dana Elcar; *Myron Green:* Michael Lerner; *Hesh:* Dick O'Neill; *Eddie the Bell Boy:* Elisha Cook; *Finley Cummins:* Val Bisoglio; *Officer Frann:* Burr DeBenning; *Johnny Parisi:* Daniel J. Travanti; *Seymour:* Joe Roman; *Hoods:* Robert Englund, Mark Thomas, Jeff Goldblum; *Fat Angie Polaterra:* Tom Pedi; *No Nose:* Joseph De Nicola; *Shippo:* George Memmoli; *Punch:* Don Hanmer; *Mike Kluszewski:* Bob Terhune; *McDuff:* Norman Palmer; *Mickey:* Walter Brook; *Chasman:* Jerome Thor; *Arab Bagman:* George Sawaya; *Procane Butler:* Glenn Robards; *Jack Boykins:* Jerry Brutsche; *Jimmy Peskoe:* Dar Robinson; *Party Girl:* Lynn Borden; *Night Clerk:* Stanley Brock; *Station Men:* Larry Martindale, Olan Soule; *Croupier:* Louis H. Kelly; *Girl at Table:* Rosalyn Marshall; *Slim:* Owen Hith Pace; *Police Sergeant:* Morris Buchanan; *Detective:* Ben Young; *Willie:* John Steadman; *Patrolman:* Benjie Bancroft; *Nurses:* Gayla Gallaway, Jill Stone; *Orderly:* Edward Cross.

CREDITS

Producers: Pancho Kohner, Stanley Canter; *Director:* J. Lee Thompson; *Assistant Directors:* Ronald L. Schwary, Ed Ledding; *Screenwriter:* Barry Beckerman; *Based on the Novel* "The Procane Chronicle" *by:* Oliver Bleeck; *Cinematographer:* Lucien Ballard: *Production Designer:* Philip M. Jeffries; *Set Decorator:* Robert De Vestel; *Special Effects:* Gene Grigg; *Musical Score:* Lalo Schifrin; *Editor:* Michael F. Anderson. *Running Time:* 94 minutes.

THE FILM

Bronson's ongoing change of pace continued win the approval of his critics in *St. Ives,* a throwback to the sort of film usually associated with Humphrey Bogart or Dick Powell in the Forties. And it put him back in contemporary necktie and jacket for the first time since *Death Wish.*

Much of the movie was shot in Los Angeles locations, where it fluctuated between being called *The Last Score* and *St. Ives' Last Score,* before settling on the succinct but unrevealing *St. Ives.* Based on Oliver Bleeck's crime novel, *The Procane Chronicle,* this Barry Beckerman script had Bronson portray an ex-crime reporter turned author, with a string of unpublished novels to his credit—and little money. He accepts a commission from a wealthy recluse (John Houseman) to retrieve five stolen ledgers. It's an assignment that leads to a web of complications, murders and betrayals.

While few of the film's critics pretended to have followed all of the plot's confused byways, nearly all applauded the movie's discreet avoidance of the sort of violence that usually accompanied a Bronson vehicle. For this, credit was given veteran director J. Lee Thompson, whose sympathetic handling of the actor would result in subsequent professional reunions for *The White Buffalo* and *Cabo Blanco.*

With Robert Englund, Jeff Goldblum, and Mark Thomas.

With Harry Guardino.

With Jacqueline Bisset.

As Raymond St. Ives.

CRITICS' CORNER

"*St. Ives* merely confirms a point: eliminate gratuitous, offensive and overdone violence from a dull and plodding film story, and all you've got left is a dull and plodding film. It is careful to show that Bronson's character doesn't need pistols; nobody would, what with other characters taking care of the (admittedly low-key and offscreen) mayhem.

"This film is another pace-change for Bronson, and in that sense additional diversification should be encouraged. Unlike many of his films, this time the script does give him an earlier life and background which provides some dimension to his character's motivation and attitudes. It's a good step in the right direction, but there's a way to go."

"Murf.," *Variety*

"The attraction of *St. Ives* is that it takes itself neither too seriously nor too lightly, its occasional wit avoids heavy parody; its action avoids heavy reliance on violence, car chases and other such mechanical paraphernalia.

"Finally, there is what must be the least explicit sex scene of the year. Miss Bisset sits down on Mr. Bronson's bed, smoldering. She puts one hand to her zipper and believe it or not, the scene ends. Miss Bisset, who does wonderful things for silly roles and once in a while is allowed to do wonderful things for good ones, makes that unpulled zipper seem like an X-rating all by itself.

"Charles Bronson, whose sagging eyes and moustache make him look more and more like Fu Manchu, is not good at a great many things, but he does a few things rather well. He manages a pleasantly tired skepticism while the bodies fall all around. He is like one of those companions on a long trip who become agreeable by not saying much. *St. Ives* does come to seem rather a long and foolish trip, but Miss Bisset and Mr. Bronson help it pass amiably enough.

Richard Eder, *The New York Times*

"One is so accustomed to seeing Charles Bronson play hard, mean men that, if nothing else, *St. Ives* represents a welcome change of pace for its star. Bronson is not playing a ninety-pound weakling, mind you, but he is playing his most sympathetic role to date. What is unique about this particular Bronson character is that he abhors violence; also, he has what might be loosely described as a sense of humor (his instant analysis of Jacqueline Bisset: "You're tough, smart and you've got a lot of great-looking bits and pieces."). That goes for *St. Ives*, too. Still, any movie that allows Bronson to do something more than bust heads together can't be all bad."

Kathleen Carroll, *The New York Daily News*

With Maximilian Schell and Jacqueline Bisset.

With Burr De Benning.

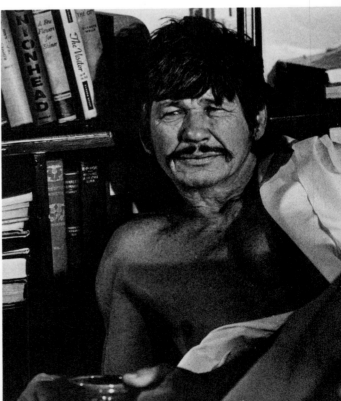

With Damon Douglas, Hector Morales, Douglas V. Fowley, and Stan Haze.

From Noon Till Three

A Frankovich-Self Production
  for United Artists / 1976
  In Deluxe Color

CAST
Graham Dorsey: Charles Bronson; *Amanda Starbuck:* Jill Ireland; *Buck Bowers:* Douglas V. Fowley; *Ape:* Stan Haze; *Boy:* Damon Douglas; *Mexican:* Hector Morales; *Sheriff:* Bert Williams; *Rev. Cabot:* William Lanteau; *Edna:* Betty Cole; *Sam:* Davis Roberts; *Postmaster Hall:* Fred Franklyn; *Dr. Finger:* Sonny Jones; *Deke:* Hoke Howell; *Mr. Foster:* Howard Brunner; *Mr. Taylor:* Larry French; *Cody Taylor:* Michael Le Clair; *Massive Woman:* Anne Ramsey; *Red Roxy:* Don "Red" Barry; *Songwriters:* Elmer Bernstein, Alan Bergman.

CREDITS
Producers: M. J. (Mike) Frankovich, William Self; *Director-Screenwriter:* Frank D. Gilroy, *Based on His Novel; Assistant Directors:* Russell Saunders, Mike Kusley; *Cinematographer:* Lucien Ballard; *Production Designer:* Robert Clatworthy; *Assistant Art Director:* Dick Lawrence; *Set Decorator:* George R. Nelson; *Special Effects:* Augie Lohman; *Musical Score:* Elmer Bernstein; *Editor:* Maury Winetrobe.
Running Time: 99 minutes.

THE FILM
From Noon Till Three, bearing the look of a civilized period-piece, marked an even greater departure for the Bronson-Ireland team: romantic comedy. At least, comedy is the prevailing mood throughout *much* of this film, written and directed by Frank D. Gilroy. Gilroy had won a Pulitzer Prize for his play *The Subject Was Roses* and critical acclaim as writer-director of the 1971 Shirley MacLaine film *Desperate Characters.* But what, at first, amuses its audience in *From Noon Till Three* eventually proves puzzling. The film's critical consensus was nearly unanimous in blaming Gilroy for its inconsistency of tone and style, and for allowing an initially intriguing premise to go wildly astray, ending on a decidedly downbeat note.

In a preface to his screenplay, Gilroy calls it "The possibly true and certainly tragic story of an outlaw and a lady whose love knows no bounds!" Which tells little, of course.

Faced with an unusual motion picture that the Bronson public might not be ready for, United Artists' advertising copywriters opted for a bit of hard-sell. Accompanying an apparently

As Graham Dorsey.

post-coital photograph of the movie's stars contentedly sharing a bed, was the following hyperbole:

"He's got a physique of tempered steel and the scarred, roadmap face of a matinee idol left out too long in a war. He looks like he can lick any man in the world and put away a quart of scotch with the other hand. He is the highest-paid movie actor in the world—legendary gunfighter, tough guy, street brawler, and all-round, guaranteed, pure box-office macho on seven continents. And now he's going to charm and delight a world full of fans as a lover, as a funny guy as good with a punchline as he is with a punch, and yes, even as the world's most unlikely coward in a great and unexpected entertainment."

According to "informed sources," Bronson was paid "somewhere in the $1,500,000 area" for this film, plus 10 percent of the gross receipts over $10,000,000, as well as (reportedly) 40 to 50 percent of the net profits. Yet, *From Noon Till Three* is said to be among the few Bronson-starred films *not* to have made a fortune.

Understandably, it is a picture that the Bronsons very much enjoyed making. And Frank Gilroy has only favorable comments on his star: "A more willing, congenial and professional actor I've never met. It took a little time to

evolve a relaxed feeling between all of us. Bronson's poverty-stricken youth doesn't inspire trust in people. Nor has he had the easiest career. Kicking around Hollywood is enough to corrode anyone. It's a wonder he's as nice as he is."

CRITICS' CORNER
"Although it's to Charles Bronson's credit that he's finally making a Herculean effort to break out of his type-cast persona of quietly violent macho heroism, his venture into romantic comedy—opposite wife Jill Ireland—proves to be a well-intentioned failure. And while Gilroy's storyline has a cute premise at its heart, his screenplay suffers from stubborn unbelievability, unaided by the uncertain tones and pacing of his first directorial assignment. When all is said and done, *From Noon Till Three* amounts to little more than a personal showcase for Mr. and Mrs. Bronson, one that probably proved far more enjoyable and worthwhile for them to make than it will for audiences to sit through."
The Independent Film Journal

"*From Noon Till Three* is neither a conventionally comic Western nor a conventional comedy, and it certainly isn't a conventional Bronson film. More than anything else, I suppose, it is an ebulliently cheerful satire of contemporary myth-making and celebrity, cast as a fable of the Old West. Not all of it is equally successful, and it takes its time making certain points, which, being made, are made again; yet its intelligence and its narrative shape are immensely satisfying.

"Mr. Gilroy has a nice, light way with irony that prevents *From Noon Till Three* from tripping over its own rather large intentions. He's also obtained two remarkably attractive, absolutely straight performances from Mr. Bronson, who is funny without ever lunging at a laugh (as Burt Reynolds often does under similar circumstances) and from Miss Ireland, whose cool, somewhat steely beauty are perfectly suited to the widow who manages almost immediately to transform a real-life experience into mass-media material with plenty of spin-off."
Vincent Canby, *The New York Times*

"Bronson fans may be disappointed, but others could be pleasantly surprised. The leads are given a chance to be more animated than usual, which will also shock those who thought Bronson and Ireland were incapable of more than one emotion. Ms. Ireland is called upon to be highly dramatic and comic, and proves to be very adept at both.''

Boxoffice

"An offbeat satiric comedy and an offbeat Charles Bronson vehicle. It's a grand takeoff on celebrity, legend-making and exploitation—and a very good, very handsome entertainment.''

Judith Crist, *TV Guide*

With Jill Ireland.

Raid on Entebbe

An Edgar J. Scherick Associates Production
    for 20th Century-Fox and the
    NBC Television Network   /   1977
In DeLuxe Color

CAST

Gen. Dan Shomron: Charles Bronson; *Prime Minister Yitzhak Rabin:* Peter Finch; *President Idi Amin:* Yaphet Kotto; *Gen. Mordecai Gur:* Jack Warden; *Chief Terrorist Wilfred Boese:* Horst Bucholz; *Capt. Michel Bacos:* Eddie Constantine; *Daniel Cooper:* Martin Balsam; *Gen. Benny Peled:* John Saxon; *Dora Bloch:* Sylvia Sidney; *Defense Minister Shimon Peres:* Tige Andrews; *Pasco Cohen:* Allan Arbus; *Yigal Allon:* Robert Loggia; *Menachem Begin:* David Opatoshu; *Gabriele Krieger:* Mariclare Costello; *Co. Yonatan "Yonni" Netanyahu:* Stephen Macht; *Yaakobi:* Warren Kemmerling; *Sammy Berg:* James Woods; *Bar Lev:* Lou Gilbert; *15th Terrorist:* Alex Colon; *Mr. Sager:* Robin Gammell; *Lt. Grut:* Aharon Ipale; *Mr. Harvey:* Harvey Lembeck; *Goldbaum:* Billy Sands; *Mrs. Loeb:* Pearl Shear; *Mrs. Sager:* Millie Slavin; *38th Terrorist:* Rene Assa; *1st Relative:* Allyne Bennet; *Mrs. Berg:* Anna Berger; *Gallili:* Stanley Brock; *Scharf:* Peter Brocco; *Uri Rosen:* Fred Cardoza; *Julie Darin:* Lauren Frost; *Mr. Berg:* Larry Gelman; *Nathan Darin:* Bill Gerber; *Meteorologist:* Dov Gottesfeld; *Mrs. Gordon:* Hanna Hertelendy; *Rachel Sager:* Dinah Manoff; *Mrs. Bennett:* Caryn Matchinga; *Air France Stewardess:* Harlee McBride; *Zadok:* George Petrie; *Delegation Member:* Louis Quinn; *Alice:* Kim Richards; *Amos Eran:* Tom Rosqui; *Jonathan Sager:* Steve Shaw; *2nd Delegation Member:* Martin Speer.

CREDITS

Producers: Edgar J. Scherick, Daniel H. Blatt; *Associate Producer:* Robin S. Clark; *Director:* Irvin Kershner; *Assistant Directors:* Mack Harding, Max Kleven, Bud S. Isaacs; *Screenwriter:* Barry Beckerman; *Cinematographer:* Bill Butler; *2nd Unit Photographer:* Terry Meade; *Production Designer:* W. Stewart Campbell; *Art Director:* Kirk Axtel; *Set Decorator:* Fred Price; *Special Effects:* Terry Frazee; *Musical Score:* David Shire; *Editors:* Bud S. Isaacs, Nick Archer, Art Seid; *Technical Advisers:* Aharon Ipale, Shmuel Erde. *Running Time:* 152 minutes.

THE FILM

The daring rescue by Israeli commandos of 103 hostages from a jetliner hijacked by pro-Palestinian revolutionaries, at Uganda's Entebbe Airport on July 4, 1976, has, to date, become the subject of two American TV-movies, an Israeli-made theatrical feature and a CBS-Television documentary. ABC-TV was first with the star-studded, hastily produced (by Warner Bros.) *Victory at Entebbe,* with a cast that included Burt Lancaster, Kirk Douglas, Elizabeth Taylor, Helen Hayes and Anthony Hopkins.

Raid on Entebbe boasted fewer luminaries, but showed more care in its script (Barry Beckerman) and production for 20th Century-Fox's television division. And it has won considerably more critical approval than either its TV predecessor or the subsequent theatrical release, *Operation Thunderbolt.*

Charles Bronson was the first name announced for *Raid on Entebbe.* Once a TV regular in the Sixties, the actor had been away from the medium for a decade, and was about to start a long-planned Vermont vacation with Jill and their children, when the offer came from *Entebbe* producer Edgar J. Scherick. "I was counting on his strong convictions about the raid," says Scherick, "to lure him back to television." And so Bronson was cast as Gen. Dan Shomron, leader of the raid. For it he was awarded special billing, with his face prominent in all of the show's advertising and publicity. Charles Bronson in a TV movie in 1977 was indeed newsworthy!

With such solid additional cast names as Martin Balsam, Peter Finch, Yaphet Kotto, Horst Bucholz, Sylvia Sidney and Jack Warden, the film went into production in October 1976 in Stockton, California, at whose airport a replica of Uganda's Entebbe Airport was created. Competition made a fast shooting-schedule necessary; *Raid on Entebbe* was completed in three weeks by filming both day and night, and at a reported cost of $2.5 million. When it debuted on television the night of January

9, 1977, it ran for three hours.

In Europe, both *Victory at Entebbe* and *Raid on Entebbe* were shown as theatrical films. In England, the two movies opened within a week of one another in January of 1977—to considerable success.

CRITICS' CORNER

"For its Sunday 'Big Event' NBC offers its version, which claims the distinction of starring Charles Bronson. Mr. Bronson may be the world's leading example of minimal art in acting but, for reasons probably best left to pop sociologists, he is big box-office.

"The story itself, the action proper, is supposed to carry all. And, in fact, it does. Although the production was filmed in California, a sense of factual place is imaginatively established as the story shifts between Uganda and Israel. The hijacking of the plane, en route from Athens to France, is efficiently depicted, and the bulk of the dramatization is devoted to detention and rescue.

"We all know the ending, of course, but the story remains gripping and thrilling. The schmaltz in this case is understandable. It is also forgivable."

John J. O'Connor, *The New York Times*

"ABC, with the recently shown *Victory at Entebbe,* won the race, but NBC, with its *Raid on Entebbe,* wins all the laurels. This drama is a realistic and honest reenactment of the courageous operation.

"Edgar J. Scherick and co-executive producer Daniel H. Blatt, with the skillful aid of director Irvin Kershner, have managed brilliantly to bring to realization the magnitude of this daring military operation, lost in the ABC film, which had a slapped-together backlot look to it. The cast are all convincing, with no grandstand players, all team members."

Kay Gardella, *The New York Daily News*

"Fortunately, the producers and scripter Barry Beckerman realized that the situation had enough built-in suspense and largely avoided the opportunity to milk it with contrived melodramatics. What unspooled was an almost semi-documentary look at how the raid evolved, with especially telling performances by Peter Finch as Israeli Prime Minister Rabin and Yaphet Kotto as Amin. *Raid* got its best entertainment mileage, however, from the preparations under the command of Gen. Shomron, the enigmatic

As Dan Shomron.

leader of the raid—a part uniquely suited to Charles Bronson. It also got an enormous boost by the underplayed conflict between German terrorist Horst Bucholz and hostage spokesman Martin Balsam, plus its sense of restraint in its cameos of hostage travail at the Entebbe airport."

"Bok.," *Variety*

"This carefully made film opts for authenticity, rather than theatricality, in re-creating Israel's stunning raid and rescue of terrorist hostages in Unganda on July 4, 1976. Charles Bronson as General Shomron, Peter Finch as Price Minister Rabin and Yaphet Kotto as Idi Amin are outstanding."

Judith Crist, *TV Guide*

The White Buffalo

A Dino De Laurentiis Production
    for United Artists   /   1977
In Technicolor

CAST

Wild Bill Hickok/James Otis: Charles Bronson; *Charlie Zane:* Jack Warden; *Crazy Horse/Worm:* Will Sampson; *Poker Jenny Schermerhorn:* Kim Novak: *Whistling Jack Kileen:* Clint Walker; *Winifred Coxy:* Stuart Whitman; *Abel Pinkney:* Slim Pickens; *Amos Briggs:* John Carradine: *Cassie Ollinger:* Cara Williams; *Tim Brady:* Shay Duffin; *Amos Bixby:* Douglas V. Fowley; *Pete Holt:* Cliff Pellow; *Capt. Tom Custer:* Ed Lauter; *Jack McCall:* Martin Kove; *Gyp Hook-Hand:* Scott Walker; *Ben Corbett:* Ed Bakey; *Corp. Kileen:* Richard Gilliland; *Kid Jelly:* David Roy Chandler; *Wes Pugh:* Philip Montgomery: *Black Shawl:* Linda Moon Redfearn; *Old Worm:* Chief Tug Smith; *Aaron Pratt:* Douglas Hume; *Johnny Varner:* Cliff Carnell; *Frozen Dog Pimp:* Ron Thompson; *Frieda:* Eve Brent; *Silky Smith:* Joe Roman; *Paddy Welsh:* Bert Williams; *Tall Man:* Dan Vadis; *Short Man:* Christopher Cary; *Cheyenne Bar Man:* Larry Martindale; *Frozen Dog Miners:* Scott Bryson, Will Walker, Gregg White.

CREDITS

Executive Producer: Dino De Laurentiis; *Producer:* Pancho Kohner; *Director:* J. Lee Thompson; *Assistant Directors:* Jack Aldworth, Pat Kehoe; *Screenwriter:* Richard Sale, *Based on His Novel;* *Cinematographer:* Paul Lohmann; *Production Designer:* Tambi Larsen; *Set Decorator:* James I. Berkey; *Special Effects:* Richard M. Parker, Roy Downey; *Buffalo Sequences:* Carlo Rambaldi; *Musical Score:* John Barry; *Editor:* Michael F. Anderson.
Running Time: 97 minutes.

THE FILM

Of all Bronson's films of the Seventies, *The White Buffalo* seems to have been, ultimately, the least successful between its inception and the final product. Behind-the-scenes names all boasted respectable professional credits, and executive producer Dino De Laurentiis surrounded Bronson with an all-pro supporting cast in a production budgeted in the neighborhood of

As Wild Bill Hickok.

$5 million. Richard Sale adapted his original novel into a screenplay directed by J. Lee Thompson, and a considerable sum was spent on special effects, including the monstrous creature of the film's title. Location filming took place in Canon City, Colorado. Yet the movie was severely criticized for its phoney-looking sets and ersatz buffalo, its darkish photography and poorly recorded sound. Coming from an established producer as slickly professional as De Laurentiis, these technical failings seem inexplicable.

The story, a sort of Western *Moby Dick,* cast Bronson as the legendary Wild Bill Hickok, here alias "James Otis," returning to the West to track down the albino buffalo that has haunted his dreams.

In a parallel story, Will Sampson portrays the equally famed Sioux Indian Chief Crazy Horse, determined to avenge the killing of his infant daughter by that same animal. The paths of these two men cross when Hickok saves the chief's life as Crow Indians threaten to kill him. Later, Crazy Horse rescues Hickok during the buffalo's charge, slaying it with his knife when the white man's rifle freezes.

In the smallish role of a frontier prostitute named "Poker Jenny," Kim Novak returned to Hollywood filmmaking for the first time in eight years—discounting a pair of quickie TV movies in 1973 and 1974. It has been reported that the actress's understandable on-the-set nervousness was soon allayed by Bronson himself—who made a pretense of fluffing his own lines until Novak's confidence returned.

CRITICS' CORNER
"Withheld for months from reviewers, *The White Buffalo* is a turkey. United Artists has had the Dino De Laurentiis pic in 'test engagements.' Pancho Kohner's production features arch scripting by Richard Sale (from his novel), stilted acting and forced direction by J. Lee Thompson. The large cast of familiar names apparently hasn't fooled the public. The residual commercial outlook is grim.

With Will Sampson.

"The trade has to wonder how a project like this gets off the ground, when the dialog is enough to invite jeers from an audience. The title beast looks like a hung-over carnival prize, despite attempts at camouflage via hokey soundtrack noise, busy John Barry scoring, murky photography and fast editing. The showmanship vision of De Laurentiis isn't always clear in contemporary subject matter, but it's positively myopic on period Americana."

"Murf.," *Variety*

"Two weeks ago it seemed unlikely that a dumber monster movie than *The Car* would turn up soon. Suddenly, there's *The White Buffalo,* which is destined for almost instant obscurity in domestic release, a consummation that can't come a minute too soon for director J. Lee Thompson, star Charles Bronson and everyone else in an exposed position on this fiasco."

Gary Arnold, *The Washington Post*

"In the 1977 inventory of producer Dino De Laurentiis, *The White Buffalo* is destined to be his white elephant of the year. It is a film that defies description. Yet its screenplay attracted many Hollywood talents who must have imagined they were contributing something significant to the cinema. What they have contributed is equal to what old buffalo hunters used to throw on their camp fires to keep them burning. Charles Bronson contributes more than his share of those 'chips' in his portrayal of Wild Bill Hickok. It is an all-time low for the indestructible Bronson, who cannot even rely on his dour-faced macho to carry him through the ineptitude of Sale's plot and murkiness of Paul Lohmann's cinematography."

John Stanley, *The San Francisco Chronicle*

"*The White Buffalo* obviously didn't turn out the way producer Dino De Laurentiis intended. Despite expensive mounting plus a weighty production team and cast, something failed to spark between the drawing board and its final commitment to celluloid. United Artists seems to agree; the picture is now being quickly dumped on the market in major cities, despite the potent name of Charles Bronson above the title.

"The cast, headed by macho Bronson, is fine; it's also a pleasure to see small roles played by big actors, all doing their turns with the professional polish one would expect of them. It's too bad the final product doesn't justify their efforts, or time. Still, any picture carrying behind-camera names like director J. Lee Thompson, composer John Barry and author Richard Sale can't be completely dismissed, and *The White Buffalo* deserves better than a quick, inconspicuous burial."

Robert Osborne, *The Hollywood Reporter*

With Jack Warden.   With Kim Novak.

239

With Lee Remick.

Telefon

A Metro-Goldwyn-Mayer Production
 for United Artists / 1977
In Panavision and Metrocolor

CAST

Grigori Borzov: Charles Bronson; *Barbara:* Lee Remick; *Nicolai Dalchimsky:* Donald Pleasence; *Dorothy Putterman:* Tyne Daly; *Col. Malchenko:* Alan Badel; *Gen. Strelsky:* Patrick Magee; *Marie Wills:* Sheree North; *Harley Sandburg:* Frank Marth; *Emma Stark:* Helen Page Camp; *Doug Stark:* Roy Jenson; *Mrs. Hassler:* Jacqueline Scott; *Carl Hassler:* Ed Bakey; *Harry Bascom:* John Mitchum; *Father Stuart Diller:* Iggie Wolfington; *Mrs. Maloney:* Kathleen O'Malley; *Lt. Alexandrov:* Ake Lindman; *Dalchimsky's Mother:* Ansa Konen; *William Enders:* Hank Brandt; *Stroller:* John Carter; *TV Newsman:* John Hambrick; *TV Reporter:* Henry Alfaro; *TV Anchor Woman:* Glenda Wina; *Appliance Store Clerk:* Jim Nolan; *Gas Station Attendant:* Burton Gilliam; *Doctor:* Regis J. Cordic; *Hotel Receptionist:* George Petrie; *Maitre D':* Jeff David; *Nurse:* Carmen Zapata; *Navy Lieutenant:* Carl Byrd; *Petty Officer:* Lew Brown; *Radar Operator:* Peter Weiss; *Highway Patrolmen:* Robert Phillips, Cliff Emmich; *Martin Callender:* Alex Sharp; *Airport Clerk:* Margaret Hall Baron; *Taxi Driver:* Al Dunlap; *Hot Rod Kid:* Sean Moloney; *Russian Steward:*

Ville Veikko Salminen; *Hockey players:* Teppo Heiskanen, Mika Levio; *Tourist Family:* Marlene Hazlett, Thomas M. Runyon, Claudia Butler, Philippe Butler; *Mrs. Wills' Children:* Stephanie Ann Rydall, Derek Rydall.

CREDITS
Producer: James B. Harris; *Associate Producer:* Carol Rydall; *Director:* Don Siegel; *Assistant Directors:* David Hamburger, Luigi Alfano, Stephen Lim, Alan Brimfield; *Screenwriters:* Peter Hyams, Stirling Silliphant; *Based on the Novel by:* Walter Wager; *Cinematographer:* Michael Butler; *Production Designer:* Ted Haworth; *Art Director:* William F. O'Brien; *Set Decorator:* Robert Benton; *Special Effects:* Joe Day; *Musical Score:* Lalo Schifrin; *Editor:* Douglas Stewart.
Running Time: 103 minutes.

THE FILM
Looking a bit craggier and grayer (understandable, at fifty-six), Bronson was back with gun in hand in *Telefon,* but with a difference: as a hard-boiled Russian KGB agent on a mission to preserve East-West cordiality. Donald Pleasence portrayed the villain of the piece, an anti-detente Stalinist bent on setting off a network of deep-cover agents — human time bombs programmed twenty years earlier to blow up U.S. military installations.

Perhaps his questionable successes of recent years with old-familiar producers and directors now prompted Bronson to throw in his lot with strangers, producer James B. Harris and director Don Siegel. However, since neither Harris nor Siegel were exactly newcomers to films — and the latter had enjoyed a series of successful collaborations with actor Clint Eastwood (*Dirty Harry,* et al.) — Bronson had every right to expect high-class results from *Telefon.* With Lee Remick as his co-star (in a role where we reasonably have expected to find Jill Ireland) and an intriguing plot, based on Walter Wager's novel, by accomplished screenwriters Peter Hyams and Stirling Silliphant, Bronson's third and final 1977 vehicle boded well.

The results proved a mixed bag, attractive

With Lee Remick.

to the Bronson public (heavy U.S. television promotion helped a series of widespread simultaneous openings for the Christmas holiday season), but hardly impressive to the film's critics.

For sequences representing Russia, director Siegel took his cast and crew to Finland, where Helsinki pinch-hit for Moscow, with areas of the Finnish capital variously doubling for KGB headquarters, and a Moscow apartment house and skating rink.

CRITICS' CORNER

"*Telefon* is pleasant escapism for fast playoff in the international market. Remick's teaming with Bronson is a graceful one for both players, since she polishes some of the rough and remote edges of his screen presence (thereby humanizing the character), and he provides a match for her charisma (which often seems much too secure and strong for other actors to contend with)."

"Murf.," *Variety*

"Charles Bronson turns Russian for this espionage yarn. Can you picture him as Grigori Borzov, secret agent for the KGB? No matter. Nothing really changes; Bronson plays Bronson, and he's still the good guy. The action moves from Moscow to various U.S. cities, and while the film is busy, it is also dull and ridiculous."

William Wolf, *Cue*

"There are a lot of things working against Don Siegel's *Telefon,* including its title, which as easily suggests one of Jerry Lewis's marathon television specials as it does the material with which skillets are lined so that the eggs won't stick. *Telefon,* of course, has to do with neither. It's the Russian code name for a sabotage plan so unbelievable that the actors, when they must explain it to us in the course of the film, actually seem to be embarrassed. They know that we know that they know that it's tall-tale-time in the Kremlin—shared knowledge that has the effect of disarming solemn criticism and inviting us to succumb to the breathless nonsense as co-conspirators.

"Mr. Bronson is a movie actor of the old school. He doesn't seem to act (though that is what he's doing) as much as he inhabits a film with his particular, massive presence, giving the film much-needed ballast. Without him, *Telefon* would fly up to the ceiling and just hang there."

Vincent Canby, *The New York Times*

"*Telefon* is one of Don Siegel's best films, an intriguing and skilfully engineered Cold War thriller that . . . keeps one guessing through most of its length, despite the most implausible plot since the, in some ways, very similar *The Manchurian Candidate*.

"Bronson and Remick play beautifully together, against all expectations. He, quietly reassuring with that craggy Slav face and suggestion of pent-up violence, she looking as if she lives on a diet of wheat germ and vanilla ice cream, and making some half-funny lines sound very funny indeed.

"I would suggest that if you take *Telefon* as a black comedy, everything will be fine. If you demand a more serious attitude to East-West relations, you would do best to stay away. Its complete contempt for either ethics or logic make it one of the most compulsive bits of action nonsense in years."

Julian Fox, *Films and Filming*

With Patrick Magee and Alan Badel.

With Lee Remick.

With Jill Ireland.

Love and Bullets

A Sir Lew Grade Presentation
   for ITC Entertainment   /   1979
   and Associated Film Distribution Corp.
   In Technivision and Technicolor

CAST
Charlie Congers: Charles Bronson; *Joe Bomposa:* Rod Steiger; *Jackie Pruit:* Jill Ireland; *Louis Monk:* Strother Martin; *Brickman:* Bradford Dillman; *Vittorio Farroni:* Henry Silva; *Huntz:* Paul Koslo; *Lobo:* Michael Gazzo; *Cook:* Sam Chew; *Caruso:* Val Avery; *Mike Durant:* Bill Gray; *FBI Agent Marty:* Andy Romano; *FBI Agent George:* Robin Clarke; *Police Captain:* Cliff Pellow; *Vittorio's Girlfriend:* Lorraine Chase.

CREDITS
Executive Producer: Sir Lew Grade; *Producer:* Pancho Kohner; *Director:* Stuart Rosenberg; *Assistant Director:* Jack Aldworth; *Screenwriters:* Wendell Mayes, John Melson; *Cinematographers:* Fred Koenekamp (U.S.), Anthony Richmond (Switzerland); *Production Designer:* John De Cuir; *Music:* Lalo Schifrin; *Editor:* Michael Anderson. *Running Time:* 95 minutes.

THE FILM
1978 was the first year in fourteen without a new Charles Bronson film—a lapse which only Sir Lew Grade could explain, since this movie completed production at the *start* of that calendar year. Grade, reportedly, had signed Bronson to a four-film contract, the first of which this was. Another was to have been *Dollar Ninety Eight,* with a story and screenplay developed by Bronson and Jill Ireland. The second Bronson-Grade teaming was announced to be *Firepower,* starring Sophia Loren, which would have reunited the actor with producer-director Michael Winner. But this never took place and, amid rumors that Bronson had withdrawn because of the producers' refusal to write in a role for Jill Ireland, the film went into production in April of 1978 with Bronson replaced by his old colleague, James Coburn. Thus the public was unable to sample the charismatic

As Charlie Congers.

Jill Ireland as Jackie Pruitt.

prospect of a Bronson-Loren teaming.

Love and Bullets, Charlie (as it was called during production) was Bronson's first movie under the direction of Stuart Rosenberg, whose output had included *Cool Hand Luke, The Laughing Policeman* and *Voyage of the Damned*. With Jill Ireland in the somewhat unusual role of a crime boss's Ozark-born girlfriend and Bronson as a plainclothes Arizona cop, this film centers on the machinations of a Mafia tycoon (Rod Steiger) corrupting a Western state, as well as a gang of Italian kidnap specialists operating out of Switzerland. In the process of trying to cope with an international network of syndicate crime, Bronson not unexpectedly falls in love with the gangster's mistress. Faced with professional frustrations at every turn, he ultimately sidesteps the law to handle the matter with typical *Death Wish* dispatch.

Love and Bullets' location backgrounds alone offered a colorful visual experience, since shooting took place in locales as varied as Zurich, Zermatt, Dallas, Washington and Chicago. The film premiered in London in March of 1979.

CRITICS' CORNER
"Charles Bronson's presence in this routine yarn about a lone cop on assignment in Switzerland is the pic's only firm selling point.

"Refreshing to report, this essentially family thriller refrains from gratuitous sadism and nudity, often seemingly employed to distract attention from a poor script, or regarded as the modern route to the public's wallet. At worst, *Love and Bullets* is bland and fails to thrill. But it's never offensive."

"Simo.," *Variety*

"Charles Bronson is on TV almost every night this week in one movie or another from *Rider on the Rain* to his ascendancy as top international star in run-of-the-mill action movies like *The*

Rod Steiger as Joe Bomposa.

With Strother Martin.

Stone Killer. The movies are a frightening reminder of just how soft this once bearish ethnic rival to Clint Eastwood has gone in all his recent films since *Hard Times,* especially in his latest, *Love and Bullets.* You can almost sense all the contracted, on-location luxuries that Bronson demanded before filming. *Love and Bullets* is a genre chase film with no rough edges, and a minimal sense of physical exertion on Bronson's part. Gone is the glowering that made Bronson the last mug you'd want to go against in a dark alley.

"The only distractions from Mr. and Mrs. Bronson's amiable chatting and ambling through the touristy Alps are side trips to Rod Steiger, chewing the scenery as a stuttering, maudlinly sentimental Don. More bullets and less love, Charlie."

Tom Allen, *The Village Voice*

"Mr. Bronson spends most of his time escorting Miss Ireland onto trains, into hotels and across the snow. This is all very chivalrous, but it's also dull. The British-born Miss Ireland has no luck in affecting a hillbilly accent, and as a comic presence she's simply not there. However, she and Mr. Bronson approach each other with an appealing ease, which would be more appealing if it were not the movie's only selling point.

Mr. Bronson grows ever more coolly dependable with each new film, but *Love and Bullets* is too clumsy to show him off to much advantage."

Janet Maslin, *The New York Times*

"Director Stuart Rosenberg provides an abundance of Alpine scenery, Bronson his customary tight-lipped heroics. Boring."

William Wolf, *Cue*

"Charles Bronson is back in the slaughterhouse with *Love and Bullets,* as a Phoenix police official sent by the FBI to Switzerland to bring back a mobster's girlfriend for questioning about the mobster's activities. Improbable is the key word for the movie, which opens with an extraneous bangup car chase to hype audience attention. Which should be a clue."

Ernest Leogrande, *The New York Daily News*

"*Love and Bullets* may not be the worst, but it is a relatively dismaying example of the Lew Grade entertainment formula: as locations, production values and cliched set-pieces proliferate, scripts increasingly look like shaggy-dog stories desperately in search of a point, and actors are left to do their own thing as their characters disintegrate.

"Rod Steiger is given his most outrageously enjoyable opportunity for some time to cut some Method capers, playing Mafia leader Bomposa as if he were a parody of a Sylvester Stallone character. The incongruous appeals which Bomposa makes to our sympathy stand in stark contrast to the totally negative impact of Charles Bronson's putative hero. Since the slim point of the whole enterprise seems to be the emotional attachment which Bronson forms to the dumb blonde he is trying to save from various sets of gangsters at the behest of the FBI, it is unfortunate that Bronson's persona just fades greyly into the wallpaper in those scenes where he is not called on for tight-lipped derring-do.

"The film is a slackly organized sequence of chases and betrayals, with Stuart Rosenberg not surprisingly failing to find a tone that can accommodate Steiger's self-parody as well as Bronson's self-indulgence, but veteran screenwriter Wendell Mayes more unexpectedly falling in with the cynically overinflated, hit-or-miss approach."

Richard Combs, *Monthly Film Bulletin*

248

As Giff Hoyt.

Cabo Blanco

A Hool/Joseph Presentation
   for Cabo Productions   /   1980
In Technivision and Technicolor

CAST
Giff Hoyt: Charles Bronson; *Marie Alessandri:*
Dominique Sanda; *Gunther Beckdorff:* Jason
Robards; *Terredo:* Fernando Rey; *Hera:* Camilla
Sparv; *Jim Clarkson:* Simon MacCorkindale; *Dr.*

Ramirez: Gilbert Roland; *Horst:* Denny Miller; *Pete:* Ernest Esparza; *Lupo:* Danny Ades; *Lorrimer:* Clifton James; *John Bunce:* James Booth.

CREDITS
Executive Producers: Martin V. Smith, Pancho Kohner; *Producers:* Lance Hool, Paul A. Joseph; *Associate Producer:* Alan Conrad Hool; *Director:* J. Lee Thompson; *Assistant Director:* Jesus Marin; *Screenwriter:* Milton Gelman; *Based on an Original Story by:* James Granby Hunter and Lance Hool; *Cinematographer:* Alex Phillips, Jr.; *Art Director:* Jose Rodriguez Granada; *Special Effects:* Laurencio Cordero; *Underwater Effects:* Genaro Hurtado; *Editor:* Michael Anderson.

THE FILM
As this book went to press, the $10 million independent production of *Cabo Blanco* was in the final stages of filming in Barra de Navidad, a small town on Mexico's western coast (pinch-hitting for Peru).

According to producer Lance Hool, Bronson's casting fulfilled their search for "someone with the strength and sex appeal of Fairbanks, Flynn or Bogart." His role: that of an American expatriate adventurer, one of several strangers whose paths cross in 1949 over the search for a World War II ship sunken off the coast of Cabo Blanco, a tiny Peruvian fishing village.

Two-time Oscar winner Jason Robards portrays the film's villain, an ex-Nazi officer with a special interest in that ship, and the cast boasts a pair of blonde beauties — neither of which is Jill Ireland! French actress Dominique Sanda, seen to best advantage in *The Conformist* and *The Garden of the Finzi-Continis,* is on the scene to investigate the fate of her wartime lover; Camilla Sparv, Robert Redford's leading lady in *Downhill Racer,* plays Robards' mistress (and Bronson's ex-flame). The scene is obviously set for romance, intrigue and adventure in the old Hollywood tradition.

The movie's producers have seen fit to advise the trade press that *Cabo Blanco* is not a remake of 1942's Oscar-winning Best Picture, *Casablanca,* despite the similarity of titles. Whatever the results, this marks Charles Bronson's third film with director J. Lee Thompson.

With director J. Lee Thompson (seated) on location at Barra de Navidad, Mexico.

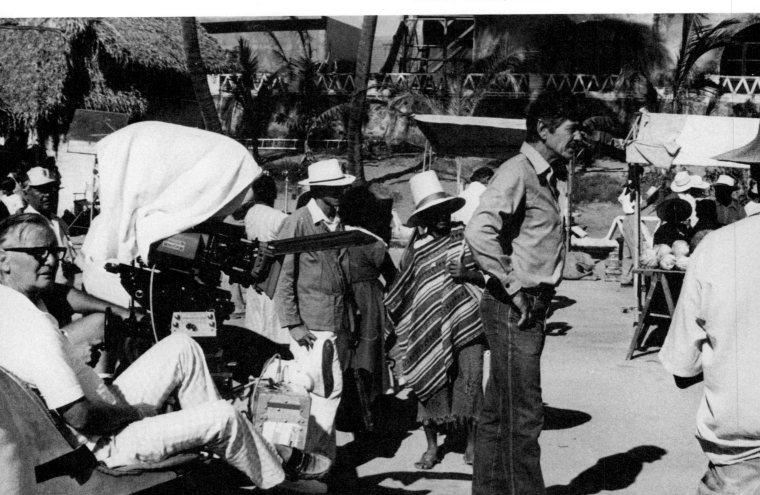

With Dominique Sanda and Jason Robards.

With Dominique Sanda.

Charles Bronson on Television

As Charles Buchinsky

The Doctor: "Take the Odds" 1/18/53 NBC
Playhouse: "Adventure in Java" 7/8/54 NBC
Four Star Playhouse "The Witness" 7/22/54 CBS

As Charles Bronson

Medic: "My Brother Joe" 10/25/54 NBC
Lux Video Theatre: "A Bell for Adano" 2/10/55 NBC
Man Behind the Badge: "The Case of the Invisible Mark" 2/19/55 CBS
Stage 7: "Debt of Honor" 2/20/55 CBS
Public Defender: "Cornered" 3/24/55 CBS
Treasury Men in Action: "The Case of the Deadly Dilemma" 3/24/55 ABC
Stage 7: "The Time of Day" 5/29/55 CBS
Treasury Men in Action: "The Case of the Shot in the Dark" 6/9/55 ABC
Polly Bergen Playhouse: "Woman in the Mine" 6/12/55 ABC
Crusader: "A Boxing Match" 10/21/55 CBS
Cavalcade Theater: "Chain of Hearts" 11/1/55 ABC
General Electric Theater: "Prosper's Old Mother" 11/20/55 CBS
Alfred Hitchcock Presents: "And So Died Riabouchinska" 2/12/56 CBS
The Crusader: "Freeze Out" 2/17/56 CBS
Medic: "Who Search for Truth" 2/27/56 NBC
Alfred Hitchcock Presents: "There Was an Old Woman" 3/18/56 CBS
Warner Bros. Presents: "Explosion" 3/27/56 ABC
Gunsmoke: "The Killer" 5/26/56 CBS
The Millionaire: "The Story of Jerry Bell" 2/27/57 CBS
Hey, Jeannie: "Jeannie the Policewoman" 3/2/57 CBS
Studio 57: "Outpost" 9/1/57 Non-network syndication
Richard Diamond, Private Detective: "The Peter Rocco Case" 9/9/57 CBS

With Estelle Windwood in "There Was an Old Woman" on *Alfred Hitchcock Presents* (1956).

As Mike Kovac in the *Man with a Camera* series (1958-60).

Have Gun, Will Travel: "The Outlaw"
9/21/57 CBS
Colt .45: "Young Gun" 12/13/57 ABC
Suspicion: "Doomsday" 12/16/57 NBC
The Court of Last Resort: "The Steve
Hrdlika Case" 1/24/58 NBC
M-Squad: "Fight" 4/18/58 NBC
Sugarfoot: "The Bullet and the Cross"
5/27/58 ABC
Have Gun, Will Travel: "Gunsmuggler"
9/27/58 CBS
Man with a Camera: "Second Avenue
Assassin" 10/10/58 ABC
Tales of Wells Fargo: "Butch Cassidy"
10/13/58 NBC
Man with a Camera: "The Warning"
10/17/58 ABC
"Profile of a Killer" 10/24/58 ABC
Gunsmoke: "Lost Rifle" 11/1/58 CBS
Man with a Camera: "Turntable" 11/7/58
ABC
"Close-up on Violence" 11/14/58
"Double Negative" 11/21/58
"Another Barrier" 11/28/58
"Blind Spot" 12/5/58
"Two Strings of Pearls" 12/12/58
"Six Faces of Satan" 12/19/58
"Lady on the Loose" 12/26/58
"Last Portrait" 1/2/59
"Face of Murder" 1/9/59
"Mute Evidence" 1/16/59
"The Big Squeeze" 1/23/59
U.S. Marshal: "Pursuit" 5/25/59 NBC
Playhouse 90: "The Rank and File" 5/28/59
CBS
Man with a Camera: "The Killer" 10/19/59
ABC
"Eyewitness" 10/26/59
"The Man Below" 11/2/59
"Black Light" 11/9/59
"The Positive Negative" 11/16/59
"Missing" 11/23/59
"Light Target" 12/7/59
"Girl in the Dark" 12/14/59

With Abby Dalton on the *Hennesey* series (1960).

With Ryan O'Neal in "Seven Days on Rough Street" on
the *Empire* series (1963).

"The Bride" 12/21/59
"The Picture War" 1/4/60
"Touch Off" 1/11/60
"Hot Ice Cream" 1/25/60
"Fragment of a Murder" 2/1/60
"Kangaroo Court" 2/8/60
Playhouse 90: "The Cruel Day" 2/24/60 CBS
Laramie: "Street of Hate" 3/1/60 NBC
Hennesey: "Hennesey a la Gun" 10/17/60
   CBS
The Aquanauts: "The Cave Divers"
   12/7/60 CBS
Riverboat: "Zigzag" 12/26/60 NBC
General Electric Theater: "Memory in
   White" 1/8/61 CBS
Alcoa Premiere: "The Last Round" 1/10/61
   ABC
The Islanders: "The Generous Politician"
   1/15/61 ABC
The Loretta Young Show: "Wood Lot"
   3/26/61 NBC
Laramie: "Run of the Hunted" 4/4/61 NBC
Hennesey: "The Nogoodnik" 4/17/61 CBS
Twilight Zone: "Two" 9/15/61 CBS
Have Gun, Will Travel: "A Proof of Love"
   10/14/61 CBS
"Ben Jalisco" 11/18/61
Cain's Hundred: "Dead Load" 11/21/61
   NBC
The New Breed: "The Valley of the Three
   Charlies" 12/15/61 ABC
Adventures in Paradise: "Survival" 12/31/61
   ABC
Alfred Hitchcock Presents: "The Woman
   Who Wanted to Live" 2/6/62 NBC
The Untouchables: "The Death Tree"
   2/15/62 ABC
The Bob Newhart Show 4/11/62 NBC
Here's Hollywood 8/8/62 NBC
Empire: "The Day the Empire Stood Still"
   (Premiere) 9/25/62 NBC
Have Gun, Will Travel: "Brotherhood"
   1/5/63 CBS
Empire: "Seven Days on Rough Street"
   2/26/63 NBC
"A House in Order" 3/5/63

With Kurt Russell in "The Day of the Misfits" on *The Travels of Jaimie McPheeters* (1964).

In "Nobility of Kings" from the *Virginian* series (1965).

"Down There the World" 3/12/63
"Burnout" 3/19/63
"Hidden Asset" 3/26/63
"Arrow in the Sky" 4/9/63
"Nobody Dies on Saturday" 4/16/63
"65 Miles Is a Long, Long Way" 4/23/63
"Duet for Eight Wheels" 4/30/63
"Between Friday and Monday" 5/7/63
"The Convention" 5/14/63
Doctor Kildare: "Who Ever Heard of a Two-Headed Doll?" 9/26/63 NBC
The Travels of Jaimie McPheeters: "The Day of the Killer" 11/17/63 ABC
"The Day of the Homeless" 11/24/63
"The Day of the Misfits" 12/15/63
"The Day of the Toll Takers" 1/5/64
Your First Impression (game show) 1/8/64 NBC
The Travels of Jaimie McPheeters: "The Day of the Wizard" 1/12/64 NBC
"The Day of the Search" 1/19/64
"The Day of the Haunted Trail" 1/26/64
"The Day of the Tin Trumpet" 2/2/64
"The Day of the Lame Duck" 2/9/64
"The Day of the 12 Candles" 2/23/64
"The Day of the Pretenders" 3/1/64
"The Day of Reckoning" 3/15/64
You Don't Say (game show) 8/31/64 & 9/4/64 NBC
Bonanza: "The Underdog" 12/13/64 NBC
Combat: "Heritage" 4/13/65 ABC
Vacation Playhouse: "Luke and the Tenderfoot" 8/13/65 CBS
The Big Valley: "Earthquake" 11/10/65 ABC
The Virginian: "Nobility of Kings" 11/10/65 NBC
Rawhide: "Duel at Daybreak" 11/16/65 CBS
The Legend of Jesse James: "The Chase" 3/7/66 ABC
The F.B.I.: "The Animal" 4/17/66 ABC
The Fugitive: 1/17/67 ABC
The Virginian: "The Reckoning" 9/13/67 NBC
Dundee and the Culhane: "The Cat in the Bag Brief" 9/13/67 CBS
Raid on Entebbe 1/9/77 NBC (TV movie)

In "The Chase" on the series *The Legend of Jesse James* (1966).

A rare TV appearance: Bronson and Ireland on the *Dinah!* show.